LES MISERABLES

CONTENTS

BOOK FIRST—A JUST MAN

BOOK SECOND—THE FALL

BOOK FIFTH.—THE DESCENT.

BOOK SIXTH.—JAVERT

BOOK SEVENTH.—THE CHAMPMATHIEU AFFAIR

BOOK EIGHTH.—A COUNTER-BLOW

PREFACE

So long as there shall exist, by virtue of law and custom, decrees of damnation pronounced by society, artificially creating hells amid the civilization of earth, and adding the element of human fate to divine destiny; so long as the three great problems of the century—the degradation of man through pauperism, the corruption of woman through hunger, the crippling of children through lack of light—are unsolved; so long as social asphyxia is possible in any part of the world;—in other words, and with a still wider significance, so long as ignorance and poverty exist on earth, books of the nature of Les Miserables cannot fail to be of use.

HAUTEVILLE HOUSE, 1862.

BOOK FIRST

A JUST MAN

CHAPTER I

M. MYRIEL

In 1815, M. Charles-Francois-Bienvenu Myriel was Bishop of D—He was an old man of about seventy-five years of age; he had occupied the see of D—since 1806.

Although this detail has no connection whatever with the real substance of what we are about to relate, it will not be superfluous, if merely for the sake of exactness in all points, to mention here the various rumors and remarks which had been in circulation about him from the very moment when he arrived in the diocese. True or false, that which is said of men often occupies as important a place in their lives, and above all in their destinies, as that which they do. M. Myriel was the son of a councillor of the Parliament of Aix; hence he belonged to the nobility of the bar. It was said that his father, destining him to be the heir of his own post, had married him at a very early age, eighteen or twenty, in accordance with a custom which is rather widely prevalent in parliamentary families. In spite of this marriage, however, it was said that Charles Myriel created a great deal of talk. He was well formed, though rather short in stature, elegant, graceful, intelligent; the whole of the first portion of his life had been devoted to the world and to gallantry.

The Revolution came; events succeeded each other with precipitation; the parliamentary families, decimated, pursued, hunted down, were dispersed. M. Charles Myriel emigrated to Italy at the very beginning of the Revolution. There his wife died of a malady of the chest, from which she had long suffered. He had no children. What took place next in the fate of M. Myriel? The ruin of the French society of the olden days, the fall of his own family, the tragic spectacles of '93, which were, perhaps, even more alarming to the emigrants who viewed them from a distance, with the magnifying powers of terror,—did these cause the ideas of renunciation and solitude to germinate in him? Was he, in the midst of these distractions, these affections which absorbed his life, suddenly smitten with one of those mysterious and terrible blows which sometimes overwhelm, by striking to his heart, a man whom public catastrophes would not shake, by striking at his existence and his fortune? No one could have told: all that was known was, that when he returned from Italy he was a priest.

In 1804, M. Myriel was the Cure of B—[Brignolles]. He was already advanced in years, and lived in a very retired manner.

About the epoch of the coronation, some petty affair connected with his curacy—just what, is not precisely known—took him to Paris. Among other powerful persons to whom he went to solicit aid for his parishioners was M. le Cardinal Fesch. One day, when the Emperor had come to visit his uncle, the worthy Cure, who was waiting in the anteroom, found himself present when His Majesty passed. Napoleon, on finding himself observed with a certain curiosity by this old man, turned round and said abruptly:—

"Who is this good man who is staring at me?"

"Sire," said M. Myriel, "you are looking at a good man, and I at a great man. Each of us can profit by it."

That very evening, the Emperor asked the Cardinal the name of the Cure, and some time afterwards M. Myriel was utterly astonished to learn that he had been appointed Bishop of D—

What truth was there, after all, in the stories which were invented as to the early portion of M. Myriel's life? No one knew. Very few families had been acquainted with the Myriel family before the Revolution.

M. Myriel had to undergo the fate of every newcomer in a little town, where there are many mouths which talk, and very few heads which think. He was obliged to undergo it although he was a bishop, and because he was a bishop. But after all, the rumors with which his name was connected were rumors only,—noise, sayings, words; less than words—palabres, as the energetic language of the South expresses it.

However that may be, after nine years of episcopal power and of residence in D—, all the stories and subjects of conversation which engross petty towns and petty people at the outset had fallen into profound oblivion. No one would have dared to mention them; no one would have dared to recall them.

M. Myriel had arrived at D—accompanied by an elderly spinster, Mademoiselle Baptistine, who was his sister, and ten years his junior.

Their only domestic was a female servant of the same age as Mademoiselle Baptistine, and named Madame Magloire, who, after having been the servant of M. le Cure, now assumed the double title of maid to Mademoiselle and housekeeper to Monseigneur.

Mademoiselle Baptistine was a long, pale, thin, gentle creature; she realized the ideal expressed by the word "respectable"; for it seems that a woman must needs be a mother in order to be venerable. She had never been pretty; her whole life, which had been nothing but a succession of holy deeds, had finally conferred upon her a sort of pallor and transparency; and as she advanced in years she had acquired what may be called the beauty of goodness. What had been leanness in her youth had become transparency in her maturity; and this diaphaneity allowed the angel to be seen. She was a soul rather than a virgin. Her person seemed made of a shadow; there was hardly sufficient body to provide for sex; a little matter enclosing a light; large eyes forever drooping;—a mere pretext for a soul's remaining on the earth.

Madame Magloire was a little, fat, white old woman, corpulent and bustling; always out of breath,—in the first place, because of her activity, and in the next, because of her asthma.

On his arrival, M. Myriel was installed in the episcopal palace with the honors required by the Imperial decrees, which class a bishop immediately after a major-general. The mayor and the president paid the first call on him, and he, in turn, paid the first call on the general and the prefect.

The installation over, the town waited to see its bishop at work.

CHAPTER II

M. MYRIEL BECOMES M. WELCOME

The episcopal palace of D—adjoins the hospital.

The episcopal palace was a huge and beautiful house, built of stone at the beginning of the last century by M. Henri Puget, Doctor of Theology of the Faculty of Paris, Abbe of Simore, who had been Bishop of D—in 1712. This palace was a genuine seignorial residence. Everything about it had a grand air,—the apartments of the Bishop, the drawing-rooms, the chambers, the principal courtyard, which was very large, with walks encircling it under arcades in the old Florentine fashion, and gardens planted with magnificent trees. In the dining-room, a long and superb gallery which was situated on the ground-floor and opened on the gardens, M. Henri Puget had entertained in state, on July 29, 1714, My Lords Charles Brulart de Genlis, archbishop; Prince d'Embrun; Antoine de Mesgrigny, the capuchin, Bishop of Grasse; Philippe de Vendome, Grand Prior of France, Abbe of Saint Honore de Lerins; Francois de Berton de Crillon, bishop, Baron de Vence; Cesar de Sabran de Forcalquier, bishop, Seignor of Glandeve; and Jean Soanen, Priest of the Oratory, preacher in ordinary to the king, bishop, Seignor of Senez. The portraits of these seven reverend personages decorated this apartment; and this memorable date, the 29th of July, 1714, was there engraved in letters of gold on a table of white marble.

The hospital was a low and narrow building of a single story, with a small garden.

Three days after his arrival, the Bishop visited the hospital. The visit ended, he had the director requested to be so good as to come to his house.

"Monsieur the director of the hospital," said he to him, "how many sick people have you at the present moment?"

"Twenty-six, Monseigneur."

"That was the number which I counted," said the Bishop.

"The beds," pursued the director, "are very much crowded against each other."

"That is what I observed."

"The halls are nothing but rooms, and it is with difficulty that the air can be changed in them."

"So it seems to me."

"And then, when there is a ray of sun, the garden is very small for the convalescents."

"That was what I said to myself."

"In case of epidemics,—we have had the typhus fever this year; we had the sweating sickness two years ago, and a hundred patients at times,—we know not what to do."

"That is the thought which occurred to me."

"What would you have, Monseigneur?" said the director. "One must resign one's self."

This conversation took place in the gallery dining-room on the ground-floor.

The Bishop remained silent for a moment; then he turned abruptly to the director of the hospital.

"Monsieur," said he, "how many beds do you think this hall alone would hold?"

"Monseigneur's dining-room?" exclaimed the stupefied director.

The Bishop cast a glance round the apartment, and seemed to be taking measures and calculations with his eyes.

"It would hold full twenty beds," said he, as though speaking to himself. Then, raising his voice:—

"Hold, Monsieur the director of the hospital, I will tell you something. There is evidently a mistake here. There are thirty-six of you, in five or six small rooms. There are three of us here, and we have room for sixty. There is some mistake, I tell you; you have my house, and I have yours. Give me back my house; you are at home here."

On the following day the thirty-six patients were installed in the Bishop's palace, and the Bishop was settled in the hospital.

M. Myriel had no property, his family having been ruined by the Revolution. His sister was in receipt of a yearly income of five hundred francs, which sufficed for her personal wants at the vicarage. M. Myriel received from the State, in his quality of bishop, a salary of fifteen thousand francs. On the very day when he took up his abode in the hospital, M. Myriel settled on the disposition of this sum once for all, in the following manner. We transcribe here a note made by his own hand:—

NOTE ON THE REGULATION OF
MY HOUSEHOLD EXPENSES.

For the little seminary	1,500	livres
Society of the mission	100	"
For the Lazarists of Montdidier	100	"
Seminary for foreign missions in Paris	200	"
Congregation of the Holy Spirit	150	"
Religious establishments of the Holy Land	100	"
Charitable maternity societies	300	"
Extra, for that of Arles	50	"
Work for the amelioration of prisons	400	"
Work for the relief and delivery of prisoners	500	"
To liberate fathers of families incarcerated for debt	1,000	"

Addition to the salary of the poor teachers of the diocese	2,000	"
Public granary of the Hautes-Alpes	100	"
Congregation of the ladies of D——, of Manosque, and of Sisteron, for the gratuitous instruction of poor girls	1,500	"
For the poor	6,000	"
My personal expenses	1,000	"
Total	15,000	"

M. Myriel made no change in this arrangement during the entire period that he occupied the see of D——As has been seen, he called it regulating his household expenses.

This arrangement was accepted with absolute submission by Mademoiselle Baptistine. This holy woman regarded Monseigneur of D——as at one and the same time her brother and her bishop, her friend according to the flesh and her superior according to the Church. She simply loved and venerated him. When he spoke, she bowed; when he acted, she yielded her adherence. Their only servant, Madame Magloire, grumbled a little. It will be observed that Monsieur the Bishop had reserved for himself only one thousand livres, which, added to the pension of Mademoiselle Baptistine, made fifteen hundred francs a year. On these fifteen hundred francs these two old women and the old man subsisted.

And when a village curate came to D——, the Bishop still found means to entertain him, thanks to the severe economy of Madame Magloire, and to the intelligent administration of Mademoiselle Baptistine.

One day, after he had been in D——about three months, the Bishop said:—

"And still I am quite cramped with it all!"

"I should think so!" exclaimed Madame Magloire. "Monseigneur has not even claimed the allowance which the department owes him for the expense of his carriage in town, and for his journeys about the diocese. It was customary for bishops in former days."

"Hold!" cried the Bishop, "you are quite right, Madame Magloire."

And he made his demand.

Some time afterwards the General Council took this demand under consideration, and voted him an annual sum of three thousand francs, under this heading: Allowance to M. the Bishop for expenses of carriage, expenses of posting, and expenses of pastoral visits.

This provoked a great outcry among the local burgesses; and a senator of the Empire, a former member of the Council of the Five Hundred which favored the 18 Brumaire, and who was provided with a magnificent senatorial office in the vicinity of the town of D——, wrote to M. Bigot de Preameneu, the minister of public worship, a very angry and confidential note on the subject, from which we extract these authentic lines:—

"Expenses of carriage? What can be done with it in a town of less than four thousand inhabitants? Expenses of journeys? What is the use of these trips, in the first place? Next, how can the posting be accomplished in these mountainous parts? There are no roads. No one travels otherwise than on horseback. Even the bridge between Durance and Chateau-Arnoux can barely support ox-teams. These priests are all thus, greedy and avaricious. This man played the good priest when he first came. Now he does like the rest; he must have a carriage and a posting-chaise, he must have luxuries, like the bishops of the olden days. Oh, all this priesthood! Things will not go well, M. le Comte, until the Emperor has freed us from these black-capped rascals. Down with the Pope! [Matters were getting embroiled with Rome.] For my part, I am for Caesar alone." Etc., etc.

On the other hand, this affair afforded great delight to Madame Magloire. "Good," said she to Mademoiselle Baptistine; "Monseigneur began with other people, but he has had to wind up with himself, after all. He has regulated all his charities. Now here are three thousand francs for us! At last!"

That same evening the Bishop wrote out and handed to his sister a memorandum conceived in the following terms:—

EXPENSES OF CARRIAGE AND CIRCUIT.

For furnishing meat soup to the patients in the hospital.	1,500	livres
For the maternity charitable society of Aix.	250	”
For the maternity charitable society of Draguignan	250	”
For foundlings	500	”
For orphans.	500	”
Total.	3,000	”

Such was M. Myriel's budget.

As for the chance episcopal perquisites, the fees for marriage bans, dispensations, private baptisms, sermons, benedictions, of churches or chapels, marriages, etc., the Bishop levied them on the wealthy with all the more asperity, since he bestowed them on the needy.

After a time, offerings of money flowed in. Those who had and those who lacked knocked at M. Myriel's door,—the latter in search of the alms which the former came to deposit. In less than a year the Bishop had become the treasurer of all benevolence and the cashier of all those in distress. Considerable sums of money passed through his hands, but nothing could induce him to make any change whatever in his mode of life, or add anything superfluous to his bare necessities.

Far from it. As there is always more wretchedness below than there is brotherhood above, all was given away, so to speak, before it was received. It was like water on dry soil; no matter how much money he received, he never had any. Then he stripped himself.

The usage being that bishops shall announce their baptismal names at the head of their charges and their pastoral letters, the poor people of the country-side had selected, with a sort of affectionate instinct, among the names and prenomens of their bishop, that which had a meaning for them; and they never called him anything except Monseigneur Bienvenu [Welcome]. We will follow their example, and will also call him thus when we have occasion to name him. Moreover, this appellation pleased him.

"I like that name," said he. "Bienvenu makes up for the Monseigneur."

We do not claim that the portrait herewith presented is probable; we confine ourselves to stating that it resembles the original.

CHAPTER III

A HARD BISHOPRIC FOR A GOOD BISHOP

The Bishop did not omit his pastoral visits because he had converted his carriage into alms. The diocese of D—is a fatiguing one. There are very few plains and a great many mountains; hardly any roads, as we have just seen; thirty-two curacies, forty-one vicarships, and two hundred and eighty-five auxiliary chapels. To visit all these is quite a task.

The Bishop managed to do it. He went on foot when it was in the neighborhood, in a tilted spring-cart when it was on the plain, and on a donkey in the mountains. The two old women accompanied him. When the trip was too hard for them, he went alone.

One day he arrived at Senez, which is an ancient episcopal city. He was mounted on an ass. His purse, which was very dry at that moment, did not permit him any other equipage. The mayor of the town came to receive him at the gate of the town, and watched him dismount from his ass, with scandalized eyes. Some of the citizens were laughing around him. "Monsieur the Mayor," said the Bishop, "and Messieurs Citizens, I perceive that I shock you. You think it very arrogant in a poor priest to ride an animal which was used by Jesus Christ. I have done so from necessity, I assure you, and not from vanity."

In the course of these trips he was kind and indulgent, and talked rather than preached. He never went far in search of his arguments and his examples. He quoted to the inhabitants of one district the example of a neighboring district. In the cantons where they were harsh to the poor, he said: "Look at the people of Briancon! They have conferred on the poor, on widows and orphans, the right to have their meadows mown three days in advance of every one else. They rebuild their houses for them gratuitously when they are ruined. Therefore it is a country which is blessed by God. For a whole century, there has not been a single murderer among them."

In villages which were greedy for profit and harvest, he said: "Look at the people of Embrun! If, at the harvest season, the father of a family has his son away on service in the army, and his daughters at service in the town, and if he is ill and incapacitated, the cure recommends him to the prayers of the congregation; and on Sunday, after the mass, all the inhabitants of the village—men, women, and children—go to the poor man's field and do his harvesting for him, and carry his straw and his grain to his granary." To families divided by questions of money and inheritance he said: "Look at the mountaineers of Devolny, a country so wild that the nightingale is not heard there once in fifty years. Well, when the father of a family dies, the boys go off to seek their fortunes, leaving the property to the girls, so that they may find husbands." To the cantons which had a taste for lawsuits, and where the farmers ruined themselves in stamped paper, he said: "Look at those good peasants in the valley of Queyras! There are three thousand souls of them. Mon Dieu! it is like a little republic. Neither judge nor bailiff is known there. The mayor does everything. He allots the imposts, taxes each person conscientiously, judges quarrels for nothing, divides inheritances without charge, pronounces sentences gratuitously; and he is obeyed, because he is a just man among simple men." To villages where he found no schoolmaster, he quoted once more the people of Queyras: "Do you know how they manage?" he said. "Since a little country of a dozen or fifteen hearths cannot always support a teacher, they have school-masters who are paid by the whole valley, who make the round of the villages, spending a week in this one, ten days in that, and instruct them. These teachers go to the fairs. I have seen them there. They are to be recognized by the quill pens which they

27

wear in the cord of their hat. Those who teach reading only have one pen; those who teach reading and reckoning have two pens; those who teach reading, reckoning, and Latin have three pens. But what a disgrace to be ignorant! Do like the people of Queyras!"

Thus he discoursed gravely and paternally; in default of examples, he invented parables, going directly to the point, with few phrases and many images, which characteristic formed the real eloquence of Jesus Christ. And being convinced himself, he was persuasive.

CHAPTER IV

WORKS CORRESPONDING TO WORDS

His conversation was gay and affable. He put himself on a level with the two old women who had passed their lives beside him. When he laughed, it was the laugh of a schoolboy. Madame Magloire liked to call him Your Grace [Votre Grandeur]. One day he rose from his arm-chair, and went to his library in search of a book. This book was on one of the upper shelves. As the bishop was rather short of stature, he could not reach it. "Madame Magloire," said he, "fetch me a chair. My greatness [grandeur] does not reach as far as that shelf."

One of his distant relatives, Madame la Comtesse de Lo, rarely allowed an opportunity to escape of enumerating, in his presence, what she designated as "the expectations" of her three sons. She had numerous relatives, who were very old and near to death, and of whom her sons were the natural heirs. The youngest of the three was to receive from a grand-aunt a good hundred thousand livres of income; the second was the heir by entail to the title of the Duke, his uncle; the eldest was to succeed to the peerage of his grandfather. The Bishop was accustomed to listen in silence to these innocent and pardonable maternal boasts. On one occasion, however, he appeared to be more thoughtful than usual, while Madame de Lo was relating once again the details of all these inheritances and all these "expectations." She interrupted herself impatiently: "Mon Dieu, cousin! What are you thinking about?" "I am thinking," replied the Bishop, "of a singular remark, which is to be found,

I believe, in St. Augustine,—'Place your hopes in the man from whom you do not inherit.'"

At another time, on receiving a notification of the decease of a gentleman of the country-side, wherein not only the dignities of the dead man, but also the feudal and noble qualifications of all his relatives, spread over an entire page: "What a stout back Death has!" he exclaimed. "What a strange burden of titles is cheerfully imposed on him, and how much wit must men have, in order thus to press the tomb into the service of vanity!"

He was gifted, on occasion, with a gentle raillery, which almost always concealed a serious meaning. In the course of one Lent, a youthful vicar came to D—, and preached in the cathedral. He was tolerably eloquent. The subject of his sermon was charity. He urged the rich to give to the poor, in order to avoid hell, which he depicted in the most frightful manner of which he was capable, and to win paradise, which he represented as charming and desirable. Among the audience there was a wealthy retired merchant, who was somewhat of a usurer, named M. Geborand, who had amassed two millions in the manufacture of coarse cloth, serges, and woollen galloons. Never in his whole life had M. Geborand bestowed alms on any poor wretch. After the delivery of that sermon, it was observed that he gave a sou every Sunday to the poor old beggar-women at the door of the cathedral. There were six of them to share it. One day the Bishop caught sight of him in the act of bestowing this charity, and said to his sister, with a smile, "There is M. Geborand purchasing paradise for a sou."

When it was a question of charity, he was not to be rebuffed even by a refusal, and on such occasions he gave utterance to remarks which induced reflection. Once he was begging for the poor in a drawing-room of the town; there was present the Marquis de Champtercier, a wealthy and avaricious old man, who contrived to be, at one and the same time, an ultra-royalist and an ultra-Voltairian. This variety of man has actually existed. When the Bishop came to him, he touched his arm, "You must give me something, M. le Marquis." The Marquis turned round and answered dryly, "I have poor people of my own, Monseigneur." "Give them to me," replied the Bishop.

One day he preached the following sermon in the cathedral:—

"My very dear brethren, my good friends, there are thirteen hundred and twenty thousand peasants' dwellings in France which have but three openings; eighteen hundred and seventeen thousand hovels which have but two openings, the door and one window; and three hundred and forty-six thousand cabins besides which have but one opening, the door. And this arises from a thing which is called the tax on doors and windows. Just put poor families, old women and little children, in those buildings, and behold the fevers and maladies which result! Alas! God gives air to men; the law sells it to them. I do not blame the law, but I bless God. In the department of the Isere, in the Var, in the two departments of the Alpes, the Hautes, and the Basses, the peasants have not even wheelbarrows; they transport their manure on the backs of men; they have no candles, and they burn resinous sticks, and bits of rope dipped in pitch. That is the state of affairs throughout the whole of the hilly country of Dauphine. They make bread for six months at one time; they bake it with dried cow-dung. In the winter they break this bread up with an axe, and they soak it for twenty-four hours, in order to render it eatable. My brethren, have pity! behold the suffering on all sides of you!"

Born a Provencal, he easily familiarized himself with the dialect of the south. He said, "En be! moussu, ses sage?" as in lower Languedoc; "Onte anaras passa?" as in the Basses-Alpes; "Puerte un bouen moutu embe un bouen fromage grase," as in upper Dauphine. This pleased the people extremely, and contributed not a little to win him access to all spirits. He was perfectly at home in the thatched cottage and in the mountains. He understood how to say the grandest things in the most vulgar of idioms. As he spoke all tongues, he entered into all hearts.

Moreover, he was the same towards people of the world and towards the lower classes. He condemned nothing in haste and without taking circumstances into account. He said, "Examine the road over which the fault has passed."

Being, as he described himself with a smile, an ex-sinner, he had none of the asperities of austerity, and he professed, with a good deal of distinctness, and without the frown of the ferociously virtuous, a doctrine which may be summed up as follows:—

"Man has upon him his flesh, which is at once his burden and his temptation. He drags it with him and yields to it. He must watch it, check it, repress it, and obey it only at the last extremity. There may be some fault even in this obedience; but the fault thus committed is venial; it is a fall, but a fall on the knees which may terminate in prayer.

"To be a saint is the exception; to be an upright man is the rule. Err, fall, sin if you will, but be upright.

"The least possible sin is the law of man. No sin at all is the dream of the angel. All which is terrestrial is subject to sin. Sin is a gravitation."

When he saw everyone exclaiming very loudly, and growing angry very quickly, "Oh! oh!" he said, with a smile; "to all appearance, this is a great crime which all the world commits. These are hypocrisies which have taken fright, and are in haste to make protest and to put themselves under shelter."

He was indulgent towards women and poor people, on whom the burden of human society rest. He said, "The faults of women, of children, of the feeble, the indigent, and the ignorant, are the fault of the husbands, the fathers, the masters, the strong, the rich, and the wise."

He said, moreover, "Teach those who are ignorant as many things as possible; society is culpable, in that it does not afford instruction gratis; it is responsible for the night which it produces. This soul is full of shadow; sin is therein committed. The guilty one is not the person who has committed the sin, but the person who has created the shadow."

It will be perceived that he had a peculiar manner of his own of judging things: I suspect that he obtained it from the Gospel.

One day he heard a criminal case, which was in preparation and on the point of trial, discussed in a drawing-room. A wretched man, being at the end of his resources, had coined counterfeit money, out of love for a woman, and for the child which he had had by her. Counterfeiting was still punishable with death at that epoch. The woman had been arrested in the act of passing the first false piece made by the man. She was held, but there were no proofs except against her. She alone could accuse her lover, and destroy him by her confession. She denied; they insisted. She persisted in her denial. Thereupon an idea occurred to the attorney for the crown. He invented an infidelity on the part of the lover, and succeeded, by means of fragments of letters cunningly presented, in persuading the unfortunate woman that she had a rival, and that the man was deceiving her. Thereupon, exasperated by jealousy, she denounced her lover, confessed all, proved all.

The man was ruined. He was shortly to be tried at Aix with his accomplice. They were relating the matter, and each one was expressing enthusiasm over the cleverness of the magistrate. By bringing jealousy into play, he had caused the truth to burst forth in wrath, he had educed the justice of revenge. The Bishop listened to all this in silence. When they had finished, he inquired,—

"Where are this man and woman to be tried?"

"At the Court of Assizes."

He went on, "And where will the advocate of the crown be tried?"

A tragic event occurred at D—A man was condemned to death for murder. He was a wretched fellow, not exactly educated, not exactly ignorant, who had been a mountebank at fairs, and a writer for the public. The town took a great interest in the trial. On the eve of the day fixed for the execution of the condemned man, the chaplain of the prison fell ill. A priest was needed to attend the criminal in his last moments. They sent for the cure. It seems that he refused to come, saying, "That is no affair of mine. I have nothing to do with that unpleasant task, and with that mountebank: I, too, am ill; and besides, it is not my place." This reply was reported to the Bishop, who said, "Monsieur le Cure is right: it is not his place; it is mine."

He went instantly to the prison, descended to the cell of the "mountebank," called him by name, took him by the hand, and spoke to him. He passed the entire day with him, forgetful of food and sleep, praying to God for the soul of the condemned man, and praying the condemned man for his own. He told him the best truths, which are also the most simple. He was father, brother, friend; he was bishop only to bless. He taught him everything, encouraged and consoled him. The man was on the point of dying in despair. Death was an abyss to him. As he stood trembling on its mournful brink, he recoiled with horror. He was not sufficiently ignorant to be absolutely indifferent. His condemnation, which had been a profound shock, had, in a manner, broken through, here and there, that wall which separates us from the mystery of things, and which we call life. He gazed incessantly beyond this world through these fatal breaches, and beheld only darkness. The Bishop made him see light.

On the following day, when they came to fetch the unhappy wretch, the Bishop was still there. He followed him, and exhibited himself to the eyes of the crowd in his purple camail and with his episcopal cross upon his neck, side by side with the criminal bound with cords.

He mounted the tumbril with him, he mounted the scaffold with him. The sufferer, who had been so gloomy and cast down on the preceding day, was radiant. He felt that his soul was reconciled, and he hoped in God. The Bishop embraced him, and at the moment when the knife was about to fall, he said to him: "God raises from the dead him whom man slays; he whom his brothers have rejected finds his Father once more. Pray, believe, enter into life: the Father is there." When he descended from the scaffold, there was something in his look which made the people draw aside to let him pass. They did not know which was most worthy of admiration, his pallor or his serenity. On his return to the humble dwelling, which he designated, with a smile, as his palace, he said to his sister, "I have just officiated pontifically."

Since the most sublime things are often those which are the least understood, there were people in the town who said, when commenting on this conduct of the Bishop, "It is affectation."

This, however, was a remark which was confined to the drawing-rooms. The populace, which perceives no jest in holy deeds, was touched, and admired him.

As for the Bishop, it was a shock to him to have beheld the guillotine, and it was a long time before he recovered from it.

In fact, when the scaffold is there, all erected and prepared, it has something about it which produces hallucination. One may feel a certain indifference to the death penalty, one may refrain from pronouncing upon it, from saying yes or no, so long as one has not seen a guillotine with one's own eyes: but if one encounters one of them, the shock is violent; one is forced to decide, and to take part for or against. Some admire it, like de Maistre; others execrate it, like Beccaria. The guillotine is the concretion of the law; it is called vindicte; it is not neutral, and it does not permit you to remain neutral. He who sees it shivers with the most mysterious of shivers. All social problems erect their interrogation point around this chopping-knife. The scaffold is a vision. The scaffold is not a piece of carpentry; the scaffold is not a machine; the scaffold is not an inert bit of mechanism constructed of wood, iron and cords.

It seems as though it were a being, possessed of I know not what sombre initiative; one would say that this piece of carpenter's work saw, that this machine heard, that this mechanism understood, that this wood, this iron, and these cords were possessed of will. In the frightful meditation into which its presence casts the soul the scaffold appears in terrible guise, and as though taking part in what is going on. The scaffold is the accomplice of the executioner; it devours, it eats flesh, it drinks blood; the scaffold is a sort of monster fabricated by the judge and the carpenter, a spectre which seems to live with a horrible vitality composed of all the death which it has inflicted.

Therefore, the impression was terrible and profound; on the day following the execution, and on many succeeding days, the Bishop appeared to be crushed. The almost violent serenity of the funereal moment had disappeared; the phantom of social justice tormented him. He, who generally returned from all his deeds with a radiant satisfaction, seemed to be reproaching himself. At times he talked to himself, and stammered lugubrious monologues in a low voice. This is one which his sister overheard one evening and preserved: "I did not think that it was so monstrous. It is wrong to become absorbed in the divine law to such a degree as not to perceive human law. Death belongs to God alone. By what right do men touch that unknown thing?"

In course of time these impressions weakened and probably vanished. Nevertheless, it was observed that the Bishop thenceforth avoided passing the place of execution.

M. Myriel could be summoned at any hour to the bedside of the sick and dying. He did not ignore the fact that therein lay his greatest duty and his greatest labor. Widowed and orphaned families had no need to summon him; he came of his own accord. He understood how to sit down and hold his peace for long hours beside the man who had lost the wife of his love, of the mother who had lost her child. As he knew the moment for silence he knew also the moment for speech. Oh, admirable consoler! He sought not to efface sorrow by forgetfulness, but to magnify and dignify it by hope. He said:—

"Have a care of the manner in which you turn towards the dead. Think not of that which perishes. Gaze steadily. You will perceive the living light of your well-beloved dead in the depths of heaven." He knew that faith is wholesome. He sought to counsel and calm the despairing man, by pointing out to him the resigned man, and to transform the grief which gazes upon a grave by showing him the grief which fixes its gaze upon a star.

CHAPTER V

MONSEIGNEUR BIENVENU MADE HIS
CASSOCKS LAST TOO LONG

The private life of M. Myriel was filled with the same thoughts as his public life. The voluntary poverty in which the Bishop of D—lived, would have been a solemn and charming sight for any one who could have viewed it close at hand.

Like all old men, and like the majority of thinkers, he slept little. This brief slumber was profound. In the morning he meditated for an hour, then he said his mass, either at the cathedral or in his own house. His mass said, he broke his fast on rye bread dipped in the milk of his own cows. Then he set to work.

A Bishop is a very busy man: he must every day receive the secretary of the bishopric, who is generally a canon, and nearly every day his vicars-general. He has congregations to reprove, privileges to grant, a whole ecclesiastical library to examine,—prayer-books, diocesan catechisms, books of hours, etc.,—charges to write, sermons to authorize, cures and mayors to reconcile, a clerical correspondence, an administrative correspondence; on one side the State, on the other the Holy See; and a thousand matters of business.

What time was left to him, after these thousand details of business, and his offices and his breviary, he bestowed first on the necessitous, the sick, and the afflicted; the time which was left to him from the afflicted, the sick, and the necessitous, he devoted to work. Sometimes he dug in his garden; again, he read or wrote. He had but one word for both these kinds of toil; he called them gardening. "The mind is a garden," said he.

Towards mid-day, when the weather was fine, he went forth and took a stroll in the country or in town, often entering lowly dwellings. He was seen walking alone, buried in his own thoughts, his eyes cast down, supporting himself on his long cane, clad in his wadded purple garment of silk, which was very warm, wearing purple stockings inside his coarse shoes, and surmounted by a flat hat which allowed three golden tassels of large bullion to droop from its three points.

It was a perfect festival wherever he appeared. One would have said that his presence had something warming and luminous about it. The children and the old people came out to the doorsteps for the Bishop as for the sun. He bestowed his blessing, and they blessed him. They pointed out his house to any one who was in need of anything.

Here and there he halted, accosted the little boys and girls, and smiled upon the mothers. He visited the poor so long as he had any money; when he no longer had any, he visited the rich.

As he made his cassocks last a long while, and did not wish to have it noticed, he never went out in the town without his wadded purple cloak. This inconvenienced him somewhat in summer.

On his return, he dined. The dinner resembled his breakfast.

At half-past eight in the evening he supped with his sister, Madame Magloire standing behind them and serving them at table. Nothing could be more frugal than this repast. If, however, the Bishop had one of his cures to supper, Madame Magloire took advantage of the opportunity to serve Monseigneur with some excellent fish from the lake, or with some fine game from the mountains. Every cure furnished the pretext for a good meal: the Bishop did not interfere. With that exception, his ordinary diet consisted only of vegetables boiled in water, and oil soup. Thus it was said in the town, when the Bishop does not indulge in the cheer of a cure, he indulges in the cheer of a trappist.

After supper he conversed for half an hour with Mademoiselle Baptistine and Madame Magloire; then he retired to his own room and set to writing, sometimes on loose sheets, and again on the margin of some folio. He was a man of letters and rather learned. He left behind him five or six very curious manuscripts; among others, a dissertation on this verse in Genesis, In the beginning, the spirit of God floated upon the waters. With this verse he compares three texts: the Arabic verse which says, The winds of God blew; Flavius Josephus who says, A wind from above was precipitated upon the earth; and finally, the Chaldaic paraphrase of Onkelos, which renders it, A wind coming from God blew upon the face of the waters. In another dissertation, he examines the theological works of Hugo, Bishop of Ptolemais, great-grand-uncle to the writer of this book, and establishes the fact, that to this bishop must be attributed the divers little works published during the last century, under the pseudonym of Barleycourt.

Sometimes, in the midst of his reading, no matter what the book might be which he had in his hand, he would suddenly fall into a profound meditation, whence he only emerged to write a few lines on the pages of the volume itself. These lines have often no connection whatever with the book which contains them. We now have under our eyes a note written by him on the margin of a quarto entitled Correspondence of Lord Germain with Generals Clinton, Cornwallis, and the Admirals on the American station. Versailles, Poincot, book-seller; and Paris, Pissot, bookseller, Quai des Augustins.

Here is the note:—

"Oh, you who are!

"Ecclesiastes calls you the All-powerful; the Maccabees call you the Creator; the Epistle to the Ephesians calls you liberty; Baruch calls you Immensity; the Psalms call you Wisdom and Truth; John calls you Light; the Books of Kings call you Lord; Exodus calls you Providence; Leviticus, Sanctity; Esdras, Justice; the creation calls you God; man calls you Father;

but Solomon calls you Compassion, and that is the most beautiful of all your names."

Toward nine o'clock in the evening the two women retired and betook themselves to their chambers on the first floor, leaving him alone until morning on the ground floor.

It is necessary that we should, in this place, give an exact idea of the dwelling of the Bishop of D—

CHAPTER VI

WHO GUARDED HIS HOUSE FOR HIM

The house in which he lived consisted, as we have said, of a ground floor, and one story above; three rooms on the ground floor, three chambers on the first, and an attic above. Behind the house was a garden, a quarter of an acre in extent. The two women occupied the first floor; the Bishop was lodged below. The first room, opening on the street, served him as dining-room, the second was his bedroom, and the third his oratory. There was no exit possible from this oratory, except by passing through the bedroom, nor from the bedroom, without passing through the dining-room. At the end of the suite, in the oratory, there was a detached alcove with a bed, for use in cases of hospitality. The Bishop offered this bed to country curates whom business or the requirements of their parishes brought to D——

The pharmacy of the hospital, a small building which had been added to the house, and abutted on the garden, had been transformed into a kitchen and cellar. In addition to this, there was in the garden a stable, which had formerly been the kitchen of the hospital, and in which the Bishop kept two cows. No matter what the quantity of milk they gave, he invariably sent half of it every morning to the sick people in the hospital. "I am paying my tithes," he said.

His bedroom was tolerably large, and rather difficult to warm in bad weather. As wood is extremely dear at D——, he hit upon the idea of having a compartment of boards constructed in the cow-shed. Here he passed his evenings during seasons of severe cold: he called it his winter salon.

In this winter salon, as in the dining-room, there was no other furniture than a square table in white wood, and four straw-seated chairs. In addition to this the dining-room was ornamented with an antique sideboard, painted pink, in water colors. Out of a similar sideboard, properly draped with white napery and imitation lace, the Bishop had constructed the altar which decorated his oratory.

His wealthy penitents and the sainted women of D—had more than once assessed themselves to raise the money for a new altar for Monseigneur's oratory; on each occasion he had taken the money and had given it to the poor. "The most beautiful of altars," he said, "is the soul of an unhappy creature consoled and thanking God."

In his oratory there were two straw prie-Dieu, and there was an arm-chair, also in straw, in his bedroom. When, by chance, he received seven or eight persons at one time, the prefect, or the general, or the staff of the regiment in garrison, or several pupils from the little seminary, the chairs had to be fetched from the winter salon in the stable, the prie-Dieu from the oratory, and the arm-chair from the bedroom: in this way as many as eleven chairs could be collected for the visitors. A room was dismantled for each new guest.

It sometimes happened that there were twelve in the party; the Bishop then relieved the embarrassment of the situation by standing in front of the chimney if it was winter, or by strolling in the garden if it was summer.

There was still another chair in the detached alcove, but the straw was half gone from it, and it had but three legs, so that it was of service only when propped against the wall. Mademoiselle Baptistine had also in her own room a very large easy-chair of wood, which had formerly been gilded, and which was covered with flowered pekin; but they had been obliged to hoist this bergere up to the first story through the window, as the staircase was too narrow; it could not, therefore, be reckoned among the possibilities in the way of furniture.

Mademoiselle Baptistine's ambition had been to be able to purchase a set of drawing-room furniture in yellow Utrecht velvet, stamped with a rose pattern, and with mahogany in swan's neck style, with a sofa. But this would have cost five hundred francs at least, and in view of the fact that she had only been able to lay by forty-two francs and ten sous for this purpose in the course of five years, she had ended by renouncing the idea. However, who is there who has attained his ideal?

Nothing is more easy to present to the imagination than the Bishop's bedchamber. A glazed door opened on the garden; opposite this was the bed,—a hospital bed of iron, with a canopy of green serge; in the shadow of the bed, behind a curtain, were the utensils of the toilet, which still betrayed the elegant habits of the man of the world: there were two doors, one near the chimney, opening into the oratory; the other near the bookcase, opening into the dining-room. The bookcase was a large cupboard with glass doors filled with books; the chimney was of wood painted to represent marble, and habitually without fire. In the chimney stood a pair of firedogs of iron, ornamented above with two garlanded vases, and flutings which had formerly been silvered with silver leaf, which was a sort of episcopal luxury; above the chimney-piece hung a crucifix of copper, with the silver worn off, fixed on a background of threadbare velvet in a wooden frame from which the gilding had fallen; near the glass door a large table with an inkstand, loaded with a confusion of papers and with huge volumes; before the table an arm-chair of straw; in front of the bed a prie-Dieu, borrowed from the oratory.

Two portraits in oval frames were fastened to the wall on each side of the bed. Small gilt inscriptions on the plain surface of the cloth at the side of these figures indicated that the portraits represented, one the Abbe of Chaliot, bishop of Saint Claude; the other, the Abbe Tourteau, vicar-general of Agde, abbe of Grand-Champ, order of Citeaux, diocese of Chartres. When the Bishop succeeded to this apartment, after the hospital patients, he had found these portraits there, and had left them. They were priests, and probably donors—two reasons for respecting them. All that he knew about these two persons was, that they had been appointed by the king, the one to his bishopric, the other to his benefice, on the same day, the 27th of April, 1785. Madame Magloire having taken the pictures down to dust, the Bishop had discovered these particulars written in whitish ink on a little square of paper, yellowed by time, and attached to the back of the portrait of the Abbe of Grand-Champ with four wafers.

At his window he had an antique curtain of a coarse woollen stuff, which finally became so old, that, in order to avoid the expense of a new one, Madame Magloire was forced to take a large seam in the very middle of it. This seam took the form of a cross. The Bishop often called attention to it: "How delightful that is!" he said.

All the rooms in the house, without exception, those on the ground floor as well as those on the first floor, were white-washed, which is a fashion in barracks and hospitals.

However, in their latter years, Madame Magloire discovered beneath the paper which had been washed over, paintings, ornamenting the apartment of Mademoiselle Baptistine, as we shall see further on. Before becoming a hospital, this house had been the ancient parliament house of the Bourgeois. Hence this decoration. The chambers were paved in red bricks, which were washed every week, with straw mats in front of all the beds. Altogether, this dwelling, which was attended to by the two women, was exquisitely clean from top to bottom. This was the sole luxury which the Bishop permitted. He said, "That takes nothing from the poor."

It must be confessed, however, that he still retained from his former possessions six silver knives and forks and a soup-ladle, which Madame Magloire contemplated every day with delight, as they glistened splendidly upon the coarse linen cloth. And since we are now painting the Bishop of D—as he was in reality, we must add that he had said more than once, "I find it difficult to renounce eating from silver dishes."

To this silverware must be added two large candlesticks of massive silver, which he had inherited from a great-aunt. These candlesticks held two wax candles, and usually figured on the Bishop's chimney-piece. When he had any one to dinner, Madame Magloire lighted the two candles and set the candlesticks on the table.

In the Bishop's own chamber, at the head of his bed, there was a small cupboard, in which Madame Magloire locked up the six silver knives and forks and the big spoon every night. But it is necessary to add, that the key was never removed.

The garden, which had been rather spoiled by the ugly buildings which we have mentioned, was composed of four alleys in cross-form, radiating from a tank. Another walk made the circuit of the garden, and skirted the white wall which enclosed it. These alleys left behind them four square plots rimmed with box. In three of these, Madame Magloire cultivated vegetables; in the fourth, the Bishop had planted some flowers; here and there stood a few fruit-trees. Madame Magloire had once remarked, with a sort of gentle malice: "Monseigneur, you who turn everything to account, have, nevertheless, one useless plot. It would be better to grow salads there than bouquets." "Madame Magloire," retorted the Bishop, "you are mistaken. The beautiful is as useful as the useful." He added after a pause, "More so, perhaps."

This plot, consisting of three or four beds, occupied the Bishop almost as much as did his books. He liked to pass an hour or two there, trimming, hoeing, and making holes here and there in the earth, into which he dropped seeds. He was not as hostile to insects as a gardener could have wished to see him. Moreover, he made no pretensions to botany; he ignored groups and consistency; he made not the slightest effort to decide between Tournefort and the natural method; he took part neither with the buds against the cotyledons, nor with Jussieu against Linnaeus. He did not study plants; he loved flowers. He respected learned men greatly; he respected the ignorant still more; and, without ever failing in these two respects, he watered his flower-beds every summer evening with a tin watering-pot painted green.

The house had not a single door which could be locked. The door of the dining-room, which, as we have said, opened directly on the cathedral square, had formerly been ornamented with locks and bolts like the door of a prison. The Bishop had had all this ironwork removed, and this door was never fastened, either by night or by day, with anything except the latch. All that the first passerby had to do at any hour, was to give it a push. At first, the two women had been very much tried by this door, which was never fastened, but Monsieur de D——had said to them, "Have bolts put on your rooms, if that will please you." They had ended by sharing his confidence, or by at least acting as though they shared it. Madame Magloire alone had frights from time to time. As for the Bishop, his thought can be found explained, or at least indicated, in the three lines which he wrote on the margin of a Bible, "This is the shade of difference: the door of the physician should never be shut, the door of the priest should always be open."

On another book, entitled Philosophy of the Medical Science, he had written this other note: "Am not I a physician like them? I also have my patients, and then, too, I have some whom I call my unfortunates."

Again he wrote: "Do not inquire the name of him who asks a shelter of you. The very man who is embarrassed by his name is the one who needs shelter."

It chanced that a worthy cure, I know not whether it was the cure of Couloubroux or the cure of Pompierry, took it into his head to ask him one day, probably at the instigation of Madame Magloire, whether Monsieur was sure that he was not committing an indiscretion, to a certain extent, in leaving his door unfastened day and night, at the mercy of any one who should choose to enter, and whether, in short, he did not fear lest some misfortune might occur in a house so little guarded. The Bishop touched his shoulder, with gentle gravity, and said to him, "Nisi Dominus custodierit domum, in vanum vigilant qui custodiunt eam," Unless the Lord guard the house, in vain do they watch who guard it.

Then he spoke of something else.

He was fond of saying, "There is a bravery of the priest as well as the bravery of a colonel of dragoons,—only," he added, "ours must be tranquil."

CHAPTER VII

CRAVATTE

It is here that a fact falls naturally into place, which we must not omit, because it is one of the sort which show us best what sort of a man the Bishop of D—was.

After the destruction of the band of Gaspard Bes, who had infested the gorges of Ollioules, one of his lieutenants, Cravatte, took refuge in the mountains. He concealed himself for some time with his bandits, the remnant of Gaspard Bes's troop, in the county of Nice; then he made his way to Piedmont, and suddenly reappeared in France, in the vicinity of Barcelonette. He was first seen at Jauziers, then at Tuiles. He hid himself in the caverns of the Joug-de-l'Aigle, and thence he descended towards the hamlets and villages through the ravines of Ubaye and Ubayette.

He even pushed as far as Embrun, entered the cathedral one night, and despoiled the sacristy. His highway robberies laid waste the country-side. The gendarmes were set on his track, but in vain. He always escaped; sometimes he resisted by main force. He was a bold wretch. In the midst of all this terror the Bishop arrived. He was making his circuit to Chastelar. The mayor came to meet him, and urged him to retrace his steps. Cravatte was in possession of the mountains as far as Arche, and beyond; there was danger even with an escort; it merely exposed three or four unfortunate gendarmes to no purpose.

"Therefore," said the Bishop, "I intend to go without escort."

"You do not really mean that, Monseigneur!" exclaimed the mayor.

"I do mean it so thoroughly that I absolutely refuse any gendarmes, and shall set out in an hour."

"Set out?"

"Set out."

"Alone?"

"Alone."

"Monseigneur, you will not do that!"

"There exists yonder in the mountains," said the Bishop, "a tiny community no bigger than that, which I have not seen for three years. They are my good friends, those gentle and honest shepherds. They own one goat out of every thirty that they tend. They make very pretty woollen cords of various colors, and they play the mountain airs on little flutes with six holes. They need to be told of the good God now and then. What would they say to a bishop who was afraid? What would they say if I did not go?"

"But the brigands, Monseigneur?"

"Hold," said the Bishop, "I must think of that. You are right. I may meet them. They, too, need to be told of the good God."

"But, Monseigneur, there is a band of them! A flock of wolves!"

"Monsieur le maire, it may be that it is of this very flock of wolves that Jesus has constituted me the shepherd. Who knows the ways of Providence?"

"They will rob you, Monseigneur."

"I have nothing."

"They will kill you."

"An old goodman of a priest, who passes along mumbling his prayers? Bah! To what purpose?"

"Oh, mon Dieu! what if you should meet them!"

"I should beg alms of them for my poor."

"Do not go, Monseigneur. In the name of Heaven! You are risking your life!"

"Monsieur le maire," said the Bishop, "is that really all? I am not in the world to guard my own life, but to guard souls."

They had to allow him to do as he pleased. He set out, accompanied only by a child who offered to serve as a guide. His obstinacy was bruited about the country-side, and caused great consternation.

He would take neither his sister nor Madame Magloire. He traversed the mountain on mule-back, encountered no one, and arrived safe and sound at the residence of his "good friends," the shepherds. He remained there for a fortnight, preaching, administering the sacrament, teaching, exhorting. When the time of his departure approached, he resolved to chant a Te Deum pontifically. He mentioned it to the cure. But what was to be done? There were no episcopal ornaments. They could only place at his disposal a wretched village sacristy, with a few ancient chasubles of threadbare damask adorned with imitation lace.

"Bah!" said the Bishop. "Let us announce our Te Deum from the pulpit, nevertheless, Monsieur le Cure. Things will arrange themselves."

They instituted a search in the churches of the neighborhood. All the magnificence of these humble parishes combined would not have sufficed to clothe the chorister of a cathedral properly.

While they were thus embarrassed, a large chest was brought and deposited in the presbytery for the Bishop, by two unknown horsemen, who departed on the instant. The chest was opened; it contained a cope of cloth of gold, a mitre ornamented with diamonds, an archbishop's cross, a magnificent crosier,—all the pontifical vestments which had been stolen a month previously from the treasury of Notre Dame d'Embrun. In the chest was a paper, on which these words were written, "From Cravatte to Monseigneur Bienvenu."

"Did not I say that things would come right of themselves?" said the Bishop. Then he added, with a smile, "To him who contents himself with the surplice of a curate, God sends the cope of an archbishop."

"Monseigneur," murmured the cure, throwing back his head with a smile. "God—or the Devil."

The Bishop looked steadily at the cure, and repeated with authority, "God!"

49

When he returned to Chastelar, the people came out to stare at him as at a curiosity, all along the road. At the priest's house in Chastelar he rejoined Mademoiselle Baptistine and Madame Magloire, who were waiting for him, and he said to his sister: "Well! was I in the right? The poor priest went to his poor mountaineers with empty hands, and he returns from them with his hands full. I set out bearing only my faith in God; I have brought back the treasure of a cathedral."

That evening, before he went to bed, he said again: "Let us never fear robbers nor murderers. Those are dangers from without, petty dangers. Let us fear ourselves. Prejudices are the real robbers; vices are the real murderers. The great dangers lie within ourselves. What matters it what threatens our head or our purse! Let us think only of that which threatens our soul."

Then, turning to his sister: "Sister, never a precaution on the part of the priest, against his fellow-man. That which his fellow does, God permits. Let us confine ourselves to prayer, when we think that a danger is approaching us. Let us pray, not for ourselves, but that our brother may not fall into sin on our account."

However, such incidents were rare in his life. We relate those of which we know; but generally he passed his life in doing the same things at the same moment. One month of his year resembled one hour of his day.

As to what became of "the treasure" of the cathedral of Embrun, we should be embarrassed by any inquiry in that direction. It consisted of very handsome things, very tempting things, and things which were very well adapted to be stolen for the benefit of the unfortunate. Stolen they had already been elsewhere. Half of the adventure was completed; it only remained to impart a new direction to the theft, and to cause it to take a short trip in the direction of the poor. However, we make no assertions on this point. Only, a rather obscure note was found among the Bishop's papers, which may bear some relation to this matter, and which is couched in these terms, "The question is, to decide whether this should be turned over to the cathedral or to the hospital."

CHAPTER VIII

PHILOSOPHY AFTER DRINKING

The senator above mentioned was a clever man, who had made his own way, heedless of those things which present obstacles, and which are called conscience, sworn faith, justice, duty: he had marched straight to his goal, without once flinching in the line of his advancement and his interest. He was an old attorney, softened by success; not a bad man by any means, who rendered all the small services in his power to his sons, his sons-in-law, his relations, and even to his friends, having wisely seized upon, in life, good sides, good opportunities, good windfalls. Everything else seemed to him very stupid. He was intelligent, and just sufficiently educated to think himself a disciple of Epicurus; while he was, in reality, only a product of Pigault-Lebrun. He laughed willingly and pleasantly over infinite and eternal things, and at the "Crotchets of that good old fellow the Bishop." He even sometimes laughed at him with an amiable authority in the presence of M. Myriel himself, who listened to him.

On some semi-official occasion or other, I do not recollect what, Count*** [this senator] and M. Myriel were to dine with the prefect. At dessert, the senator, who was slightly exhilarated, though still perfectly dignified, exclaimed:—

"Egad, Bishop, let's have a discussion. It is hard for a senator and a bishop to look at each other without winking. We are two augurs. I am going to make a confession to you. I have a philosophy of my own."

"And you are right," replied the Bishop. "As one makes one's philosophy, so one lies on it. You are on the bed of purple, senator."

The senator was encouraged, and went on:—

"Let us be good fellows."

"Good devils even," said the Bishop.

"I declare to you," continued the senator, "that the Marquis d'Argens, Pyrrhon, Hobbes, and M. Naigeon are no rascals. I have all the philosophers in my library gilded on the edges."

"Like yourself, Count," interposed the Bishop.

The senator resumed:—

"I hate Diderot; he is an ideologist, a declaimer, and a revolutionist, a believer in God at bottom, and more bigoted than Voltaire. Voltaire made sport of Needham, and he was wrong, for Needham's eels prove that God is useless. A drop of vinegar in a spoonful of flour paste supplies the fiat lux. Suppose the drop to be larger and the spoonful bigger; you have the world. Man is the eel. Then what is the good of the Eternal Father? The Jehovah hypothesis tires me, Bishop. It is good for nothing but to produce shallow people, whose reasoning is hollow. Down with that great All, which torments me! Hurrah for Zero which leaves me in peace! Between you and me, and in order to empty my sack, and make confession to my pastor, as it behooves me to do, I will admit to you that I have good sense. I am not enthusiastic over your Jesus, who preaches renunciation and sacrifice to the last extremity. 'Tis the counsel of an avaricious man to beggars. Renunciation; why? Sacrifice; to what end? I do not see one wolf immolating himself for the happiness of another wolf. Let us stick to nature, then. We are at the top; let us have a superior philosophy. What is the advantage of being at the top, if one sees no further than the end of other people's noses? Let us live merrily. Life is all. That man has another future elsewhere, on high, below, anywhere, I don't believe; not one single word of it. Ah! sacrifice and renunciation are recommended to me; I must take heed to everything I do; I must cudgel my brains over good and evil, over the just and the unjust, over the fas and the nefas. Why? Because I shall have to render an account of my actions. When? After death. What a fine dream! After my death it will be a very clever person who can catch me. Have a handful of dust seized by a shadow-hand, if you can. Let us tell the truth, we who are initiated, and who have raised the veil of Isis: there is no such thing as either good or evil; there is vegetation. Let us seek the real. Let us get to the bottom of it. Let us go into it thoroughly. What the deuce! let us go to the bottom of it! We must scent out the truth; dig in the earth for it, and seize it. Then it gives you exquisite joys. Then you grow strong, and you laugh. I am square on the bottom, I am. Immortality, Bishop, is a chance, a waiting for dead men's shoes. Ah! what a charming promise! trust to it, if you like! What a fine lot Adam has! We are souls, and we shall be angels, with blue wings on our shoulder-blades. Do come to my assistance: is it not Tertullian who says that the blessed shall travel from star to star? Very well. We shall be the grasshoppers of the stars. And then, besides, we shall see God. Ta, ta, ta! What twaddle all these paradises are! God is a nonsensical monster. I would not say that in the Moniteur, egad! but I may whisper it among friends. Inter pocula. To sacrifice the world to paradise is to let slip the prey for the shadow. Be the dupe of the infinite! I'm not such a fool. I am a nought. I call myself Monsieur le Comte Nought, senator. Did I exist before my birth? No. Shall I exist after death? No. What am I? A little dust collected in an organism. What am I to do on this earth? The choice rests with me: suffer or enjoy. Whither will suffering lead me? To nothingness; but I shall have suffered. Whither will enjoyment lead me? To nothingness; but I shall have enjoyed myself. My choice is made. One must eat or be eaten. I shall eat. It is better to be the tooth than the grass. Such is my wisdom. After which, go whither I push thee, the grave-digger is there; the Pantheon for some of us: all falls into the great hole. End. Finis. Total liquidation. This is the vanishing-point. Death is death, believe me. I laugh at the idea of there being any one who has anything to tell me on that subject. Fables of nurses; bugaboo for children; Jehovah for men. No; our tomorrow is the night. Beyond the tomb there is nothing but equal nothingness. You have been Sardanapalus, you have been Vincent de Paul—it makes no difference. That is the truth. Then live your life, above all things. Make use of your *I* while you have it. In truth, Bishop, I tell you that I have a philosophy of my own, and I have my philosophers. I don't let myself be taken in with that nonsense. Of course, there must be something for those who are down,—for the barefooted beggars, knife-grinders, and miserable wretches. Legends, chimeras, the soul, immortality, paradise, the stars, are provided for them to swallow. They gobble it down. They spread it on their dry bread. He who has nothing else has the good. God. That is the least he can have. I oppose no objection to that; but I reserve Monsieur Naigeon for myself. The good God is good for the populace."

The Bishop clapped his hands.

"That's talking!" he exclaimed. "What an excellent and really marvellous thing is this materialism! Not every one who wants it can have it. Ah! when one does have it, one is no longer a dupe, one does not stupidly allow one's self to be exiled like Cato, nor stoned like Stephen, nor burned alive like Jeanne d'Arc. Those who have succeeded in procuring this admirable materialism have the joy of feeling themselves irresponsible, and of thinking that they can devour everything without uneasiness,— places, sinecures, dignities, power, whether well or ill acquired, lucrative recantations, useful treacheries, savory capitulations of conscience,— and that they shall enter the tomb with their digestion accomplished. How agreeable that is! I do not say that with reference to you, senator. Nevertheless, it is impossible for me to refrain from congratulating you. You great lords have, so you say, a philosophy of your own, and for yourselves, which is exquisite, refined, accessible to the rich alone, good for all sauces, and which seasons the voluptuousness of life admirably. This philosophy has been extracted from the depths, and unearthed by special seekers. But you are good-natured princes, and you do not think it a bad thing that belief in the good God should constitute the philosophy of the people, very much as the goose stuffed with chestnuts is the truffled turkey of the poor."

CHAPTER IX

THE BROTHER AS DEPICTED
BY THE SISTER

In order to furnish an idea of the private establishment of the Bishop of D——, and of the manner in which those two sainted women subordinated their actions, their thoughts, their feminine instincts even, which are easily alarmed, to the habits and purposes of the Bishop, without his even taking the trouble of speaking in order to explain them, we cannot do better than transcribe in this place a letter from Mademoiselle Baptistine to Madame the Vicomtess de Boischevron, the friend of her childhood. This letter is in our possession.

D——, Dec. 16, 18——.

MY GOOD MADAM: Not a day passes without our speaking of you. It is our established custom; but there is another reason besides. Just imagine, while washing and dusting the ceilings and walls, Madam Magloire has made some discoveries; now our two chambers hung with antique paper whitewashed over, would not discredit a chateau in the style of yours. Madam Magloire has pulled off all the paper. There were things beneath. My drawing-room, which contains no furniture, and which we use for spreading out the linen after washing, is fifteen feet in height, eighteen square, with a ceiling which was formerly painted and gilded, and with beams, as in yours. This was covered with a cloth while this was the hospital. And the woodwork was of the era of our grandmothers. But my room is the one you ought to see. Madam Magloire has discovered, under at least ten thicknesses of paper pasted on top, some paintings, which without being good are very tolerable. The subject is Telemachus being knighted by Minerva in some gardens, the name of which escapes me. In short, where the Roman ladies repaired on one single night. What shall I say to you? I have Romans, and Roman ladies [here occurs an illegible word], and the whole train. Madam Magloire has cleaned it all off; this summer she is going to have some small injuries repaired, and the whole revarnished, and my chamber will be a regular museum. She has also found in a corner of the attic two wooden pier-tables of ancient fashion. They asked us two crowns of six francs each to regild them, but it is much better to give the money to the poor; and they are very ugly besides, and I should much prefer a round table of mahogany.

I am always very happy. My brother is so good. He gives all he has to the poor and sick. We are very much cramped. The country is trying in the winter, and we really must do something for those who are in need. We are almost comfortably lighted and warmed. You see that these are great treats.

My brother has ways of his own. When he talks, he says that a bishop ought to be so. Just imagine! the door of our house is never fastened. Whoever chooses to enter finds himself at once in my brother's room. He fears nothing, even at night. That is his sort of bravery, he says.

He does not wish me or Madame Magloire feel any fear for him. He exposes himself to all sorts of dangers, and he does not like to have us even seem to notice it. One must know how to understand him.

He goes out in the rain, he walks in the water, he travels in winter. He fears neither suspicious roads nor dangerous encounters, nor night.

Last year he went quite alone into a country of robbers. He would not take us. He was absent for a fortnight. On his return nothing had happened to him; he was thought to be dead, but was perfectly well, and said, "This is the way I have been robbed!" And then he opened a trunk full of jewels, all the jewels of the cathedral of Embrun, which the thieves had given him.

When he returned on that occasion, I could not refrain from scolding him a little, taking care, however, not to speak except when the carriage was making a noise, so that no one might hear me.

At first I used to say to myself, "There are no dangers which will stop him; he is terrible." Now I have ended by getting used to it. I make a sign to Madam Magloire that she is not to oppose him. He risks himself as he sees fit. I carry off Madam Magloire, I enter my chamber, I pray for him and fall asleep. I am at ease, because I know that if anything were to happen to him, it would be the end of me. I should go to the good God with my brother and my bishop. It has cost Madam Magloire more trouble than it did me to accustom herself to what she terms his imprudences. But now the habit has been acquired. We pray together, we tremble together, and we fall asleep. If the devil were to enter this house, he would be allowed to do so. After all, what is there for us to fear in this house? There is always some one with us who is stronger than we. The devil may pass through it, but the good God dwells here.

This suffices me. My brother has no longer any need of saying a word to me. I understand him without his speaking, and we abandon ourselves to the care of Providence. That is the way one has to do with a man who possesses grandeur of soul.

I have interrogated my brother with regard to the information which you desire on the subject of the Faux family. You are aware that he knows everything, and that he has memories, because he is still a very good royalist. They really are a very ancient Norman family of the generalship of Caen. Five hundred years ago there was a Raoul de Faux, a Jean de Faux, and a Thomas de Faux, who were gentlemen, and one of whom was a seigneur de Rochefort. The last was Guy-Etienne-Alexandre, and was commander of a regiment, and something in the light horse of Bretagne. His daughter, Marie-Louise, married Adrien-Charles de Gramont, son of the Duke Louis de Gramont, peer of France, colonel of the French guards, and lieutenant-general of the army. It is written Faux, Fauq, and Faoucq.

Good Madame, recommend us to the prayers of your sainted relative, Monsieur the Cardinal. As for your dear Sylvanie, she has done well in not wasting the few moments which she passes with you in writing to me. She is well, works as you would wish, and loves me.

That is all that I desire. The souvenir which she sent through you reached me safely, and it makes me very happy. My health is not so very bad, and yet I grow thinner every day. Farewell; my paper is at an end, and this forces me to leave you. A thousand good wishes.

BAPTISTINE.

P.S. Your grand nephew is charming. Do you know that he will soon be five years old? Yesterday he saw some one riding by on horseback who had on knee-caps, and he said, "What has he got on his knees?" He is a charming child! His little brother is dragging an old broom about the room, like a carriage, and saying, "Hu!"

As will be perceived from this letter, these two women understood how to mould themselves to the Bishop's ways with that special feminine genius which comprehends the man better than he comprehends himself. The Bishop of D——, in spite of the gentle and candid air which never deserted him, sometimes did things that were grand, bold, and magnificent, without seeming to have even a suspicion of the fact. They trembled, but they let him alone. Sometimes Madame Magloire essayed a remonstrance in advance, but never at the time, nor afterwards. They never interfered with him by so much as a word or sign, in any action once entered upon. At certain moments, without his having occasion to mention it, when he was not even conscious of it himself in all probability, so perfect was his simplicity, they vaguely felt that he was acting as a bishop; then they were nothing more than two shadows in the house. They served him passively; and if obedience consisted in disappearing, they disappeared. They understood, with an admirable delicacy of instinct, that certain cares may be put under constraint. Thus, even when believing him to be in peril, they understood, I will not say his thought, but his nature, to such a degree that they no longer watched over him. They confided him to God.

Moreover, Baptistine said, as we have just read, that her brother's end would prove her own. Madame Magloire did not say this, but she knew it.

CHAPTER X

THE BISHOP IN THE PRESENCE OF AN UNKNOWN LIGHT

At an epoch a little later than the date of the letter cited in the preceding pages, he did a thing which, if the whole town was to be believed, was even more hazardous than his trip across the mountains infested with bandits.

In the country near D—a man lived quite alone. This man, we will state at once, was a former member of the Convention. His name was G—

Member of the Convention, G—was mentioned with a sort of horror in the little world of D—A member of the Convention—can you imagine such a thing? That existed from the time when people called each other thou, and when they said "citizen." This man was almost a monster. He had not voted for the death of the king, but almost. He was a quasi-regicide. He had been a terrible man. How did it happen that such a man had not been brought before a provost's court, on the return of the legitimate princes? They need not have cut off his head, if you please; clemency must be exercised, agreed; but a good banishment for life. An example, in short, etc. Besides, he was an atheist, like all the rest of those people. Gossip of the geese about the vulture.

Was G—a vulture after all? Yes; if he were to be judged by the element of ferocity in this solitude of his. As he had not voted for the death of the king, he had not been included in the decrees of exile, and had been able to remain in France.

He dwelt at a distance of three-quarters of an hour from the city, far from any hamlet, far from any road, in some hidden turn of a very wild valley, no one knew exactly where. He had there, it was said, a sort of field, a hole, a lair. There were no neighbors, not even passers-by. Since he had dwelt in that valley, the path which led thither had disappeared under a growth of grass. The locality was spoken of as though it had been the dwelling of a hangman.

Nevertheless, the Bishop meditated on the subject, and from time to time he gazed at the horizon at a point where a clump of trees marked the valley of the former member of the Convention, and he said, "There is a soul yonder which is lonely."

And he added, deep in his own mind, "I owe him a visit."

But, let us avow it, this idea, which seemed natural at the first blush, appeared to him after a moment's reflection, as strange, impossible, and almost repulsive. For, at bottom, he shared the general impression, and the old member of the Convention inspired him, without his being clearly conscious of the fact himself, with that sentiment which borders on hate, and which is so well expressed by the word estrangement.

Still, should the scab of the sheep cause the shepherd to recoil? No. But what a sheep!

The good Bishop was perplexed. Sometimes he set out in that direction; then he returned.

Finally, the rumor one day spread through the town that a sort of young shepherd, who served the member of the Convention in his hovel, had come in quest of a doctor; that the old wretch was dying, that paralysis was gaining on him, and that he would not live over night.— "Thank God!" some added.

The Bishop took his staff, put on his cloak, on account of his too threadbare cassock, as we have mentioned, and because of the evening breeze which was sure to rise soon, and set out.

The sun was setting, and had almost touched the horizon when the Bishop arrived at the excommunicated spot. With a certain beating of the heart, he recognized the fact that he was near the lair. He strode over a ditch, leaped a hedge, made his way through a fence of dead boughs, entered a neglected paddock, took a few steps with a good deal of boldness, and suddenly, at the extremity of the waste land, and behind lofty brambles, he caught sight of the cavern.

It was a very low hut, poor, small, and clean, with a vine nailed against the outside.

Near the door, in an old wheel-chair, the arm-chair of the peasants, there was a white-haired man, smiling at the sun.

Near the seated man stood a young boy, the shepherd lad. He was offering the old man a jar of milk.

While the Bishop was watching him, the old man spoke: "Thank you," he said, "I need nothing." And his smile quitted the sun to rest upon the child.

The Bishop stepped forward. At the sound which he made in walking, the old man turned his head, and his face expressed the sum total of the surprise which a man can still feel after a long life.

"This is the first time since I have been here," said he, "that any one has entered here. Who are you, sir?"

The Bishop answered:—

"My name is Bienvenu Myriel."

"Bienvenu Myriel? I have heard that name. Are you the man whom the people call Monseigneur Welcome?"

"I am."

The old man resumed with a half-smile

"In that case, you are my bishop?"

"Something of that sort."

"Enter, sir."

The member of the Convention extended his hand to the Bishop, but the Bishop did not take it. The Bishop confined himself to the remark:—

"I am pleased to see that I have been misinformed. You certainly do not seem to me to be ill."

"Monsieur," replied the old man, "I am going to recover."

He paused, and then said:—

"I shall die three hours hence."

Then he continued:—

"I am something of a doctor; I know in what fashion the last hour draws on. Yesterday, only my feet were cold; today, the chill has ascended to my knees; now I feel it mounting to my waist; when it reaches the heart, I shall stop. The sun is beautiful, is it not? I had myself wheeled out here to take a last look at things. You can talk to me; it does not fatigue me. You have done well to come and look at a man who is on the point of death. It is well that there should be witnesses at that moment. One has one's caprices; I should have liked to last until the dawn, but I know that I shall hardly live three hours. It will be night then. What does it matter, after all? Dying is a simple affair. One has no need of the light for that. So be it. I shall die by starlight."

The old man turned to the shepherd lad:—

"Go to thy bed; thou wert awake all last night; thou art tired."

The child entered the hut.

The old man followed him with his eyes, and added, as though speaking to himself:—

"I shall die while he sleeps. The two slumbers may be good neighbors."

The Bishop was not touched as it seems that he should have been. He did not think he discerned God in this manner of dying; let us say the whole, for these petty contradictions of great hearts must be indicated like the rest: he, who on occasion, was so fond of laughing at "His Grace," was rather shocked at not being addressed as Monseigneur, and he was almost tempted to retort "citizen." He was assailed by a fancy for peevish familiarity, common enough to doctors and priests, but which was not habitual with him. This man, after all, this member of the Convention, this representative of the people, had been one of the powerful ones of the earth; for the first time in his life, probably, the Bishop felt in a mood to be severe.

Meanwhile, the member of the Convention had been surveying him with a modest cordiality, in which one could have distinguished, possibly, that humility which is so fitting when one is on the verge of returning to dust.

The Bishop, on his side, although he generally restrained his curiosity, which, in his opinion, bordered on a fault, could not refrain from examining the member of the Convention with an attention which, as it did not have its course in sympathy, would have served his conscience as a matter of reproach, in connection with any other man. A member of the Convention produced on him somewhat the effect of being outside the pale of the law, even of the law of charity. G——, calm, his body almost upright, his voice vibrating, was one of those octogenarians who form the subject of astonishment to the physiologist. The Revolution had many of these men, proportioned to the epoch. In this old man one was conscious of a man put to the proof. Though so near to his end, he preserved all the gestures of health. In his clear glance, in his firm tone, in the robust movement of his shoulders, there was something calculated to disconcert death. Azrael, the Mohammedan angel of the sepulchre, would have turned back, and thought that he had mistaken the door. G——seemed to be dying because he willed it so. There was freedom in his agony. His legs alone were motionless. It was there that the shadows held him fast. His feet were cold and dead, but his head survived with all the power of life, and seemed full of light. G——, at this solemn moment, resembled the king in that tale of the Orient who was flesh above and marble below.

There was a stone there. The Bishop sat down. The exordium was abrupt.

"I congratulate you," said he, in the tone which one uses for a reprimand. "You did not vote for the death of the king, after all."

64

The old member of the Convention did not appear to notice the bitter meaning underlying the words "after all." He replied. The smile had quite disappeared from his face.

"Do not congratulate me too much, sir. I did vote for the death of the tyrant."

It was the tone of austerity answering the tone of severity.

"What do you mean to say?" resumed the Bishop.

"I mean to say that man has a tyrant,—ignorance. I voted for the death of that tyrant. That tyrant engendered royalty, which is authority falsely understood, while science is authority rightly understood. Man should be governed only by science."

"And conscience," added the Bishop.

"It is the same thing. Conscience is the quantity of innate science which we have within us."

Monseigneur Bienvenu listened in some astonishment to this language, which was very new to him.

The member of the Convention resumed:—

"So far as Louis XVI. was concerned, I said 'no.' I did not think that I had the right to kill a man; but I felt it my duty to exterminate evil. I voted the end of the tyrant, that is to say, the end of prostitution for woman, the end of slavery for man, the end of night for the child. In voting for the Republic, I voted for that. I voted for fraternity, concord, the dawn. I have aided in the overthrow of prejudices and errors. The crumbling away of prejudices and errors causes light. We have caused the fall of the old world, and the old world, that vase of miseries, has become, through its upsetting upon the human race, an urn of joy."

"Mixed joy," said the Bishop.

"You may say troubled joy, and today, after that fatal return of the past, which is called 1814, joy which has disappeared! Alas! The work was incomplete, I admit: we demolished the ancient regime in deeds; we were not able to suppress it entirely in ideas. To destroy abuses is not sufficient; customs must be modified. The mill is there no longer; the wind is still there."

"You have demolished. It may be of use to demolish, but I distrust a demolition complicated with wrath."

"Right has its wrath, Bishop; and the wrath of right is an element of progress. In any case, and in spite of whatever may be said, the French Revolution is the most important step of the human race since the advent of Christ. Incomplete, it may be, but sublime. It set free all the unknown social quantities; it softened spirits, it calmed, appeased, enlightened; it caused the waves of civilization to flow over the earth. It was a good thing. The French Revolution is the consecration of humanity."

The Bishop could not refrain from murmuring:—

"Yes? '93!"

The member of the Convention straightened himself up in his chair with an almost lugubrious solemnity, and exclaimed, so far as a dying man is capable of exclamation:—

"Ah, there you go; '93! I was expecting that word. A cloud had been forming for the space of fifteen hundred years; at the end of fifteen hundred years it burst. You are putting the thunderbolt on its trial."

The Bishop felt, without, perhaps, confessing it, that something within him had suffered extinction. Nevertheless, he put a good face on the matter. He replied:—

"The judge speaks in the name of justice; the priest speaks in the name of pity, which is nothing but a more lofty justice. A thunderbolt should commit no error." And he added, regarding the member of the Convention steadily the while, "Louis XVII.?"

The conventionary stretched forth his hand and grasped the Bishop's arm.

"Louis XVII.! let us see. For whom do you mourn? is it for the innocent child? very good; in that case I mourn with you. Is it for the royal child? I demand time for reflection. To me, the brother of Cartouche, an innocent child who was hung up by the armpits in the Place de Greve, until death

66

ensued, for the sole crime of having been the brother of Cartouche, is no less painful than the grandson of Louis XV., an innocent child, martyred in the tower of the Temple, for the sole crime of having been grandson of Louis XV."

"Monsieur," said the Bishop, "I like not this conjunction of names."

"Cartouche? Louis XV.? To which of the two do you object?"

A momentary silence ensued. The Bishop almost regretted having come, and yet he felt vaguely and strangely shaken.

The conventionary resumed:—

"Ah, Monsieur Priest, you love not the crudities of the true. Christ loved them. He seized a rod and cleared out the Temple. His scourge, full of lightnings, was a harsh speaker of truths. When he cried, 'Sinite parvulos,' he made no distinction between the little children. It would not have embarrassed him to bring together the Dauphin of Barabbas and the Dauphin of Herod. Innocence, Monsieur, is its own crown. Innocence has no need to be a highness. It is as august in rags as in fleurs de lys."

"That is true," said the Bishop in a low voice.

"I persist," continued the conventionary G—"You have mentioned Louis XVII. to me. Let us come to an understanding. Shall we weep for all the innocent, all martyrs, all children, the lowly as well as the exalted? I agree to that. But in that case, as I have told you, we must go back further than '93, and our tears must begin before Louis XVII. I will weep with you over the children of kings, provided that you will weep with me over the children of the people."

"I weep for all," said the Bishop.

"Equally!" exclaimed conventionary G—; "and if the balance must incline, let it be on the side of the people. They have been suffering longer."

Another silence ensued. The conventionary was the first to break it. He raised himself on one elbow, took a bit of his cheek between his thumb and his forefinger, as one does mechanically when one interrogates and judges, and appealed to the Bishop with a gaze full of all the forces of the death agony. It was almost an explosion.

"Yes, sir, the people have been suffering a long while. And hold! that is not all, either; why have you just questioned me and talked to me about Louis XVII.? I know you not. Ever since I have been in these parts I have dwelt in this enclosure alone, never setting foot outside, and seeing no one but that child who helps me. Your name has reached me in a confused manner, it is true, and very badly pronounced, I must admit; but that signifies nothing: clever men have so many ways of imposing on that honest goodman, the people. By the way, I did not hear the sound of your carriage; you have left it yonder, behind the coppice at the fork of the roads, no doubt. I do not know you, I tell you. You have told me that you are the Bishop; but that affords me no information as to your moral personality. In short, I repeat my question. Who are you? You are a bishop; that is to say, a prince of the church, one of those gilded men with heraldic bearings and revenues, who have vast prebends,—the bishopric of D—fifteen thousand francs settled income, ten thousand in perquisites; total, twenty-five thousand francs,—who have kitchens, who have liveries, who make good cheer, who eat moor-hens on Friday, who strut about, a lackey before, a lackey behind, in a gala coach, and who have palaces, and who roll in their carriages in the name of Jesus Christ who went barefoot! You are a prelate,—revenues, palace, horses, servants, good table, all the sensualities of life; you have this like the rest, and like the rest, you enjoy it; it is well; but this says either too much or too little; this does not enlighten me upon the intrinsic and essential value of the man who comes with the probable intention of bringing wisdom to me. To whom do I speak? Who are you?"

The Bishop hung his head and replied, "Vermis sum—I am a worm."

"A worm of the earth in a carriage?" growled the conventionary.

It was the conventionary's turn to be arrogant, and the Bishop's to be humble.

The Bishop resumed mildly:—

"So be it, sir. But explain to me how my carriage, which is a few paces off behind the trees yonder, how my good table and the moorhens which I eat on Friday, how my twenty-five thousand francs income, how my palace and my lackeys prove that clemency is not a duty, and that '93 was not inexorable."

The conventionary passed his hand across his brow, as though to sweep away a cloud.

"Before replying to you," he said, "I beseech you to pardon me. I have just committed a wrong, sir. You are at my house, you are my guest, I owe you courtesy. You discuss my ideas, and it becomes me to confine myself to combating your arguments. Your riches and your pleasures are advantages which I hold over you in the debate; but good taste dictates that I shall not make use of them. I promise you to make no use of them in the future."

"I thank you," said the Bishop.

G—resumed.

"Let us return to the explanation which you have asked of me. Where were we? What were you saying to me? That '93 was inexorable?"

"Inexorable; yes," said the Bishop. "What think you of Marat clapping his hands at the guillotine?"

"What think you of Bossuet chanting the Te Deum over the dragonnades?"

The retort was a harsh one, but it attained its mark with the directness of a point of steel. The Bishop quivered under it; no reply occurred to him; but he was offended by this mode of alluding to Bossuet. The best of minds will have their fetiches, and they sometimes feel vaguely wounded by the want of respect of logic.

The conventionary began to pant; the asthma of the agony which is mingled with the last breaths interrupted his voice; still, there was a perfect lucidity of soul in his eyes. He went on:—

"Let me say a few words more in this and that direction; I am willing. Apart from the Revolution, which, taken as a whole, is an immense human affirmation, '93 is, alas! a rejoinder. You think it inexorable, sir; but what of the whole monarchy, sir? Carrier is a bandit; but what name do you give to Montrevel? Fouquier-Tainville is a rascal; but what is your opinion as to Lamoignon-Baville? Maillard is terrible; but Saulx-Tavannes, if you please? Duchene senior is ferocious; but what epithet will you allow me for the elder Letellier? Jourdan-Coupe-Tete is a monster; but not so great a one as M. the Marquis de Louvois. Sir, sir, I am sorry for Marie Antoinette, archduchess and queen; but I am also sorry for that poor Huguenot woman, who, in 1685, under Louis the Great, sir, while with a nursing infant, was bound, naked to the waist, to a stake, and the child kept at a distance; her breast swelled with milk and her heart with anguish; the little one, hungry and pale, beheld that breast and cried and agonized; the executioner said to the woman, a mother and a nurse, 'Abjure!' giving her her choice between the death of her infant and the death of her conscience. What say you to that torture of Tantalus as applied to a mother? Bear this well in mind sir: the French Revolution had its reasons for existence; its wrath will be absolved by the future; its result is the world made better. From its most terrible blows there comes forth a caress for the human race. I abridge, I stop, I have too much the advantage; moreover, I am dying."

And ceasing to gaze at the Bishop, the conventionary concluded his thoughts in these tranquil words:—

"Yes, the brutalities of progress are called revolutions. When they are over, this fact is recognized,—that the human race has been treated harshly, but that it has progressed."

The conventionary doubted not that he had successively conquered all the inmost intrenchments of the Bishop. One remained, however, and from this intrenchment, the last resource of Monseigneur Bienvenu's resistance, came forth this reply, wherein appeared nearly all the harshness of the beginning:—

"Progress should believe in God. Good cannot have an impious servitor. He who is an atheist is but a bad leader for the human race."

The former representative of the people made no reply. He was seized with a fit of trembling. He looked towards heaven, and in his glance a tear gathered slowly. When the eyelid was full, the tear trickled down his livid cheek, and he said, almost in a stammer, quite low, and to himself, while his eyes were plunged in the depths:—

"O thou! O ideal! Thou alone existest!"

The Bishop experienced an indescribable shock.

After a pause, the old man raised a finger heavenward and said:—

"The infinite is. He is there. If the infinite had no person, person would be without limit; it would not be infinite; in other words, it would not exist. There is, then, an *I*. That *I* of the infinite is God."

The dying man had pronounced these last words in a loud voice, and with the shiver of ecstasy, as though he beheld some one. When he had spoken, his eyes closed. The effort had exhausted him. It was evident that he had just lived through in a moment the few hours which had been left to him. That which he had said brought him nearer to him who is in death. The supreme moment was approaching.

The Bishop understood this; time pressed; it was as a priest that he had come: from extreme coldness he had passed by degrees to extreme emotion; he gazed at those closed eyes, he took that wrinkled, aged and ice-cold hand in his, and bent over the dying man.

"This hour is the hour of God. Do you not think that it would be regrettable if we had met in vain?"

The conventionary opened his eyes again. A gravity mingled with gloom was imprinted on his countenance.

"Bishop," said he, with a slowness which probably arose more from his dignity of soul than from the failing of his strength, "I have passed my life in meditation, study, and contemplation. I was sixty years of age when my country called me and commanded me to concern myself with its affairs. I obeyed. Abuses existed, I combated them; tyrannies existed, I destroyed them; rights and principles existed, I proclaimed and confessed them. Our territory was invaded, I defended it; France was

71

menaced, I offered my breast. I was not rich; I am poor. I have been one of the masters of the state; the vaults of the treasury were encumbered with specie to such a degree that we were forced to shore up the walls, which were on the point of bursting beneath the weight of gold and silver; I dined in Dead Tree Street, at twenty-two sous. I have succored the oppressed, I have comforted the suffering. I tore the cloth from the altar, it is true; but it was to bind up the wounds of my country. I have always upheld the march forward of the human race, forward towards the light, and I have sometimes resisted progress without pity. I have, when the occasion offered, protected my own adversaries, men of your profession. And there is at Peteghem, in Flanders, at the very spot where the Merovingian kings had their summer palace, a convent of Urbanists, the Abbey of Sainte Claire en Beaulieu, which I saved in 1793. I have done my duty according to my powers, and all the good that I was able. After which, I was hunted down, pursued, persecuted, blackened, jeered at, scorned, cursed, proscribed. For many years past, I with my white hair have been conscious that many people think they have the right to despise me; to the poor ignorant masses I present the visage of one damned. And I accept this isolation of hatred, without hating any one myself. Now I am eighty-six years old; I am on the point of death. What is it that you have come to ask of me?"

"Your blessing," said the Bishop.

And he knelt down.

When the Bishop raised his head again, the face of the conventionary had become august. He had just expired.

The Bishop returned home, deeply absorbed in thoughts which cannot be known to us. He passed the whole night in prayer. On the following morning some bold and curious persons attempted to speak to him about member of the Convention G——; he contented himself with pointing heavenward.

From that moment he redoubled his tenderness and brotherly feeling towards all children and sufferers.

72

Any allusion to "that old wretch of a G—" caused him to fall into a singular preoccupation. No one could say that the passage of that soul before his, and the reflection of that grand conscience upon his, did not count for something in his approach to perfection.

This "pastoral visit" naturally furnished an occasion for a murmur of comment in all the little local coteries.

"Was the bedside of such a dying man as that the proper place for a bishop? There was evidently no conversion to be expected. All those revolutionists are backsliders. Then why go there? What was there to be seen there? He must have been very curious indeed to see a soul carried off by the devil."

One day a dowager of the impertinent variety who thinks herself spiritual, addressed this sally to him, "Monseigneur, people are inquiring when Your Greatness will receive the red cap!"—"Oh! oh! that's a coarse color," replied the Bishop. "It is lucky that those who despise it in a cap revere it in a hat."

CHAPTER XI

A RESTRICTION

We should incur a great risk of deceiving ourselves, were we to conclude from this that Monseigneur Welcome was "a philosophical bishop," or a "patriotic cure." His meeting, which may almost be designated as his union, with conventionary G——, left behind it in his mind a sort of astonishment, which rendered him still more gentle. That is all.

Although Monseigneur Bienvenu was far from being a politician, this is, perhaps, the place to indicate very briefly what his attitude was in the events of that epoch, supposing that Monseigneur Bienvenu ever dreamed of having an attitude.

Let us, then, go back a few years.

Some time after the elevation of M. Myriel to the episcopate, the Emperor had made him a baron of the Empire, in company with many other bishops. The arrest of the Pope took place, as every one knows, on the night of the 5th to the 6th of July, 1809; on this occasion, M. Myriel was summoned by Napoleon to the synod of the bishops of France and Italy convened at Paris. This synod was held at Notre-Dame, and assembled for the first time on the 15th of June, 1811, under the presidency of Cardinal Fesch. M. Myriel was one of the ninety-five bishops who attended it. But he was present only at one sitting and at three or four private conferences. Bishop of a mountain diocese, living so very close to nature, in rusticity and deprivation, it appeared that he imported among these eminent personages, ideas which altered the temperature of the assembly. He very soon returned to D—He was interrogated as to this speedy return, and he replied: "I embarrassed them. The outside air penetrated to them through me. I produced on them the effect of an open door."

On another occasion he said, "What would you have? Those gentlemen are princes. I am only a poor peasant bishop."

The fact is that he displeased them. Among other strange things, it is said that he chanced to remark one evening, when he found himself at the house of one of his most notable colleagues: "What beautiful clocks! What beautiful carpets! What beautiful liveries! They must be a great trouble. I would not have all those superfluities, crying incessantly in my ears: 'There are people who are hungry! There are people who are cold! There are poor people! There are poor people!'"

Let us remark, by the way, that the hatred of luxury is not an intelligent hatred. This hatred would involve the hatred of the arts. Nevertheless, in churchmen, luxury is wrong, except in connection with representations and ceremonies. It seems to reveal habits which have very little that is charitable about them. An opulent priest is a contradiction. The priest must keep close to the poor. Now, can one come in contact incessantly night and day with all this distress, all these misfortunes, and this poverty, without having about one's own person a little of that misery, like the dust of labor? Is it possible to imagine a man near a brazier who is not warm? Can one imagine a workman who is working near a furnace, and who has neither a singed hair, nor blackened nails, nor a drop of sweat, nor a speck of ashes on his face? The first proof of charity in the priest, in the bishop especially, is poverty.

This is, no doubt, what the Bishop of D—thought.

It must not be supposed, however, that he shared what we call the "ideas of the century" on certain delicate points. He took very little part in the theological quarrels of the moment, and maintained silence on questions in which Church and State were implicated; but if he had been strongly pressed, it seems that he would have been found to be an ultramontane rather than a gallican. Since we are making a portrait, and since we do not wish to conceal anything, we are forced to add that he was glacial towards Napoleon in his decline. Beginning with 1813, he gave in his adherence to or applauded all hostile manifestations. He refused to see him, as he passed through on his return from the island of Elba, and he abstained from ordering public prayers for the Emperor in his diocese during the Hundred Days.

Besides his sister, Mademoiselle Baptistine, he had two brothers, one a general, the other a prefect. He wrote to both with tolerable frequency. He was harsh for a time towards the former, because, holding a command in Provence at the epoch of the disembarkation at Cannes, the general had put himself at the head of twelve hundred men and had pursued the Emperor as though the latter had been a person whom one is desirous of allowing to escape. His correspondence with the other brother, the ex-prefect, a fine, worthy man who lived in retirement at Paris, Rue Cassette, remained more affectionate.

Thus Monseigneur Bienvenu also had his hour of party spirit, his hour of bitterness, his cloud. The shadow of the passions of the moment traversed this grand and gentle spirit occupied with eternal things. Certainly, such a man would have done well not to entertain any political opinions. Let there be no mistake as to our meaning: we are not confounding what is called "political opinions" with the grand aspiration for progress, with the sublime faith, patriotic, democratic, humane, which in our day should be the very foundation of every generous intellect. Without going deeply into questions which are only indirectly connected with the subject of this book, we will simply say this: It would have been well if Monseigneur Bienvenu had not been a Royalist, and if his glance had never been, for a single instant, turned away from that serene contemplation in which is distinctly discernible, above the fictions and the hatreds of this world, above the stormy vicissitudes of human things, the beaming of those three pure radiances, truth, justice, and charity.

While admitting that it was not for a political office that God created Monseigneur Welcome, we should have understood and admired his protest in the name of right and liberty, his proud opposition, his just but perilous resistance to the all-powerful Napoleon. But that which pleases us in people who are rising pleases us less in the case of people who are falling. We only love the fray so long as there is danger, and in any case, the combatants of the first hour have alone the right to be the exterminators of the last. He who has not been a stubborn accuser in prosperity should hold his peace in the face of ruin. The denunciator of success is the only legitimate executioner of the fall. As for us, when Providence intervenes and strikes, we let it work. 1812 commenced to disarm us. In 1813 the cowardly breach of silence of that taciturn legislative body, emboldened by catastrophe, possessed only traits which aroused indignation. And it was a crime to applaud, in 1814, in the presence of those marshals who betrayed; in the presence of that senate which passed from one dunghill to another, insulting after having deified; in the presence of that idolatry which was loosing its footing and spitting on its idol,—it was a duty to turn aside the head. In 1815, when the supreme disasters filled the air, when France was seized with a shiver at their sinister approach, when Waterloo could be dimly discerned opening before Napoleon, the mournful acclamation of the army and the people to the condemned of destiny had nothing laughable in it, and, after making all allowance for the despot, a heart like that of the Bishop of D——, ought not perhaps to have failed to recognize the august and touching features presented by the embrace of a great nation and a great man on the brink of the abyss.

With this exception, he was in all things just, true, equitable, intelligent, humble and dignified, beneficent and kindly, which is only another sort of benevolence. He was a priest, a sage, and a man. It must be admitted, that even in the political views with which we have just reproached him, and which we are disposed to judge almost with severity, he was tolerant and easy, more so, perhaps, than we who are speaking here. The porter of the town-hall had been placed there by the Emperor. He was an old non-commissioned officer of the old guard, a member of the Legion of Honor at Austerlitz, as much of a Bonapartist as the eagle. This poor fellow occasionally let slip inconsiderate remarks, which the law then stigmatized as seditious speeches. After the imperial profile disappeared from the Legion of Honor, he never dressed himself in his regimentals, as he said, so that he should not be obliged to wear his cross. He had himself devoutly removed the imperial effigy from the cross which Napoleon had given him; this made a hole, and he would not put anything in its place. "I will die," he said, "rather than wear the three frogs upon my heart!" He liked to scoff aloud at Louis XVIII. "The gouty old creature in English gaiters!" he said; "let him take himself off to Prussia with that queue of his." He was happy to combine in the same imprecation the two things which he most detested, Prussia and England. He did it so often that he lost his place. There he was, turned out of the house, with his wife and children, and without bread. The Bishop sent for him, reproved him gently, and appointed him beadle in the cathedral.

In the course of nine years Monseigneur Bienvenu had, by dint of holy deeds and gentle manners, filled the town of D—with a sort of tender and filial reverence. Even his conduct towards Napoleon had been accepted and tacitly pardoned, as it were, by the people, the good and weakly flock who adored their emperor, but loved their bishop.

CHAPTER XII

THE SOLITUDE OF
MONSEIGNEUR WELCOME

A bishop is almost always surrounded by a full squadron of little abbes, just as a general is by a covey of young officers. This is what that charming Saint Francois de Sales calls somewhere "les pretres blancs-becs," callow priests. Every career has its aspirants, who form a train for those who have attained eminence in it. There is no power which has not its dependents. There is no fortune which has not its court. The seekers of the future eddy around the splendid present. Every metropolis has its staff of officials. Every bishop who possesses the least influence has about him his patrol of cherubim from the seminary, which goes the round, and maintains good order in the episcopal palace, and mounts guard over monseigneur's smile. To please a bishop is equivalent to getting one's foot in the stirrup for a sub-diaconate. It is necessary to walk one's path discreetly; the apostleship does not disdain the canonship.

Just as there are bigwigs elsewhere, there are big mitres in the Church. These are the bishops who stand well at Court, who are rich, well endowed, skilful, accepted by the world, who know how to pray, no doubt, but who know also how to beg, who feel little scruple at making a whole diocese dance attendance in their person, who are connecting links between the sacristy and diplomacy, who are abbes rather than priests, prelates rather than bishops. Happy those who approach them! Being persons of influence, they create a shower about them, upon the assiduous and the favored, and upon all the young men who understand the art of pleasing, of large parishes, prebends, archidiaconates, chaplaincies, and cathedral posts, while awaiting episcopal honors. As they advance themselves, they cause their satellites to progress also; it is a whole solar system on the march. Their radiance casts a gleam of purple over their suite. Their prosperity is crumbled up behind the scenes, into nice little promotions. The larger the diocese of the patron, the fatter the curacy for the favorite. And then, there is Rome. A bishop who understands how to become an archbishop, an archbishop who knows how to become a cardinal, carries you with him as conclavist; you enter a court of papal jurisdiction, you receive the pallium, and behold! you are an auditor, then a papal chamberlain, then monsignor, and from a Grace to an Eminence is only a step, and between the Eminence and the Holiness there is but the smoke of a ballot. Every skull-cap may dream of the tiara. The priest is nowadays the only man who can become a king in a regular manner; and what a king! the supreme king. Then what a nursery of aspirations is a seminary! How many blushing choristers, how many youthful abbes bear on their heads Perrette's pot of milk! Who knows how easy it is for ambition to call itself vocation? in good faith, perchance, and deceiving itself, devotee that it is.

Monseigneur Bienvenu, poor, humble, retiring, was not accounted among the big mitres. This was plain from the complete absence of young priests about him. We have seen that he "did not take" in Paris. Not a single future dreamed of engrafting itself on this solitary old man. Not a single sprouting ambition committed the folly of putting forth its foliage in his shadow. His canons and grand-vicars were good old men, rather vulgar like himself, walled up like him in this diocese, without exit to a cardinalship, and who resembled their bishop, with this difference, that they were finished and he was completed. The impossibility of growing great under Monseigneur Bienvenu was so well understood, that no sooner had the young men whom he ordained left the seminary than they got themselves recommended to the archbishops of Aix or of Auch, and went off in a great hurry. For, in short, we repeat it, men wish to be pushed. A saint who dwells in a paroxysm of abnegation is a dangerous neighbor; he might communicate to you, by contagion, an incurable poverty, an anchylosis of the joints, which are useful in advancement, and in short, more renunciation than you desire; and this infectious virtue is avoided. Hence the isolation of Monseigneur Bienvenu. We live in the midst of a gloomy society. Success; that is the lesson which falls drop by drop from the slope of corruption.

Be it said in passing, that success is a very hideous thing. Its false resemblance to merit deceives men. For the masses, success has almost the same profile as supremacy. Success, that Menaechmus of talent, has one dupe,—history. Juvenal and Tacitus alone grumble at it. In our day, a philosophy which is almost official has entered into its service, wears the livery of success, and performs the service of its antechamber. Succeed: theory. Prosperity argues capacity. Win in the lottery, and behold! you are a clever man. He who triumphs is venerated. Be born with a silver spoon in your mouth! everything lies in that. Be lucky, and you will have all the rest; be happy, and people will think you great. Outside of five or six immense exceptions, which compose the splendor of a century, contemporary admiration is nothing but short-sightedness. Gilding is gold. It does no harm to be the first arrival by pure chance, so long as you do arrive. The common herd is an old Narcissus who adores himself, and who applauds the vulgar herd. That enormous ability by virtue of which one is Moses, Aeschylus, Dante, Michael Angelo, or Napoleon, the multitude awards on the spot, and by acclamation, to whomsoever attains his object, in whatsoever it may consist. Let a notary transfigure himself into a deputy: let a false Corneille compose Tiridate; let a eunuch come to possess a harem; let a military Prudhomme accidentally win the decisive battle of an epoch; let an apothecary invent cardboard shoe-soles for the army of the Sambre-and-Meuse, and construct for himself, out of this cardboard, sold as leather, four hundred thousand francs of income; let a pork-packer espouse usury, and cause it to bring forth seven or eight millions, of which he is the father and of which it is the mother; let a preacher become a bishop by force of his nasal drawl; let the steward of a fine family be so rich on retiring from service that he is made minister of finances,—and men call that Genius, just as they call the face of Mousqueton Beauty, and the mien of Claude Majesty. With the constellations of space they confound the stars of the abyss which are made in the soft mire of the puddle by the feet of ducks.

CHAPTER XIII

WHAT HE BELIEVED

We are not obliged to sound the Bishop of D—on the score of orthodoxy. In the presence of such a soul we feel ourselves in no mood but respect. The conscience of the just man should be accepted on his word. Moreover, certain natures being given, we admit the possible development of all beauties of human virtue in a belief that differs from our own.

What did he think of this dogma, or of that mystery? These secrets of the inner tribunal of the conscience are known only to the tomb, where souls enter naked. The point on which we are certain is, that the difficulties of faith never resolved themselves into hypocrisy in his case. No decay is possible to the diamond. He believed to the extent of his powers. "Credo in Patrem," he often exclaimed. Moreover, he drew from good works that amount of satisfaction which suffices to the conscience, and which whispers to a man, "Thou art with God!"

The point which we consider it our duty to note is, that outside of and beyond his faith, as it were, the Bishop possessed an excess of love. In was in that quarter, *quia multum amavit*,—because he loved much—that he was regarded as vulnerable by "serious men," "grave persons" and "reasonable people"; favorite locutions of our sad world where egotism takes its word of command from pedantry. What was this excess of love? It was a serene benevolence which overflowed men, as we have already pointed out, and which, on occasion, extended even to things. He lived without disdain. He was indulgent towards God's creation. Every man, even the best, has within him a thoughtless harshness which he reserves for animals. The Bishop of D—had none of that harshness, which is peculiar to many priests, nevertheless. He did not go as far as the Brahmin, but he seemed to have weighed this saying of Ecclesiastes: "Who knoweth whither the soul of the animal goeth?" Hideousness of aspect, deformity of instinct, troubled him not, and did not arouse his indignation. He was touched, almost softened by them. It seemed as though he went thoughtfully away to seek beyond the bounds of life which is apparent, the cause, the explanation, or the excuse for them. He seemed at times to be asking God to commute these penalties. He examined without wrath, and with the eye of a linguist who is deciphering a palimpsest, that portion of chaos which still exists in nature. This revery sometimes caused him to utter odd sayings. One morning he was in his garden, and thought himself alone, but his sister was walking behind him, unseen by him: suddenly he paused and gazed at something on the ground; it was a large, black, hairy, frightful spider. His sister heard him say:—

"Poor beast! It is not its fault!"

Why not mention these almost divinely childish sayings of kindness? Puerile they may be; but these sublime puerilities were peculiar to Saint Francis d'Assisi and of Marcus Aurelius. One day he sprained his ankle in his effort to avoid stepping on an ant. Thus lived this just man. Sometimes he fell asleep in his garden, and then there was nothing more venerable possible.

Monseigneur Bienvenu had formerly been, if the stories anent his youth, and even in regard to his manhood, were to be believed, a passionate, and, possibly, a violent man. His universal suavity was less an instinct of nature than the result of a grand conviction which had filtered into his heart through the medium of life, and had trickled there slowly, thought by thought; for, in a character, as in a rock, there may exist apertures made by drops of water. These hollows are uneffaceable; these formations are indestructible.

In 1815, as we think we have already said, he reached his seventy-fifth birthday, but he did not appear to be more than sixty. He was not tall; he was rather plump; and, in order to combat this tendency, he was fond of taking long strolls on foot; his step was firm, and his form was but slightly bent, a detail from which we do not pretend to draw any conclusion. Gregory XVI., at the age of eighty, held himself erect and smiling, which did not prevent him from being a bad bishop. Monseigneur Welcome had what the people term a "fine head," but so amiable was he that they forgot that it was fine.

When he conversed with that infantile gayety which was one of his charms, and of which we have already spoken, people felt at their ease with him, and joy seemed to radiate from his whole person. His fresh and ruddy complexion, his very white teeth, all of which he had preserved, and which were displayed by his smile, gave him that open and easy air which cause the remark to be made of a man, "He's a good fellow"; and of an old man, "He is a fine man." That, it will be recalled, was the effect which he produced upon Napoleon. On the first encounter, and to one who saw him for the first time, he was nothing, in fact, but a fine man. But if one remained near him for a few hours, and beheld him in the least degree pensive, the fine man became gradually transfigured, and took on some imposing quality, I know not what; his broad and serious brow, rendered august by his white locks, became august also by virtue of meditation; majesty radiated from his goodness, though his goodness ceased not to be radiant; one experienced something of the emotion which one would feel on beholding a smiling angel slowly unfold his wings, without ceasing to smile. Respect, an unutterable respect, penetrated you by degrees and mounted to your heart, and one felt that one had before him one of those strong, thoroughly tried, and indulgent souls where thought is so grand that it can no longer be anything but gentle.

As we have seen, prayer, the celebration of the offices of religion, alms-giving, the consolation of the afflicted, the cultivation of a bit of land, fraternity, frugality, hospitality, renunciation, confidence, study, work, filled every day of his life. Filled is exactly the word; certainly the Bishop's day was quite full to the brim, of good words and good deeds. Nevertheless, it was not complete if cold or rainy weather prevented his passing an hour or two in his garden before going to bed, and after the two women had retired. It seemed to be a sort of rite with him, to prepare himself for slumber by meditation in the presence of the grand spectacles of the nocturnal heavens. Sometimes, if the two old women were not asleep, they heard him pacing slowly along the walks at a very advanced hour of the night. He was there alone, communing with himself, peaceful, adoring, comparing the serenity of his heart with the serenity of the ether, moved amid the darkness by the visible splendor of the constellations and the invisible splendor of God, opening his heart to the thoughts which fall from the Unknown. At such moments, while he offered his heart at the hour when nocturnal flowers offer their perfume, illuminated like a lamp amid the starry night, as he poured himself out in ecstasy in the midst of the universal radiance of creation, he could not have told himself, probably, what was passing in his spirit; he felt something take its flight from him, and something descend into him. Mysterious exchange of the abysses of the soul with the abysses of the universe!

He thought of the grandeur and presence of God; of the future eternity, that strange mystery; of the eternity past, a mystery still more strange; of all the infinities, which pierced their way into all his senses, beneath his eyes; and, without seeking to comprehend the incomprehensible, he gazed upon it. He did not study God; he was dazzled by him. He considered those magnificent conjunctions of atoms, which communicate aspects to matter, reveal forces by verifying them, create individualities in unity, proportions in extent, the innumerable in the infinite, and, through light, produce beauty. These conjunctions are formed and dissolved incessantly; hence life and death.

He seated himself on a wooden bench, with his back against a decrepit vine; he gazed at the stars, past the puny and stunted silhouettes of his fruit-trees. This quarter of an acre, so poorly planted, so encumbered with mean buildings and sheds, was dear to him, and satisfied his wants.

What more was needed by this old man, who divided the leisure of his life, where there was so little leisure, between gardening in the daytime and contemplation at night? Was not this narrow enclosure, with the heavens for a ceiling, sufficient to enable him to adore God in his most divine works, in turn? Does not this comprehend all, in fact? and what is there left to desire beyond it? A little garden in which to walk, and immensity in which to dream. At one's feet that which can be cultivated and plucked; over head that which one can study and meditate upon: some flowers on earth, and all the stars in the sky.

CHAPTER XIV

WHAT HE THOUGHT

One last word.

Since this sort of details might, particularly at the present moment, and to use an expression now in fashion, give to the Bishop of D—a certain "pantheistical" physiognomy, and induce the belief, either to his credit or discredit, that he entertained one of those personal philosophies which are peculiar to our century, which sometimes spring up in solitary spirits, and there take on a form and grow until they usurp the place of religion, we insist upon it, that not one of those persons who knew Monseigneur Welcome would have thought himself authorized to think anything of the sort. That which enlightened this man was his heart. His wisdom was made of the light which comes from there.

No systems; many works. Abstruse speculations contain vertigo; no, there is nothing to indicate that he risked his mind in apocalypses. The apostle may be daring, but the bishop must be timid. He would probably have felt a scruple at sounding too far in advance certain problems which are, in a manner, reserved for terrible great minds. There is a sacred horror beneath the porches of the enigma; those gloomy openings stand yawning there, but something tells you, you, a passer-by in life, that you must not enter. Woe to him who penetrates thither!

Geniuses in the impenetrable depths of abstraction and pure speculation, situated, so to speak, above all dogmas, propose their ideas to God. Their prayer audaciously offers discussion. Their adoration interrogates. This

88

is direct religion, which is full of anxiety and responsibility for him who attempts its steep cliffs.

Human meditation has no limits. At his own risk and peril, it analyzes and digs deep into its own bedazzlement. One might almost say, that by a sort of splendid reaction, it with it dazzles nature; the mysterious world which surrounds us renders back what it has received; it is probable that the contemplators are contemplated. However that may be, there are on earth men who—are they men?—perceive distinctly at the verge of the horizons of revery the heights of the absolute, and who have the terrible vision of the infinite mountain. Monseigneur Welcome was one of these men; Monseigneur Welcome was not a genius. He would have feared those sublimities whence some very great men even, like Swedenborg and Pascal, have slipped into insanity. Certainly, these powerful reveries have their moral utility, and by these arduous paths one approaches to ideal perfection. As for him, he took the path which shortens,—the Gospel's.

He did not attempt to impart to his chasuble the folds of Elijah's mantle; he projected no ray of future upon the dark groundswell of events; he did not see to condense in flame the light of things; he had nothing of the prophet and nothing of the magician about him. This humble soul loved, and that was all.

That he carried prayer to the pitch of a superhuman aspiration is probable: but one can no more pray too much than one can love too much; and if it is a heresy to pray beyond the texts, Saint Theresa and Saint Jerome would be heretics.

He inclined towards all that groans and all that expiates. The universe appeared to him like an immense malady; everywhere he felt fever, everywhere he heard the sound of suffering, and, without seeking to solve the enigma, he strove to dress the wound. The terrible spectacle of created things developed tenderness in him; he was occupied only in finding for himself, and in inspiring others with the best way to compassionate and relieve. That which exists was for this good and rare priest a permanent subject of sadness which sought consolation.

There are men who toil at extracting gold; he toiled at the extraction of pity. Universal misery was his mine. The sadness which reigned everywhere was but an excuse for unfailing kindness. Love each other; he declared this to be complete, desired nothing further, and that was the whole of his doctrine. One day, that man who believed himself to be a "philosopher," the senator who has already been alluded to, said to the Bishop: "Just survey the spectacle of the world: all war against all; the strongest has the most wit. Your love each other is nonsense."—"Well," replied Monseigneur Welcome, without contesting the point, "if it is nonsense, the soul should shut itself up in it, as the pearl in the oyster." Thus he shut himself up, he lived there, he was absolutely satisfied with it, leaving on one side the prodigious questions which attract and terrify, the fathomless perspectives of abstraction, the precipices of metaphysics—all those profundities which converge, for the apostle in God, for the atheist in nothingness; destiny, good and evil, the way of being against being, the conscience of man, the thoughtful somnambulism of the animal, the transformation in death, the recapitulation of existences which the tomb contains, the incomprehensible grafting of successive loves on the persistent *I*, the essence, the substance, the Nile, and the Ens, the soul, nature, liberty, necessity; perpendicular problems, sinister obscurities, where lean the gigantic archangels of the human mind; formidable abysses, which Lucretius, Manou, Saint Paul, Dante, contemplate with eyes flashing lightning, which seems by its steady gaze on the infinite to cause stars to blaze forth there.

Monseigneur Bienvenu was simply a man who took note of the exterior of mysterious questions without scrutinizing them, and without troubling his own mind with them, and who cherished in his own soul a grave respect for darkness.

BOOK SECOND

THE FALL

CHAPTER I

THE EVENING OF A DAY OF WALKING

Early in the month of October, 1815, about an hour before sunset, a man who was travelling on foot entered the little town of D—The few inhabitants who were at their windows or on their thresholds at the moment stared at this traveller with a sort of uneasiness. It was difficult to encounter a wayfarer of more wretched appearance. He was a man of medium stature, thickset and robust, in the prime of life. He might have been forty-six or forty-eight years old. A cap with a drooping leather visor partly concealed his face, burned and tanned by sun and wind, and dripping with perspiration. His shirt of coarse yellow linen, fastened at the neck by a small silver anchor, permitted a view of his hairy breast: he had a cravat twisted into a string; trousers of blue drilling, worn and threadbare, white on one knee and torn on the other; an old gray, tattered blouse, patched on one of the elbows with a bit of green cloth sewed on with twine; a tightly packed soldier knapsack, well buckled and perfectly new, on his back; an enormous, knotty stick in his hand; iron-shod shoes on his stockingless feet; a shaved head and a long beard.

The sweat, the heat, the journey on foot, the dust, added I know not what sordid quality to this dilapidated whole. His hair was closely cut, yet bristling, for it had begun to grow a little, and did not seem to have been cut for some time.

No one knew him. He was evidently only a chance passer-by. Whence came he? From the south; from the seashore, perhaps, for he made his entrance into D—by the same street which, seven months previously, had witnessed the passage of the Emperor Napoleon on his way from Cannes to Paris. This man must have been walking all day. He seemed very much fatigued. Some women of the ancient market town which is situated below the city had seen him pause beneath the trees of the boulevard Gassendi, and drink at the fountain which stands at the end of the promenade. He must have been very thirsty: for the children who followed him saw him stop again for a drink, two hundred paces further on, at the fountain in the market-place.

On arriving at the corner of the Rue Poichevert, he turned to the left, and directed his steps toward the town-hall. He entered, then came out a quarter of an hour later. A gendarme was seated near the door, on the stone bench which General Drouot had mounted on the 4th of March to read to the frightened throng of the inhabitants of D—the proclamation of the Gulf Juan. The man pulled off his cap and humbly saluted the gendarme.

The gendarme, without replying to his salute, stared attentively at him, followed him for a while with his eyes, and then entered the town-hall.

There then existed at D—a fine inn at the sign of the Cross of Colbas. This inn had for a landlord a certain Jacquin Labarre, a man of consideration in the town on account of his relationship to another Labarre, who kept the inn of the Three Dauphins in Grenoble, and had served in the Guides. At the time of the Emperor's landing, many rumors had circulated throughout the country with regard to this inn of the Three Dauphins. It was said that General Bertrand, disguised as a carter, had made frequent trips thither in the month of January, and that he had distributed crosses of honor to the soldiers and handfuls of gold to the citizens. The truth is, that when the Emperor entered Grenoble he had refused to install himself at the hotel of the prefecture; he had thanked the mayor, saying, "I am going to the house of a brave man of my acquaintance"; and he had betaken himself to the Three Dauphins.

This glory of the Labarre of the Three Dauphins was reflected upon the Labarre of the Cross of Colbas, at a distance of five and twenty leagues. It was said of him in the town, "That is the cousin of the man of Grenoble."

The man bent his steps towards this inn, which was the best in the country-side. He entered the kitchen, which opened on a level with the street. All the stoves were lighted; a huge fire blazed gayly in the fireplace. The host, who was also the chief cook, was going from one stew-pan to another, very busily superintending an excellent dinner designed for the wagoners, whose loud talking, conversation, and laughter were audible from an adjoining apartment. Any one who has travelled knows that there is no one who indulges in better cheer than wagoners. A fat marmot, flanked by white partridges and heather-cocks, was turning on a long spit before the fire; on the stove, two huge carps from Lake Lauzet and a trout from Lake Alloz were cooking.

The host, hearing the door open and seeing a newcomer enter, said, without raising his eyes from his stoves:—

"What do you wish, sir?"

"Food and lodging," said the man.

"Nothing easier," replied the host. At that moment he turned his head, took in the traveller's appearance with a single glance, and added, "By paying for it."

The man drew a large leather purse from the pocket of his blouse, and answered, "I have money."

"In that case, we are at your service," said the host.

The man put his purse back in his pocket, removed his knapsack from his back, put it on the ground near the door, retained his stick in his hand, and seated himself on a low stool close to the fire. D—is in the mountains. The evenings are cold there in October.

But as the host went back and forth, he scrutinized the traveller.

"Will dinner be ready soon?" said the man.

"Immediately," replied the landlord.

While the newcomer was warming himself before the fire, with his back turned, the worthy host, Jacquin Labarre, drew a pencil from his pocket, then tore off the corner of an old newspaper which was lying on a small table near the window. On the white margin he wrote a line or two, folded it without sealing, and then intrusted this scrap of paper to a child who seemed to serve him in the capacity both of scullion and lackey. The landlord whispered a word in the scullion's ear, and the child set off on a run in the direction of the town-hall.

The traveller saw nothing of all this.

Once more he inquired, "Will dinner be ready soon?"

"Immediately," responded the host.

The child returned. He brought back the paper. The host unfolded it eagerly, like a person who is expecting a reply. He seemed to read it attentively, then tossed his head, and remained thoughtful for a moment. Then he took a step in the direction of the traveller, who appeared to be immersed in reflections which were not very serene.

"I cannot receive you, sir," said he.

The man half rose.

"What! Are you afraid that I will not pay you? Do you want me to pay you in advance? I have money, I tell you."

"It is not that."

"What then?"

"You have money—"

"Yes," said the man.

"And I," said the host, "have no room."

The man resumed tranquilly, "Put me in the stable."

"I cannot."

"Why?"

"The horses take up all the space."

"Very well!" retorted the man; "a corner of the loft then, a truss of straw. We will see about that after dinner."

"I cannot give you any dinner."

This declaration, made in a measured but firm tone, struck the stranger as grave. He rose.

"Ah! bah! But I am dying of hunger. I have been walking since sunrise. I have travelled twelve leagues. I pay. I wish to eat."

"I have nothing," said the landlord.

The man burst out laughing, and turned towards the fireplace and the stoves: "Nothing! and all that?"

"All that is engaged."

"By whom?"

"By messieurs the wagoners."

"How many are there of them?"

"Twelve."

"There is enough food there for twenty."

"They have engaged the whole of it and paid for it in advance."

The man seated himself again, and said, without raising his voice, "I am at an inn; I am hungry, and I shall remain."

Then the host bent down to his ear, and said in a tone which made him start, "Go away!"

At that moment the traveller was bending forward and thrusting some brands into the fire with the iron-shod tip of his staff; he turned quickly round, and as he opened his mouth to reply, the host gazed steadily at him and added, still in a low voice: "Stop! there's enough of that sort of talk. Do you want me to tell you your name? Your name is Jean Valjean. Now do you want me to tell you who you are? When I saw you come in I suspected something; I sent to the town-hall, and this was the reply that was sent to me. Can you read?"

So saying, he held out to the stranger, fully unfolded, the paper which had just travelled from the inn to the town-hall, and from the town-hall to the inn. The man cast a glance upon it. The landlord resumed after a pause.

"I am in the habit of being polite to every one. Go away!"

The man dropped his head, picked up the knapsack which he had deposited on the ground, and took his departure.

He chose the principal street. He walked straight on at a venture, keeping close to the houses like a sad and humiliated man. He did not turn round a single time. Had he done so, he would have seen the host of the Cross of Colbas standing on his threshold, surrounded by all the guests of his inn, and all the passers-by in the street, talking vivaciously, and pointing him out with his finger; and, from the glances of terror and distrust cast by the group, he might have divined that his arrival would speedily become an event for the whole town.

He saw nothing of all this. People who are crushed do not look behind them. They know but too well the evil fate which follows them.

Thus he proceeded for some time, walking on without ceasing, traversing at random streets of which he knew nothing, forgetful of his fatigue, as is often the case when a man is sad. All at once he felt the pangs of hunger sharply. Night was drawing near. He glanced about him, to see whether he could not discover some shelter.

The fine hostelry was closed to him; he was seeking some very humble public house, some hovel, however lowly.

Just then a light flashed up at the end of the streets; a pine branch suspended from a cross-beam of iron was outlined against the white sky of the twilight. He proceeded thither.

It proved to be, in fact, a public house. The public house which is in the Rue de Chaffaut.

The wayfarer halted for a moment, and peeped through the window into the interior of the low-studded room of the public house, illuminated by a small lamp on a table and by a large fire on the hearth. Some men were engaged in drinking there. The landlord was warming himself. An iron pot, suspended from a crane, bubbled over the flame.

The entrance to this public house, which is also a sort of an inn, is by two doors. One opens on the street, the other upon a small yard filled with manure. The traveller dare not enter by the street door. He slipped into the yard, halted again, then raised the latch timidly and opened the door.

"Who goes there?" said the master.

"Some one who wants supper and bed."

"Good. We furnish supper and bed here."

He entered. All the men who were drinking turned round. The lamp illuminated him on one side, the firelight on the other. They examined him for some time while he was taking off his knapsack.

The host said to him, "There is the fire. The supper is cooking in the pot. Come and warm yourself, comrade."

He approached and seated himself near the hearth. He stretched out his feet, which were exhausted with fatigue, to the fire; a fine odor was emitted by the pot. All that could be distinguished of his face, beneath his cap, which was well pulled down, assumed a vague appearance of comfort, mingled with that other poignant aspect which habitual suffering bestows.

It was, moreover, a firm, energetic, and melancholy profile. This physiognomy was strangely composed; it began by seeming humble, and ended by seeming severe. The eye shone beneath its lashes like a fire beneath brushwood.

One of the men seated at the table, however, was a fishmonger who, before entering the public house of the Rue de Chaffaut, had been to stable his horse at Labarre's. It chanced that he had that very morning encountered this unprepossessing stranger on the road between Bras d'Asse and—I have forgotten the name. I think it was Escoublon. Now, when he met him, the man, who then seemed already extremely weary, had requested him to take him on his crupper; to which the fishmonger had made no reply except by redoubling his gait. This fishmonger had been a member half an hour previously of the group which surrounded Jacquin Labarre, and had himself related his disagreeable encounter of the morning to the people at the Cross of Colbas. From where he sat he made an imperceptible sign to the tavern-keeper. The tavern-keeper went to him. They exchanged a few words in a low tone. The man had again become absorbed in his reflections.

The tavern-keeper returned to the fireplace, laid his hand abruptly on the shoulder of the man, and said to him:—

"You are going to get out of here."

The stranger turned round and replied gently, "Ah! You know?—"

"Yes."

"I was sent away from the other inn."

"And you are to be turned out of this one."

"Where would you have me go?"

"Elsewhere."

The man took his stick and his knapsack and departed.

As he went out, some children who had followed him from the Cross of Colbas, and who seemed to be lying in wait for him, threw stones at him. He retraced his steps in anger, and threatened them with his stick: the children dispersed like a flock of birds.

He passed before the prison. At the door hung an iron chain attached to a bell. He rang.

The wicket opened.

"Turnkey," said he, removing his cap politely, "will you have the kindness to admit me, and give me a lodging for the night?"

A voice replied:—

"The prison is not an inn. Get yourself arrested, and you will be admitted."

The wicket closed again.

He entered a little street in which there were many gardens. Some of them are enclosed only by hedges, which lends a cheerful aspect to the street. In the midst of these gardens and hedges he caught sight of a small house of a single story, the window of which was lighted up. He peered through the pane as he had done at the public house. Within was a large whitewashed room, with a bed draped in printed cotton stuff, and a cradle in one corner, a few wooden chairs, and a double-barrelled gun hanging on the wall. A table was spread in the centre of the room. A copper lamp illuminated the tablecloth of coarse white linen, the pewter jug shining like silver, and filled with wine, and the brown, smoking soup-tureen. At this table sat a man of about forty, with a merry and open countenance, who was dandling a little child on his knees. Close by a very young woman was nursing another child. The father was laughing, the child was laughing, the mother was smiling.

The stranger paused a moment in revery before this tender and calming spectacle. What was taking place within him? He alone could have told. It is probable that he thought that this joyous house would be hospitable, and that, in a place where he beheld so much happiness, he would find perhaps a little pity.

He tapped on the pane with a very small and feeble knock.

They did not hear him.

He tapped again.

He heard the woman say, "It seems to me, husband, that some one is knocking."

"No," replied the husband.

He tapped a third time.

The husband rose, took the lamp, and went to the door, which he opened.

He was a man of lofty stature, half peasant, half artisan. He wore a huge leather apron, which reached to his left shoulder, and which a hammer, a red handkerchief, a powder-horn, and all sorts of objects which were upheld by the girdle, as in a pocket, caused to bulge out. He carried his head thrown backwards; his shirt, widely opened and turned back, displayed his bull neck, white and bare. He had thick eyelashes, enormous black whiskers, prominent eyes, the lower part of his face like a snout; and besides all this, that air of being on his own ground, which is indescribable.

"Pardon me, sir," said the wayfarer, "Could you, in consideration of payment, give me a plate of soup and a corner of that shed yonder in the garden, in which to sleep? Tell me; can you? For money?"

"Who are you?" demanded the master of the house.

The man replied: "I have just come from Puy-Moisson. I have walked all day long. I have travelled twelve leagues. Can you?—if I pay?"

"I would not refuse," said the peasant, "to lodge any respectable man who would pay me. But why do you not go to the inn?"

"There is no room."

"Bah! Impossible. This is neither a fair nor a market day. Have you been to Labarre?"

"Yes."

"Well?"

The traveller replied with embarrassment: "I do not know. He did not receive me."

"Have you been to What's-his-name's, in the Rue Chaffaut?"

The stranger's embarrassment increased; he stammered, "He did not receive me either."

The peasant's countenance assumed an expression of distrust; he surveyed the newcomer from head to feet, and suddenly exclaimed, with a sort of shudder:—

"Are you the man?—"

He cast a fresh glance upon the stranger, took three steps backwards, placed the lamp on the table, and took his gun down from the wall.

Meanwhile, at the words, Are you the man? the woman had risen, had clasped her two children in her arms, and had taken refuge precipitately behind her husband, staring in terror at the stranger, with her bosom uncovered, and with frightened eyes, as she murmured in a low tone, "Tso-maraude."[1]

1 Patois of the French Alps: chat de maraude, rascally marauder.

All this took place in less time than it requires to picture it to one's self. After having scrutinized the man for several moments, as one scrutinizes a viper, the master of the house returned to the door and said:—

102

"Clear out!"

"For pity's sake, a glass of water," said the man.

"A shot from my gun!" said the peasant.

Then he closed the door violently, and the man heard him shoot two large bolts. A moment later, the window-shutter was closed, and the sound of a bar of iron which was placed against it was audible outside.

Night continued to fall. A cold wind from the Alps was blowing. By the light of the expiring day the stranger perceived, in one of the gardens which bordered the street, a sort of hut, which seemed to him to be built of sods. He climbed over the wooden fence resolutely, and found himself in the garden. He approached the hut; its door consisted of a very low and narrow aperture, and it resembled those buildings which road-laborers construct for themselves along the roads. He thought without doubt, that it was, in fact, the dwelling of a road-laborer; he was suffering from cold and hunger, but this was, at least, a shelter from the cold. This sort of dwelling is not usually occupied at night. He threw himself flat on his face, and crawled into the hut. It was warm there, and he found a tolerably good bed of straw. He lay, for a moment, stretched out on this bed, without the power to make a movement, so fatigued was he. Then, as the knapsack on his back was in his way, and as it furnished, moreover, a pillow ready to his hand, he set about unbuckling one of the straps. At that moment, a ferocious growl became audible. He raised his eyes. The head of an enormous dog was outlined in the darkness at the entrance of the hut.

It was a dog's kennel.

He was himself vigorous and formidable; he armed himself with his staff, made a shield of his knapsack, and made his way out of the kennel in the best way he could, not without enlarging the rents in his rags.

He left the garden in the same manner, but backwards, being obliged, in order to keep the dog respectful, to have recourse to that manoeuvre with his stick which masters in that sort of fencing designate as la rose couverte.

When he had, not without difficulty, repassed the fence, and found himself once more in the street, alone, without refuge, without shelter, without a roof over his head, chased even from that bed of straw and from that miserable kennel, he dropped rather than seated himself on a stone, and it appears that a passer-by heard him exclaim, "I am not even a dog!"

He soon rose again and resumed his march. He went out of the town, hoping to find some tree or haystack in the fields which would afford him shelter.

He walked thus for some time, with his head still drooping. When he felt himself far from every human habitation, he raised his eyes and gazed searchingly about him. He was in a field. Before him was one of those low hills covered with close-cut stubble, which, after the harvest, resemble shaved heads.

The horizon was perfectly black. This was not alone the obscurity of night; it was caused by very low-hanging clouds which seemed to rest upon the hill itself, and which were mounting and filling the whole sky. Meanwhile, as the moon was about to rise, and as there was still floating in the zenith a remnant of the brightness of twilight, these clouds formed at the summit of the sky a sort of whitish arch, whence a gleam of light fell upon the earth.

The earth was thus better lighted than the sky, which produces a particularly sinister effect, and the hill, whose contour was poor and mean, was outlined vague and wan against the gloomy horizon. The whole effect was hideous, petty, lugubrious, and narrow.

There was nothing in the field or on the hill except a deformed tree, which writhed and shivered a few paces distant from the wayfarer.

This man was evidently very far from having those delicate habits of intelligence and spirit which render one sensible to the mysterious aspects of things; nevertheless, there was something in that sky, in that hill, in that plain, in that tree, which was so profoundly desolate, that after a moment of immobility and revery he turned back abruptly. There are instants when nature seems hostile.

He retraced his steps; the gates of D—were closed. D—, which had sustained sieges during the wars of religion, was still surrounded in 1815 by ancient walls flanked by square towers which have been demolished since. He passed through a breach and entered the town again.

It might have been eight o'clock in the evening. As he was not acquainted with the streets, he recommenced his walk at random.

In this way he came to the prefecture, then to the seminary. As he passed through the Cathedral Square, he shook his fist at the church.

At the corner of this square there is a printing establishment. It is there that the proclamations of the Emperor and of the Imperial Guard to the army, brought from the Island of Elba and dictated by Napoleon himself, were printed for the first time.

Worn out with fatigue, and no longer entertaining any hope, he lay down on a stone bench which stands at the doorway of this printing office.

At that moment an old woman came out of the church. She saw the man stretched out in the shadow. "What are you doing there, my friend?" said she.

He answered harshly and angrily: "As you see, my good woman, I am sleeping." The good woman, who was well worthy the name, in fact, was the Marquise de R—

"On this bench?" she went on.

"I have had a mattress of wood for nineteen years," said the man; "today I have a mattress of stone."

"You have been a soldier?"

"Yes, my good woman, a soldier."

"Why do you not go to the inn?"

"Because I have no money."

"Alas!" said Madame de R—, "I have only four sous in my purse."

"Give it to me all the same."

The man took the four sous. Madame de R—continued: "You cannot obtain lodgings in an inn for so small a sum. But have you tried? It is impossible for you to pass the night thus. You are cold and hungry, no doubt. Some one might have given you a lodging out of charity."

"I have knocked at all doors."

"Well?"

"I have been driven away everywhere."

The "good woman" touched the man's arm, and pointed out to him on the other side of the street a small, low house, which stood beside the Bishop's palace.

"You have knocked at all doors?"

"Yes."

"Have you knocked at that one?"

"No."

"Knock there."

CHAPTER II

PRUDENCE COUNSELLED TO WISDOM.

That evening, the Bishop of D—, after his promenade through the town, remained shut up rather late in his room. He was busy over a great work on Duties, which was never completed, unfortunately. He was carefully compiling everything that the Fathers and the doctors have said on this important subject. His book was divided into two parts: firstly, the duties of all; secondly, the duties of each individual, according to the class to which he belongs. The duties of all are the great duties. There are four of these. Saint Matthew points them out: duties towards God (Matt. vi.); duties towards one's self (Matt. v. 29, 30); duties towards one's neighbor (Matt. vii. 12); duties towards animals (Matt. vi. 20, 25). As for the other duties the Bishop found them pointed out and prescribed elsewhere: to sovereigns and subjects, in the Epistle to the Romans; to magistrates, to wives, to mothers, to young men, by Saint Peter; to husbands, fathers, children and servants, in the Epistle to the Ephesians; to the faithful, in the Epistle to the Hebrews; to virgins, in the Epistle to the Corinthians. Out of these precepts he was laboriously constructing a harmonious whole, which he desired to present to souls.

At eight o'clock he was still at work, writing with a good deal of inconvenience upon little squares of paper, with a big book open on his knees, when Madame Magloire entered, according to her wont, to get the silver-ware from the cupboard near his bed. A moment later, the Bishop, knowing that the table was set, and that his sister was probably waiting for him, shut his book, rose from his table, and entered the dining-room.

The dining-room was an oblong apartment, with a fireplace, which had a door opening on the street (as we have said), and a window opening on the garden.

Madame Magloire was, in fact, just putting the last touches to the table.

As she performed this service, she was conversing with Mademoiselle Baptistine.

A lamp stood on the table; the table was near the fireplace. A wood fire was burning there.

One can easily picture to one's self these two women, both of whom were over sixty years of age. Madame Magloire small, plump, vivacious; Mademoiselle Baptistine gentle, slender, frail, somewhat taller than her brother, dressed in a gown of puce-colored silk, of the fashion of 1806, which she had purchased at that date in Paris, and which had lasted ever since. To borrow vulgar phrases, which possess the merit of giving utterance in a single word to an idea which a whole page would hardly suffice to express, Madame Magloire had the air of a peasant, and Mademoiselle Baptistine that of a lady. Madame Magloire wore a white quilted cap, a gold Jeannette cross on a velvet ribbon upon her neck, the only bit of feminine jewelry that there was in the house, a very white fichu puffing out from a gown of coarse black woollen stuff, with large, short sleeves, an apron of cotton cloth in red and green checks, knotted round the waist with a green ribbon, with a stomacher of the same attached by two pins at the upper corners, coarse shoes on her feet, and yellow stockings, like the women of Marseilles. Mademoiselle Baptistine's gown was cut on the patterns of 1806, with a short waist, a narrow, sheath-like skirt, puffed sleeves, with flaps and buttons. She concealed her gray hair under a frizzed wig known as the baby wig. Madame Magloire had an intelligent, vivacious, and kindly air; the two corners of her mouth unequally raised, and her upper lip, which was larger than the lower, imparted to her a rather crabbed and imperious look. So long as Monseigneur held his peace, she talked to him resolutely with a mixture of respect and freedom; but as soon as Monseigneur began to speak, as we have seen, she obeyed passively like her mistress. Mademoiselle Baptistine did not even speak. She confined herself to obeying and pleasing him. She had never been pretty, even when she was young; she had large, blue, prominent eyes, and a long arched nose; but her whole visage, her whole person, breathed forth an ineffable goodness, as we stated in the beginning. She had always been predestined to gentleness; but faith, charity, hope, those three virtues which mildly warm the soul, had gradually elevated that gentleness to sanctity. Nature had made her a lamb, religion had made her an angel. Poor sainted virgin! Sweet memory which has vanished!

Mademoiselle Baptistine has so often narrated what passed at the episcopal residence that evening, that there are many people now living who still recall the most minute details.

At the moment when the Bishop entered, Madame Magloire was talking with considerable vivacity. She was haranguing Mademoiselle Baptistine on a subject which was familiar to her and to which the Bishop was also accustomed. The question concerned the lock upon the entrance door.

It appears that while procuring some provisions for supper, Madame Magloire had heard things in divers places. People had spoken of a prowler of evil appearance; a suspicious vagabond had arrived who must be somewhere about the town, and those who should take it into their heads to return home late that night might be subjected to unpleasant encounters. The police was very badly organized, moreover, because there was no love lost between the Prefect and the Mayor, who sought to injure each other by making things happen. It behooved wise people to play the part of their own police, and to guard themselves well, and care must be taken to duly close, bar and barricade their houses, and to fasten the doors well.

Madame Magloire emphasized these last words; but the Bishop had just come from his room, where it was rather cold. He seated himself in front of the fire, and warmed himself, and then fell to thinking of other things. He did not take up the remark dropped with design by Madame Magloire. She repeated it. Then Mademoiselle Baptistine, desirous of satisfying Madame Magloire without displeasing her brother, ventured to say timidly:—

"Did you hear what Madame Magloire is saying, brother?"

"I have heard something of it in a vague way," replied the Bishop. Then half-turning in his chair, placing his hands on his knees, and raising towards the old servant woman his cordial face, which so easily grew joyous, and which was illuminated from below by the firelight,—"Come, what is the matter? What is the matter? Are we in any great danger?"

Then Madame Magloire began the whole story afresh, exaggerating it a little without being aware of the fact. It appeared that a Bohemian, a bare-footed vagabond, a sort of dangerous mendicant, was at that moment in the town. He had presented himself at Jacquin Labarre's to obtain lodgings, but the latter had not been willing to take him in. He had been seen to arrive by the way of the boulevard Gassendi and roam about the streets in the gloaming. A gallows-bird with a terrible face.

"Really!" said the Bishop.

This willingness to interrogate encouraged Madame Magloire; it seemed to her to indicate that the Bishop was on the point of becoming alarmed; she pursued triumphantly:—

"Yes, Monseigneur. That is how it is. There will be some sort of catastrophe in this town tonight. Every one says so. And withal, the police is so badly regulated" (a useful repetition). "The idea of living in a mountainous country, and not even having lights in the streets at night! One goes out. Black as ovens, indeed! And I say, Monseigneur, and Mademoiselle there says with me—"

"I," interrupted his sister, "say nothing. What my brother does is well done."

110

Madame Magloire continued as though there had been no protest:—

"We say that this house is not safe at all; that if Monseigneur will permit, I will go and tell Paulin Musebois, the locksmith, to come and replace the ancient locks on the doors; we have them, and it is only the work of a moment; for I say that nothing is more terrible than a door which can be opened from the outside with a latch by the first passer-by; and I say that we need bolts, Monseigneur, if only for this night; moreover, Monseigneur has the habit of always saying 'come in'; and besides, even in the middle of the night, O mon Dieu! there is no need to ask permission."

At that moment there came a tolerably violent knock on the door.

"Come in," said the Bishop.

CHAPTER III

THE HEROISM OF PASSIVE OBEDIENCE.

The door opened.

It opened wide with a rapid movement, as though some one had given it an energetic and resolute push.

A man entered.

We already know the man. It was the wayfarer whom we have seen wandering about in search of shelter.

He entered, advanced a step, and halted, leaving the door open behind him. He had his knapsack on his shoulders, his cudgel in his hand, a rough, audacious, weary, and violent expression in his eyes. The fire on the hearth lighted him up. He was hideous. It was a sinister apparition.

Madame Magloire had not even the strength to utter a cry. She trembled, and stood with her mouth wide open.

Mademoiselle Baptistine turned round, beheld the man entering, and half started up in terror; then, turning her head by degrees towards the fireplace again, she began to observe her brother, and her face became once more profoundly calm and serene.

The Bishop fixed a tranquil eye on the man.

As he opened his mouth, doubtless to ask the new-comer what he desired, the man rested both hands on his staff, directed his gaze at the old man and the two women, and without waiting for the Bishop to speak, he said, in a loud voice:—

"See here. My name is Jean Valjean. I am a convict from the galleys. I have passed nineteen years in the galleys. I was liberated four days ago, and am on my way to Pontarlier, which is my destination. I have been walking for four days since I left Toulon. I have travelled a dozen leagues today on foot. This evening, when I arrived in these parts, I went to an inn, and they turned me out, because of my yellow passport, which I had shown at the town-hall. I had to do it. I went to an inn. They said to me, 'Be off,' at both places. No one would take me. I went to the prison; the jailer would not admit me. I went into a dog's kennel; the dog bit me and chased me off, as though he had been a man. One would have said that he knew who I was. I went into the fields, intending to sleep in the open air, beneath the stars. There were no stars. I thought it was going to rain, and I re-entered the town, to seek the recess of a doorway. Yonder, in the square, I meant to sleep on a stone bench. A good woman pointed out your house to me, and said to me, 'Knock there!' I have knocked. What is this place? Do you keep an inn? I have money—savings. One hundred and nine francs fifteen sous, which I earned in the galleys by my labor, in the course of nineteen years. I will pay. What is that to me? I have money. I am very weary; twelve leagues on foot; I am very hungry. Are you willing that I should remain?"

"Madame Magloire," said the Bishop, "you will set another place."

The man advanced three paces, and approached the lamp which was on the table. "Stop," he resumed, as though he had not quite understood; "that's not it. Did you hear? I am a galley-slave; a convict. I come from the galleys." He drew from his pocket a large sheet of yellow paper, which he unfolded. "Here's my passport. Yellow, as you see. This serves to expel me from every place where I go. Will you read it? I know how to read. I learned in the galleys. There is a school there for those who choose to learn. Hold, this is what they put on this passport: 'Jean Valjean, discharged convict, native of'—that is nothing to you—'has been nineteen years in the galleys: five years for house-breaking and burglary; fourteen years for having attempted to escape on four occasions. He is a very dangerous man.' There! Every one has cast me out. Are you willing to receive me? Is this an inn? Will you give me something to eat and a bed? Have you a stable?"

"Madame Magloire," said the Bishop, "you will put white sheets on the bed in the alcove." We have already explained the character of the two women's obedience.

Madame Magloire retired to execute these orders.

The Bishop turned to the man.

"Sit down, sir, and warm yourself. We are going to sup in a few moments, and your bed will be prepared while you are supping."

At this point the man suddenly comprehended. The expression of his face, up to that time sombre and harsh, bore the imprint of stupefaction, of doubt, of joy, and became extraordinary. He began stammering like a crazy man:—

"Really? What! You will keep me? You do not drive me forth? A convict! You call me sir! You do not address me as thou? 'Get out of here, you dog!' is what people always say to me. I felt sure that you would expel me, so I told you at once who I am. Oh, what a good woman that was who directed me hither! I am going to sup! A bed with a mattress and sheets, like the rest of the world! a bed! It is nineteen years since I have slept in a bed! You actually do not want me to go! You are good people. Besides, I have money. I will pay well. Pardon me, monsieur the inn-keeper, but what is your name? I will pay anything you ask. You are a fine man. You are an inn-keeper, are you not?"

"I am," replied the Bishop, "a priest who lives here."

"A priest!" said the man. "Oh, what a fine priest! Then you are not going to demand any money of me? You are the cure, are you not? the cure of this big church? Well! I am a fool, truly! I had not perceived your skull-cap."

As he spoke, he deposited his knapsack and his cudgel in a corner, replaced his passport in his pocket, and seated himself. Mademoiselle Baptistine gazed mildly at him. He continued:

"You are humane, Monsieur le Cure; you have not scorned me. A good priest is a very good thing. Then you do not require me to pay?"

"No," said the Bishop; "keep your money. How much have you? Did you not tell me one hundred and nine francs?"

"And fifteen sous," added the man.

"One hundred and nine francs fifteen sous. And how long did it take you to earn that?"

"Nineteen years."

"Nineteen years!"

The Bishop sighed deeply.

The man continued: "I have still the whole of my money. In four days I have spent only twenty-five sous, which I earned by helping unload some wagons at Grasse. Since you are an abbe, I will tell you that we had a chaplain in the galleys. And one day I saw a bishop there. Monseigneur is what they call him. He was the Bishop of Majore at Marseilles. He is the cure who rules over the other cures, you understand. Pardon me, I say that very badly; but it is such a far-off thing to me! You understand what we are! He said mass in the middle of the galleys, on an altar. He had a pointed thing, made of gold, on his head; it glittered in the bright light of midday. We were all ranged in lines on the three sides, with cannons with lighted matches facing us. We could not see very well. He spoke; but he was too far off, and we did not hear. That is what a bishop is like."

While he was speaking, the Bishop had gone and shut the door, which had remained wide open.

Madame Magloire returned. She brought a silver fork and spoon, which she placed on the table.

"Madame Magloire," said the Bishop, "place those things as near the fire as possible." And turning to his guest: "The night wind is harsh on the Alps. You must be cold, sir."

Each time that he uttered the word sir, in his voice which was so gently grave and polished, the man's face lighted up. Monsieur to a convict is like a glass of water to one of the shipwrecked of the Medusa. Ignominy thirsts for consideration.

"This lamp gives a very bad light," said the Bishop.

Madame Magloire understood him, and went to get the two silver candlesticks from the chimney-piece in Monseigneur's bed-chamber, and placed them, lighted, on the table.

"Monsieur le Cure," said the man, "you are good; you do not despise me. You receive me into your house. You light your candles for me. Yet I have not concealed from you whence I come and that I am an unfortunate man."

The Bishop, who was sitting close to him, gently touched his hand. "You could not help telling me who you were. This is not my house; it is the house of Jesus Christ. This door does not demand of him who enters whether he has a name, but whether he has a grief. You suffer, you are hungry and thirsty; you are welcome. And do not thank me; do not say that I receive you in my house. No one is at home here, except the man who needs a refuge. I say to you, who are passing by, that you are much more at home here than I am myself. Everything here is yours. What need have I to know your name? Besides, before you told me you had one which I knew."

The man opened his eyes in astonishment.

"Really? You knew what I was called?"

"Yes," replied the Bishop, "you are called my brother."

"Stop, Monsieur le Cure," exclaimed the man. "I was very hungry when I entered here; but you are so good, that I no longer know what has happened to me."

The Bishop looked at him, and said,—

"You have suffered much?"

"Oh, the red coat, the ball on the ankle, a plank to sleep on, heat, cold, toil, the convicts, the thrashings, the double chain for nothing, the cell for one word; even sick and in bed, still the chain! Dogs, dogs are happier! Nineteen years! I am forty-six. Now there is the yellow passport. That is what it is like."

"Yes," resumed the Bishop, "you have come from a very sad place. Listen. There will be more joy in heaven over the tear-bathed face of a repentant sinner than over the white robes of a hundred just men. If you emerge from that sad place with thoughts of hatred and of wrath against mankind, you are deserving of pity; if you emerge with thoughts of good-will and of peace, you are more worthy than any one of us."

In the meantime, Madame Magloire had served supper: soup, made with water, oil, bread, and salt; a little bacon, a bit of mutton, figs, a fresh cheese, and a large loaf of rye bread. She had, of her own accord, added to the Bishop's ordinary fare a bottle of his old Mauves wine.

The Bishop's face at once assumed that expression of gayety which is peculiar to hospitable natures. "To table!" he cried vivaciously. As was his custom when a stranger supped with him, he made the man sit on his right. Mademoiselle Baptistine, perfectly peaceable and natural, took her seat at his left.

The Bishop asked a blessing; then helped the soup himself, according to his custom. The man began to eat with avidity.

All at once the Bishop said: "It strikes me there is something missing on this table."

Madame Magloire had, in fact, only placed the three sets of forks and spoons which were absolutely necessary. Now, it was the usage of the house, when the Bishop had any one to supper, to lay out the whole six sets of silver on the table-cloth—an innocent ostentation. This graceful semblance of luxury was a kind of child's play, which was full of charm in that gentle and severe household, which raised poverty into dignity.

Madame Magloire understood the remark, went out without saying a word, and a moment later the three sets of silver forks and spoons demanded by the Bishop were glittering upon the cloth, symmetrically arranged before the three persons seated at the table.

CHAPTER IV

DETAILS CONCERNING THE CHEESE-DAIRIES OF PONTARLIER.

Now, in order to convey an idea of what passed at that table, we cannot do better than to transcribe here a passage from one of Mademoiselle Baptistine's letters to Madame Boischevron, wherein the conversation between the convict and the Bishop is described with ingenious minuteness.

". . . This man paid no attention to any one. He ate with the voracity of a starving man. However, after supper he said:

"'Monsieur le Cure of the good God, all this is far too good for me; but I must say that the carters who would not allow me to eat with them keep a better table than you do.'

"Between ourselves, the remark rather shocked me. My brother replied:—

"'They are more fatigued than I.'

"'No,' returned the man, 'they have more money. You are poor; I see that plainly. You cannot be even a curate. Are you really a cure? Ah, if the good God were but just, you certainly ought to be a cure!'

"'The good God is more than just,' said my brother.

"A moment later he added:—

"'Monsieur Jean Valjean, is it to Pontarlier that you are going?'

"'With my road marked out for me.'

"I think that is what the man said. Then he went on:—

"'I must be on my way by daybreak tomorrow. Travelling is hard. If the nights are cold, the days are hot.'

"'You are going to a good country,' said my brother. 'During the Revolution my family was ruined. I took refuge in Franche-Comte at first, and there I lived for some time by the toil of my hands. My will was good. I found plenty to occupy me. One has only to choose. There are paper mills, tanneries, distilleries, oil factories, watch factories on a large scale, steel mills, copper works, twenty iron foundries at least, four of which, situated at Lods, at Chatillon, at Audincourt, and at Beure, are tolerably large.'

"I think I am not mistaken in saying that those are the names which my brother mentioned. Then he interrupted himself and addressed me:—

"'Have we not some relatives in those parts, my dear sister?'

"I replied,—

"'We did have some; among others, M. de Lucenet, who was captain of the gates at Pontarlier under the old regime.'

"'Yes,' resumed my brother; 'but in '93, one had no longer any relatives, one had only one's arms. I worked. They have, in the country of Pontarlier, whither you are going, Monsieur Valjean, a truly patriarchal and truly charming industry, my sister. It is their cheese-dairies, which they call fruitieres.'

"Then my brother, while urging the man to eat, explained to him, with great minuteness, what these fruitieres of Pontarlier were; that they were divided into two classes: the big barns which belong to the rich, and where there are forty or fifty cows which produce from seven to eight thousand cheeses each summer, and the associated fruitieres, which belong to the poor; these are the peasants of mid-mountain, who hold their cows in common, and share the proceeds. 'They engage the services of a cheese-maker, whom they call the grurin; the grurin receives the milk of the associates three times a day, and marks the quantity on a double tally. It is towards the end of April that the work of the cheese-dairies begins; it is towards the middle of June that the cheese-makers drive their cows to the mountains.'

"The man recovered his animation as he ate. My brother made him drink that good Mauves wine, which he does not drink himself, because he says that wine is expensive. My brother imparted all these details with that easy gayety of his with which you are acquainted, interspersing his words with graceful attentions to me. He recurred frequently to that comfortable trade of grurin, as though he wished the man to understand, without advising him directly and harshly, that this would afford him a refuge. One thing struck me. This man was what I have told you. Well, neither during supper, nor during the entire evening, did my brother utter a single word, with the exception of a few words about Jesus when he entered, which could remind the man of what he was, nor of what my brother was. To all appearances, it was an occasion for preaching him a little sermon, and of impressing the Bishop on the convict, so that a mark of the passage might remain behind. This might have appeared to any one else who had this, unfortunate man in his hands to afford a chance to nourish his soul as well as his body, and to bestow upon him some reproach, seasoned with moralizing and advice, or a little commiseration, with an exhortation to conduct himself better in the future. My brother did not even ask him from what country he came, nor what was his history. For in his history there is a fault, and my brother seemed to avoid everything which could remind him of it. To such a point did he carry it, that at one time, when my brother was speaking of the mountaineers of Pontarlier, who exercise a gentle labor near heaven, and who, he added, are happy because they are innocent, he stopped short, fearing lest in this remark there might have escaped him something which might wound the man. By dint of reflection, I think I have comprehended what was passing in my brother's heart. He was thinking, no doubt, that this man, whose name is Jean Valjean, had his misfortune only too vividly present in his mind; that the best thing was to divert him from it, and to make him believe, if only momentarily, that he was a person like any other, by

120

treating him just in his ordinary way. Is not this indeed, to understand charity well? Is there not, dear Madame, something truly evangelical in this delicacy which abstains from sermon, from moralizing, from allusions? and is not the truest pity, when a man has a sore point, not to touch it at all? It has seemed to me that this might have been my brother's private thought. In any case, what I can say is that, if he entertained all these ideas, he gave no sign of them; from beginning to end, even to me he was the same as he is every evening, and he supped with this Jean Valjean with the same air and in the same manner in which he would have supped with M. Gedeon le Provost, or with the curate of the parish.

"Towards the end, when he had reached the figs, there came a knock at the door. It was Mother Gerbaud, with her little one in her arms. My brother kissed the child on the brow, and borrowed fifteen sous which I had about me to give to Mother Gerbaud. The man was not paying much heed to anything then. He was no longer talking, and he seemed very much fatigued. After poor old Gerbaud had taken her departure, my brother said grace; then he turned to the man and said to him, 'You must be in great need of your bed.' Madame Magloire cleared the table very promptly. I understood that we must retire, in order to allow this traveller to go to sleep, and we both went up stairs. Nevertheless, I sent Madame Magloire down a moment later, to carry to the man's bed a goat skin from the Black Forest, which was in my room. The nights are frigid, and that keeps one warm. It is a pity that this skin is old; all the hair is falling out. My brother bought it while he was in Germany, at Tottlingen, near the sources of the Danube, as well as the little ivory-handled knife which I use at table.

"Madame Magloire returned immediately. We said our prayers in the drawing-room, where we hang up the linen, and then we each retired to our own chambers, without saying a word to each other."

CHAPTER V

TRANQUILLITY

After bidding his sister good night, Monseigneur Bienvenu took one of the two silver candlesticks from the table, handed the other to his guest, and said to him,—

"Monsieur, I will conduct you to your room."

The man followed him.

As might have been observed from what has been said above, the house was so arranged that in order to pass into the oratory where the alcove was situated, or to get out of it, it was necessary to traverse the Bishop's bedroom.

At the moment when he was crossing this apartment, Madame Magloire was putting away the silverware in the cupboard near the head of the bed. This was her last care every evening before she went to bed.

The Bishop installed his guest in the alcove. A fresh white bed had been prepared there. The man set the candle down on a small table.

"Well," said the Bishop, "may you pass a good night. Tomorrow morning, before you set out, you shall drink a cup of warm milk from our cows."

"Thanks, Monsieur l'Abbe," said the man.

Hardly had he pronounced these words full of peace, when all of a sudden, and without transition, he made a strange movement, which would have frozen the two sainted women with horror, had they witnessed it. Even at this day it is difficult for us to explain what inspired him at that moment. Did he intend to convey a warning or to throw out a menace? Was he simply obeying a sort of instinctive impulse which was obscure even to himself? He turned abruptly to the old man, folded his arms, and bending upon his host a savage gaze, he exclaimed in a hoarse voice:—

"Ah! really! You lodge me in your house, close to yourself like this?"

He broke off, and added with a laugh in which there lurked something monstrous:—

"Have you really reflected well? How do you know that I have not been an assassin?"

The Bishop replied:—

"That is the concern of the good God."

Then gravely, and moving his lips like one who is praying or talking to himself, he raised two fingers of his right hand and bestowed his benediction on the man, who did not bow, and without turning his head or looking behind him, he returned to his bedroom.

When the alcove was in use, a large serge curtain drawn from wall to wall concealed the altar. The Bishop knelt before this curtain as he passed and said a brief prayer. A moment later he was in his garden, walking, meditating, contemplating, his heart and soul wholly absorbed in those grand and mysterious things which God shows at night to the eyes which remain open.

As for the man, he was actually so fatigued that he did not even profit by the nice white sheets. Snuffing out his candle with his nostrils after the manner of convicts, he dropped, all dressed as he was, upon the bed, where he immediately fell into a profound sleep.

Midnight struck as the Bishop returned from his garden to his apartment.

A few minutes later all were asleep in the little house.

CHAPTER VI

JEAN VALJEAN

Towards the middle of the night Jean Valjean woke.

Jean Valjean came from a poor peasant family of Brie. He had not learned to read in his childhood. When he reached man's estate, he became a tree-pruner at Faverolles. His mother was named Jeanne Mathieu; his father was called Jean Valjean or Vlajean, probably a sobriquet, and a contraction of viola Jean, "here's Jean."

Jean Valjean was of that thoughtful but not gloomy disposition which constitutes the peculiarity of affectionate natures. On the whole, however, there was something decidedly sluggish and insignificant about Jean Valjean in appearance, at least. He had lost his father and mother at a very early age. His mother had died of a milk fever, which had not been properly attended to. His father, a tree-pruner, like himself, had been killed by a fall from a tree. All that remained to Jean Valjean was a sister older than himself,—a widow with seven children, boys and girls. This sister had brought up Jean Valjean, and so long as she had a husband she lodged and fed her young brother.

The husband died. The eldest of the seven children was eight years old. The youngest, one.

Jean Valjean had just attained his twenty-fifth year. He took the father's place, and, in his turn, supported the sister who had brought him up. This was done simply as a duty and even a little churlishly on the part of Jean Valjean. Thus his youth had been spent in rude and ill-paid toil. He had never known a "kind woman friend" in his native parts. He had not had the time to fall in love.

He returned at night weary, and ate his broth without uttering a word. His sister, mother Jeanne, often took the best part of his repast from his bowl while he was eating,—a bit of meat, a slice of bacon, the heart of the cabbage,—to give to one of her children. As he went on eating, with his head bent over the table and almost into his soup, his long hair falling about his bowl and concealing his eyes, he had the air of perceiving nothing and allowing it. There was at Faverolles, not far from the Valjean thatched cottage, on the other side of the lane, a farmer's wife named Marie-Claude; the Valjean children, habitually famished, sometimes went to borrow from Marie-Claude a pint of milk, in their mother's name, which they drank behind a hedge or in some alley corner, snatching the jug from each other so hastily that the little girls spilled it on their aprons and down their necks. If their mother had known of this marauding, she would have punished the delinquents severely. Jean Valjean gruffly and grumblingly paid Marie-Claude for the pint of milk behind their mother's back, and the children were not punished.

In pruning season he earned eighteen sous a day; then he hired out as a hay-maker, as laborer, as neat-herd on a farm, as a drudge. He did whatever he could. His sister worked also but what could she do with seven little children? It was a sad group enveloped in misery, which was being gradually annihilated. A very hard winter came. Jean had no work. The family had no bread. No bread literally. Seven children!

One Sunday evening, Maubert Isabeau, the baker on the Church Square at Faverolles, was preparing to go to bed, when he heard a violent blow on the grated front of his shop. He arrived in time to see an arm passed through a hole made by a blow from a fist, through the grating and the glass. The arm seized a loaf of bread and carried it off. Isabeau ran out in haste; the robber fled at the full speed of his legs. Isabeau ran after him and stopped him. The thief had flung away the loaf, but his arm was still bleeding. It was Jean Valjean.

This took place in 1795. Jean Valjean was taken before the tribunals of the time for theft and breaking and entering an inhabited house at night. He had a gun which he used better than any one else in the world, he was a bit of a poacher, and this injured his case. There exists a legitimate prejudice against poachers. The poacher, like the smuggler, smacks too strongly of the brigand. Nevertheless, we will remark cursorily, there is still an abyss between these races of men and the hideous assassin of the towns. The poacher lives in the forest, the smuggler lives in the mountains or on the sea. The cities make ferocious men because they make corrupt men. The mountain, the sea, the forest, make savage men; they develop the fierce side, but often without destroying the humane side.

Jean Valjean was pronounced guilty. The terms of the Code were explicit. There occur formidable hours in our civilization; there are moments when the penal laws decree a shipwreck. What an ominous minute is that in which society draws back and consummates the irreparable abandonment of a sentient being! Jean Valjean was condemned to five years in the galleys.

On the 22d of April, 1796, the victory of Montenotte, won by the general-in-chief of the army of Italy, whom the message of the Directory to the Five Hundred, of the 2d of Floreal, year IV., calls Buona-Parte, was announced in Paris; on that same day a great gang of galley-slaves was put in chains at Bicetre. Jean Valjean formed a part of that gang. An old turnkey of the prison, who is now nearly eighty years old, still recalls perfectly that unfortunate wretch who was chained to the end of the fourth line, in the north angle of the courtyard. He was seated on the ground like the others. He did not seem to comprehend his position, except that it was horrible. It is probable that he, also, was disentangling from amid the vague ideas of a poor man, ignorant of everything, something excessive. While the bolt of his iron collar was being riveted behind his head with heavy blows from the hammer, he wept, his tears stifled him, they impeded his speech; he only managed to say from time to time, "I was a tree-pruner at Faverolles." Then still sobbing, he raised his right hand and lowered it gradually seven times, as though he were touching in succession seven heads of unequal heights, and from this gesture it was divined that the thing which he had done, whatever it was, he had done for the sake of clothing and nourishing seven little children.

He set out for Toulon. He arrived there, after a journey of twenty-seven days, on a cart, with a chain on his neck. At Toulon he was clothed in the red cassock. All that had constituted his life, even to his name, was effaced; he was no longer even Jean Valjean; he was number 24,601. What became of his sister? What became of the seven children? Who troubled himself about that? What becomes of the handful of leaves from the young tree which is sawed off at the root?

It is always the same story. These poor living beings, these creatures of God, henceforth without support, without guide, without refuge, wandered away at random,—who even knows?—each in his own direction perhaps, and little by little buried themselves in that cold mist which engulfs solitary destinies; gloomy shades, into which disappear in succession so many unlucky heads, in the sombre march of the human race. They quitted the country. The clock-tower of what had been their village forgot them; the boundary line of what had been their field forgot them; after a few years' residence in the galleys, Jean Valjean himself forgot them. In that heart, where there had been a wound, there was a scar. That is all. Only once, during all the time which he spent at Toulon, did he hear his sister mentioned. This happened, I think, towards the end of the fourth year of his captivity. I know not through what channels the news reached him. Some one who had known them in their own country had seen his sister. She was in Paris. She lived in a poor street Rear Saint-Sulpice, in the Rue du Gindre. She had with her only one child, a little boy, the youngest. Where were the other six? Perhaps she did not know herself. Every morning she went to a printing office, No. 3 Rue du Sabot, where she was a folder and stitcher. She was obliged to be there at six o'clock in the morning—long before daylight in winter. In the same building with the printing office there was a school, and to this school she took her little boy, who was seven years old. But as she entered the printing office at six, and the school only opened at seven, the child had to wait in the courtyard, for the school to open, for an hour—one hour of a winter night in the open air! They would not allow the child to come into the printing office, because he was in the way, they said. When the workmen passed in the morning, they beheld this poor little being seated on the pavement, overcome with drowsiness, and often fast asleep in the shadow, crouched down and doubled up over his basket. When it rained, an old woman, the portress, took pity on him; she took him into her den, where there was a pallet, a spinning-wheel, and two wooden chairs, and the little one slumbered in a corner, pressing himself close to the cat that he might suffer less from cold. At seven o'clock the school opened, and he entered. That is what was told to Jean Valjean.

They talked to him about it for one day; it was a moment, a flash, as though a window had suddenly been opened upon the destiny of those things whom he had loved; then all closed again. He heard nothing more forever. Nothing from them ever reached him again; he never beheld them; he never met them again; and in the continuation of this mournful history they will not be met with any more.

Towards the end of this fourth year Jean Valjean's turn to escape arrived. His comrades assisted him, as is the custom in that sad place. He escaped. He wandered for two days in the fields at liberty, if being at liberty is to be hunted, to turn the head every instant, to quake at the slightest noise, to be afraid of everything,—of a smoking roof, of a passing man, of a barking dog, of a galloping horse, of a striking clock, of the day because one can see, of the night because one cannot see, of the highway, of the path, of a bush, of sleep. On the evening of the second day he was captured. He had neither eaten nor slept for thirty-six hours. The maritime tribunal condemned him, for this crime, to a prolongation of his term for three years, which made eight years. In the sixth year his turn to escape occurred again; he availed himself of it, but could not accomplish his flight fully. He was missing at roll-call.

The cannon were fired, and at night the patrol found him hidden under the keel of a vessel in process of construction; he resisted the galley guards who seized him. Escape and rebellion. This case, provided for by a special code, was punished by an addition of five years, two of them in the double chain. Thirteen years. In the tenth year his turn came round again; he again profited by it; he succeeded no better. Three years for this fresh attempt. Sixteen years. Finally, I think it was during his thirteenth year, he made a last attempt, and only succeeded in getting retaken at the end of four hours of absence. Three years for those four hours. Nineteen years. In October, 1815, he was released; he had entered there in 1796, for having broken a pane of glass and taken a loaf of bread.

Room for a brief parenthesis. This is the second time, during his studies on the penal question and damnation by law, that the author of this book has come across the theft of a loaf of bread as the point of departure for the disaster of a destiny. Claude Gaux had stolen a loaf; Jean Valjean had stolen a loaf. English statistics prove the fact that four thefts out of five in London have hunger for their immediate cause.

Jean Valjean had entered the galleys sobbing and shuddering; he emerged impassive. He had entered in despair; he emerged gloomy.

What had taken place in that soul?

CHAPTER VII

THE INTERIOR OF DESPAIR

Let us try to say it.

It is necessary that society should look at these things, because it is itself which creates them.

He was, as we have said, an ignorant man, but he was not a fool. The light of nature was ignited in him. Unhappiness, which also possesses a clearness of vision of its own, augmented the small amount of daylight which existed in this mind. Beneath the cudgel, beneath the chain, in the cell, in hardship, beneath the burning sun of the galleys, upon the plank bed of the convict, he withdrew into his own consciousness and meditated.

He constituted himself the tribunal.

He began by putting himself on trial.

He recognized the fact that he was not an innocent man unjustly punished. He admitted that he had committed an extreme and blameworthy act; that that loaf of bread would probably not have been refused to him had he asked for it; that, in any case, it would have been better to wait until he could get it through compassion or through work; that it is not an unanswerable argument to say, "Can one wait when one is hungry?" That, in the first place, it is very rare for any one to die of hunger, literally; and next, that, fortunately or unfortunately, man is so constituted that he can suffer long and much, both morally and physically, without dying; that it is therefore necessary to have patience; that that would even have been better for those poor little children; that it had been an act of madness for him, a miserable, unfortunate wretch, to take society at large violently by the collar, and to imagine that one can escape from misery through theft; that that is in any case a poor door through which to escape from misery through which infamy enters; in short, that he was in the wrong.

Then he asked himself—

Whether he had been the only one in fault in his fatal history. Whether it was not a serious thing, that he, a laborer, out of work, that he, an industrious man, should have lacked bread. And whether, the fault once committed and confessed, the chastisement had not been ferocious and disproportioned. Whether there had not been more abuse on the part of the law, in respect to the penalty, than there had been on the part of the culprit in respect to his fault. Whether there had not been an excess of weights in one balance of the scale, in the one which contains expiation. Whether the over-weight of the penalty was not equivalent to the annihilation of the crime, and did not result in reversing the situation, of replacing the fault of the delinquent by the fault of the repression, of converting the guilty man into the victim, and the debtor into the creditor, and of ranging the law definitely on the side of the man who had violated it.

Whether this penalty, complicated by successive aggravations for attempts at escape, had not ended in becoming a sort of outrage perpetrated by the stronger upon the feebler, a crime of society against the individual, a crime which was being committed afresh every day, a crime which had lasted nineteen years.

He asked himself whether human society could have the right to force its members to suffer equally in one case for its own unreasonable lack of foresight, and in the other case for its pitiless foresight; and to seize a poor man forever between a defect and an excess, a default of work and an excess of punishment.

Whether it was not outrageous for society to treat thus precisely those of its members who were the least well endowed in the division of goods made by chance, and consequently the most deserving of consideration.

These questions put and answered, he judged society and condemned it.

He condemned it to his hatred.

He made it responsible for the fate which he was suffering, and he said to himself that it might be that one day he should not hesitate to call it to account. He declared to himself that there was no equilibrium between the harm which he had caused and the harm which was being done to him; he finally arrived at the conclusion that his punishment was not, in truth, unjust, but that it most assuredly was iniquitous.

Anger may be both foolish and absurd; one can be irritated wrongfully; one is exasperated only when there is some show of right on one's side at bottom. Jean Valjean felt himself exasperated.

And besides, human society had done him nothing but harm; he had never seen anything of it save that angry face which it calls Justice, and which it shows to those whom it strikes. Men had only touched him to bruise him. Every contact with them had been a blow. Never, since his infancy, since the days of his mother, of his sister, had he ever encountered a friendly word and a kindly glance. From suffering to suffering, he had gradually arrived at the conviction that life is a war; and that in this war he was the conquered. He had no other weapon than his hate. He resolved to whet it in the galleys and to bear it away with him when he departed.

There was at Toulon a school for the convicts, kept by the Ignorantin friars, where the most necessary branches were taught to those of the unfortunate men who had a mind for them. He was of the number who had a mind. He went to school at the age of forty, and learned to read, to write, to cipher. He felt that to fortify his intelligence was to fortify his hate. In certain cases, education and enlightenment can serve to eke out evil.

This is a sad thing to say; after having judged society, which had caused his unhappiness, he judged Providence, which had made society, and he condemned it also.

Thus during nineteen years of torture and slavery, this soul mounted and at the same time fell. Light entered it on one side, and darkness on the other.

Jean Valjean had not, as we have seen, an evil nature. He was still good when he arrived at the galleys. He there condemned society, and felt that he was becoming wicked; he there condemned Providence, and was conscious that he was becoming impious.

It is difficult not to indulge in meditation at this point.

Does human nature thus change utterly and from top to bottom? Can the man created good by God be rendered wicked by man? Can the soul be completely made over by fate, and become evil, fate being evil? Can the heart become misshapen and contract incurable deformities and infirmities under the oppression of a disproportionate unhappiness, as the vertebral column beneath too low a vault? Is there not in every human soul, was there not in the soul of Jean Valjean in particular, a first spark, a divine element, incorruptible in this world, immortal in the other, which good can develop, fan, ignite, and make to glow with splendor, and which evil can never wholly extinguish?

Grave and obscure questions, to the last of which every physiologist would probably have responded no, and that without hesitation, had he beheld at Toulon, during the hours of repose, which were for Jean Valjean hours of revery, this gloomy galley-slave, seated with folded arms upon the bar of some capstan, with the end of his chain thrust into his pocket to prevent its dragging, serious, silent, and thoughtful, a pariah of the laws which regarded the man with wrath, condemned by civilization, and regarding heaven with severity.

Certainly,—and we make no attempt to dissimulate the fact,—the observing physiologist would have beheld an irremediable misery; he would, perchance, have pitied this sick man, of the law's making; but he would not have even essayed any treatment; he would have turned aside his gaze from the caverns of which he would have caught a glimpse within this soul, and, like Dante at the portals of hell, he would have effaced from this existence the word which the finger of God has, nevertheless, inscribed upon the brow of every man,—hope.

Was this state of his soul, which we have attempted to analyze, as perfectly clear to Jean Valjean as we have tried to render it for those who read us? Did Jean Valjean distinctly perceive, after their formation, and had he seen distinctly during the process of their formation, all the elements of which his moral misery was composed? Had this rough and unlettered man gathered a perfectly clear perception of the succession of ideas through which he had, by degrees, mounted and descended to the lugubrious aspects which had, for so many years, formed the inner horizon of his spirit? Was he conscious of all that passed within him, and of all that was working there? That is something which we do not presume to state; it is something which we do not even believe. There was too much ignorance in Jean Valjean, even after his misfortune, to prevent much vagueness from still lingering there. At times he did not rightly know himself what he felt. Jean Valjean was in the shadows; he suffered in the shadows; he hated in the shadows; one might have said that he hated in advance of himself. He dwelt habitually in this shadow, feeling his way like a blind man and a dreamer. Only, at intervals, there suddenly came to him, from without and from within, an access of wrath, a surcharge of suffering, a livid and rapid flash which illuminated his whole soul, and caused to appear abruptly all around him, in front, behind, amid the gleams of a frightful light, the hideous precipices and the sombre perspective of his destiny.

The flash passed, the night closed in again; and where was he? He no longer knew. The peculiarity of pains of this nature, in which that which is pitiless—that is to say, that which is brutalizing—predominates, is to transform a man, little by little, by a sort of stupid transfiguration, into a wild beast; sometimes into a ferocious beast.

Jean Valjean's successive and obstinate attempts at escape would alone suffice to prove this strange working of the law upon the human soul. Jean Valjean would have renewed these attempts, utterly useless and foolish as they were, as often as the opportunity had presented itself, without reflecting for an instant on the result, nor on the experiences which he had already gone through. He escaped impetuously, like the wolf who finds his cage open. Instinct said to him, "Flee!" Reason would have said, "Remain!" But in the presence of so violent a temptation, reason vanished; nothing remained but instinct. The beast alone acted. When he was recaptured, the fresh severities inflicted on him only served to render him still more wild.

One detail, which we must not omit, is that he possessed a physical strength which was not approached by a single one of the denizens of the galleys. At work, at paying out a cable or winding up a capstan, Jean Valjean was worth four men. He sometimes lifted and sustained enormous weights on his back; and when the occasion demanded it, he replaced that implement which is called a jack-screw, and was formerly called orgueil [pride], whence, we may remark in passing, is derived the name of the Rue Montorgueil, near the Halles [Fishmarket] in Paris. His comrades had nicknamed him Jean the Jack-screw. Once, when they were repairing the balcony of the town-hall at Toulon, one of those admirable caryatids of Puget, which support the balcony, became loosened, and was on the point of falling. Jean Valjean, who was present, supported the caryatid with his shoulder, and gave the workmen time to arrive.

His suppleness even exceeded his strength. Certain convicts who were forever dreaming of escape, ended by making a veritable science of force and skill combined. It is the science of muscles. An entire system of mysterious statics is daily practised by prisoners, men who are forever envious of the flies and birds. To climb a vertical surface, and to find points of support where hardly a projection was visible, was play to Jean Valjean. An angle of the wall being given, with the tension of his back and legs, with his elbows and his heels fitted into the unevenness of the stone, he raised himself as if by magic to the third story. He sometimes mounted thus even to the roof of the galley prison.

He spoke but little. He laughed not at all. An excessive emotion was required to wring from him, once or twice a year, that lugubrious laugh of the convict, which is like the echo of the laugh of a demon. To all appearance, he seemed to be occupied in the constant contemplation of something terrible.

He was absorbed, in fact.

Athwart the unhealthy perceptions of an incomplete nature and a crushed intelligence, he was confusedly conscious that some monstrous thing was resting on him. In that obscure and wan shadow within which he crawled, each time that he turned his neck and essayed to raise his glance, he perceived with terror, mingled with rage, a sort of frightful accumulation of things, collecting and mounting above him, beyond the range of his vision,—laws, prejudices, men, and deeds,—whose outlines escaped him, whose mass terrified him, and which was nothing else than that prodigious pyramid which we call civilization. He distinguished, here and there in that swarming and formless mass, now near him, now afar off and on inaccessible table-lands, some group, some detail, vividly illuminated; here the galley-sergeant and his cudgel; there the gendarme and his sword; yonder the mitred archbishop; away at the top, like a sort of sun, the Emperor, crowned and dazzling. It seemed to him that these distant splendors, far from dissipating his night, rendered it more funereal and more black. All this—laws, prejudices, deeds, men, things—went and came above him, over his head, in accordance with the complicated and mysterious movement which God imparts to civilization, walking over him and crushing him with I know not what peacefulness in its cruelty and inexorability in its indifference. Souls which have fallen to the bottom of all possible misfortune, unhappy men lost in the lowest of those limbos at which no one any longer looks, the reproved of the law, feel the whole weight of this human society, so formidable for him who is without, so frightful for him who is beneath, resting upon their heads.

136

In this situation Jean Valjean meditated; and what could be the nature of his meditation?

If the grain of millet beneath the millstone had thoughts, it would, doubtless, think that same thing which Jean Valjean thought.

All these things, realities full of spectres, phantasmagories full of realities, had eventually created for him a sort of interior state which is almost indescribable.

At times, amid his convict toil, he paused. He fell to thinking. His reason, at one and the same time riper and more troubled than of yore, rose in revolt. Everything which had happened to him seemed to him absurd; everything that surrounded him seemed to him impossible. He said to himself, "It is a dream." He gazed at the galley-sergeant standing a few paces from him; the galley-sergeant seemed a phantom to him. All of a sudden the phantom dealt him a blow with his cudgel.

Visible nature hardly existed for him. It would almost be true to say that there existed for Jean Valjean neither sun, nor fine summer days, nor radiant sky, nor fresh April dawns. I know not what vent-hole daylight habitually illumined his soul.

To sum up, in conclusion, that which can be summed up and translated into positive results in all that we have just pointed out, we will confine ourselves to the statement that, in the course of nineteen years, Jean Valjean, the inoffensive tree-pruner of Faverolles, the formidable convict of Toulon, had become capable, thanks to the manner in which the galleys had moulded him, of two sorts of evil action: firstly, of evil action which was rapid, unpremeditated, dashing, entirely instinctive, in the nature of reprisals for the evil which he had undergone; secondly, of evil action which was serious, grave, consciously argued out and premeditated, with the false ideas which such a misfortune can furnish. His deliberate deeds passed through three successive phases, which natures of a certain stamp can alone traverse,—reasoning, will, perseverance. He had for moving causes his habitual wrath, bitterness of soul, a profound sense of indignities suffered, the reaction even against the good, the innocent, and the just, if there are any such. The point of departure, like the point of arrival, for all his thoughts, was hatred of human law; that hatred which, if it be not arrested in its development by some providential incident, becomes, within a given time, the hatred of society, then the hatred of the human race, then the hatred of creation, and which manifests itself by a vague, incessant, and brutal desire to do harm to some living being, no matter whom. It will be perceived that it was not without reason that Jean Valjean's passport described him as a very dangerous man.

From year to year this soul had dried away slowly, but with fatal sureness. When the heart is dry, the eye is dry. On his departure from the galleys it had been nineteen years since he had shed a tear.

CHAPTER VIII

BILLOWS AND SHADOWS

A man overboard!

What matters it? The vessel does not halt. The wind blows. That sombre ship has a path which it is forced to pursue. It passes on.

The man disappears, then reappears; he plunges, he rises again to the surface; he calls, he stretches out his arms; he is not heard. The vessel, trembling under the hurricane, is wholly absorbed in its own workings; the passengers and sailors do not even see the drowning man; his miserable head is but a speck amid the immensity of the waves. He gives vent to desperate cries from out of the depths. What a spectre is that retreating sail! He gazes and gazes at it frantically. It retreats, it grows dim, it diminishes in size. He was there but just now, he was one of the crew, he went and came along the deck with the rest, he had his part of breath and of sunlight, he was a living man. Now, what has taken place? He has slipped, he has fallen; all is at an end.

He is in the tremendous sea. Under foot he has nothing but what flees and crumbles. The billows, torn and lashed by the wind, encompass him hideously; the tossings of the abyss bear him away; all the tongues of water dash over his head; a populace of waves spits upon him; confused openings half devour him; every time that he sinks, he catches glimpses of precipices filled with night; frightful and unknown vegetations seize him, knot about his feet, draw him to them; he is conscious that he is becoming an abyss, that he forms part of the foam; the waves toss him from one to another; he drinks in the bitterness; the cowardly ocean attacks him furiously, to drown him; the enormity plays with his agony. It seems as though all that water were hate.

Nevertheless, he struggles.

He tries to defend himself; he tries to sustain himself; he makes an effort; he swims. He, his petty strength all exhausted instantly, combats the inexhaustible.

Where, then, is the ship? Yonder. Barely visible in the pale shadows of the horizon.

The wind blows in gusts; all the foam overwhelms him. He raises his eyes and beholds only the lividness of the clouds. He witnesses, amid his death-pangs, the immense madness of the sea. He is tortured by this madness; he hears noises strange to man, which seem to come from beyond the limits of the earth, and from one knows not what frightful region beyond.

There are birds in the clouds, just as there are angels above human distresses; but what can they do for him? They sing and fly and float, and he, he rattles in the death agony.

He feels himself buried in those two infinities, the ocean and the sky, at one and the same time: the one is a tomb; the other is a shroud.

Night descends; he has been swimming for hours; his strength is exhausted; that ship, that distant thing in which there were men, has vanished; he is alone in the formidable twilight gulf; he sinks, he stiffens himself, he twists himself; he feels under him the monstrous billows of the invisible; he shouts.

There are no more men. Where is God?

He shouts. Help! Help! He still shouts on.

Nothing on the horizon; nothing in heaven.

He implores the expanse, the waves, the seaweed, the reef; they are deaf. He beseeches the tempest; the imperturbable tempest obeys only the infinite.

Around him darkness, fog, solitude, the stormy and nonsentient tumult, the undefined curling of those wild waters. In him horror and fatigue. Beneath him the depths. Not a point of support. He thinks of the gloomy adventures of the corpse in the limitless shadow. The bottomless cold paralyzes him. His hands contract convulsively; they close, and grasp nothingness. Winds, clouds, whirlwinds, gusts, useless stars! What is to be done? The desperate man gives up; he is weary, he chooses the alternative of death; he resists not; he lets himself go; he abandons his grip; and then he tosses forevermore in the lugubrious dreary depths of engulfment.

Oh, implacable march of human societies! Oh, losses of men and of souls on the way! Ocean into which falls all that the law lets slip! Disastrous absence of help! Oh, moral death!

The sea is the inexorable social night into which the penal laws fling their condemned. The sea is the immensity of wretchedness.

The soul, going down stream in this gulf, may become a corpse. Who shall resuscitate it?

CHAPTER IX

NEW TROUBLES

When the hour came for him to take his departure from the galleys, when Jean Valjean heard in his ear the strange words, Thou art free! the moment seemed improbable and unprecedented; a ray of vivid light, a ray of the true light of the living, suddenly penetrated within him. But it was not long before this ray paled. Jean Valjean had been dazzled by the idea of liberty. He had believed in a new life. He very speedily perceived what sort of liberty it is to which a yellow passport is provided.

And this was encompassed with much bitterness. He had calculated that his earnings, during his sojourn in the galleys, ought to amount to a hundred and seventy-one francs. It is but just to add that he had forgotten to include in his calculations the forced repose of Sundays and festival days during nineteen years, which entailed a diminution of about eighty francs. At all events, his hoard had been reduced by various local levies to the sum of one hundred and nine francs fifteen sous, which had been counted out to him on his departure. He had understood nothing of this, and had thought himself wronged. Let us say the word—robbed.

On the day following his liberation, he saw, at Grasse, in front of an orange-flower distillery, some men engaged in unloading bales. He offered his services. Business was pressing; they were accepted. He set to work. He was intelligent, robust, adroit; he did his best; the master seemed pleased. While he was at work, a gendarme passed, observed him, and demanded his papers. It was necessary to show him the yellow passport. That done, Jean Valjean resumed his labor. A little while before he had questioned one of the workmen as to the amount which they earned each day at this occupation; he had been told thirty sous. When evening arrived, as he was forced to set out again on the following day, he presented himself to the owner of the distillery and requested to be paid. The owner did not utter a word, but handed him fifteen sous. He objected. He was told, "That is enough for thee." He persisted. The master looked him straight between the eyes, and said to him "Beware of the prison."

There, again, he considered that he had been robbed.

Society, the State, by diminishing his hoard, had robbed him wholesale. Now it was the individual who was robbing him at retail.

Liberation is not deliverance. One gets free from the galleys, but not from the sentence.

That is what happened to him at Grasse. We have seen in what manner he was received at D—

CHAPTER X

THE MAN AROUSED

As the Cathedral clock struck two in the morning, Jean Valjean awoke.

What woke him was that his bed was too good. It was nearly twenty years since he had slept in a bed, and, although he had not undressed, the sensation was too novel not to disturb his slumbers.

He had slept more than four hours. His fatigue had passed away. He was accustomed not to devote many hours to repose.

He opened his eyes and stared into the gloom which surrounded him; then he closed them again, with the intention of going to sleep once more.

When many varied sensations have agitated the day, when various matters preoccupy the mind, one falls asleep once, but not a second time. Sleep comes more easily than it returns. This is what happened to Jean Valjean. He could not get to sleep again, and he fell to thinking.

He was at one of those moments when the thoughts which one has in one's mind are troubled. There was a sort of dark confusion in his brain. His memories of the olden time and of the immediate present floated there pell-mell and mingled confusedly, losing their proper forms, becoming disproportionately large, then suddenly disappearing, as in a muddy and perturbed pool. Many thoughts occurred to him; but there was one which kept constantly presenting itself afresh, and which drove away all others. We will mention this thought at once: he had observed the six sets of silver forks and spoons and the ladle which Madame Magloire had placed on the table.

Those six sets of silver haunted him.—They were there.—A few paces distant.—Just as he was traversing the adjoining room to reach the one in which he then was, the old servant-woman had been in the act of placing them in a little cupboard near the head of the bed.—He had taken careful note of this cupboard.—On the right, as you entered from the dining-room.—They were solid.—And old silver.—From the ladle one could get at least two hundred francs.—Double what he had earned in nineteen years.—It is true that he would have earned more if "the administration had not robbed him."

His mind wavered for a whole hour in fluctuations with which there was certainly mingled some struggle. Three o'clock struck. He opened his eyes again, drew himself up abruptly into a sitting posture, stretched out his arm and felt of his knapsack, which he had thrown down on a corner of the alcove; then he hung his legs over the edge of the bed, and placed his feet on the floor, and thus found himself, almost without knowing it, seated on his bed.

He remained for a time thoughtfully in this attitude, which would have been suggestive of something sinister for any one who had seen him thus in the dark, the only person awake in that house where all were sleeping. All of a sudden he stooped down, removed his shoes and placed them softly on the mat beside the bed; then he resumed his thoughtful attitude, and became motionless once more.

Throughout this hideous meditation, the thoughts which we have above indicated moved incessantly through his brain; entered, withdrew, re-entered, and in a manner oppressed him; and then he thought, also, without knowing why, and with the mechanical persistence of revery, of a convict named Brevet, whom he had known in the galleys, and whose trousers had been upheld by a single suspender of knitted cotton. The checkered pattern of that suspender recurred incessantly to his mind.

145

He remained in this situation, and would have so remained indefinitely, even until daybreak, had not the clock struck one—the half or quarter hour. It seemed to him that that stroke said to him, "Come on!"

He rose to his feet, hesitated still another moment, and listened; all was quiet in the house; then he walked straight ahead, with short steps, to the window, of which he caught a glimpse. The night was not very dark; there was a full moon, across which coursed large clouds driven by the wind. This created, outdoors, alternate shadow and gleams of light, eclipses, then bright openings of the clouds; and indoors a sort of twilight. This twilight, sufficient to enable a person to see his way, intermittent on account of the clouds, resembled the sort of livid light which falls through an air-hole in a cellar, before which the passersby come and go. On arriving at the window, Jean Valjean examined it. It had no grating; it opened in the garden and was fastened, according to the fashion of the country, only by a small pin. He opened it; but as a rush of cold and piercing air penetrated the room abruptly, he closed it again immediately. He scrutinized the garden with that attentive gaze which studies rather than looks. The garden was enclosed by a tolerably low white wall, easy to climb. Far away, at the extremity, he perceived tops of trees, spaced at regular intervals, which indicated that the wall separated the garden from an avenue or lane planted with trees.

Having taken this survey, he executed a movement like that of a man who has made up his mind, strode to his alcove, grasped his knapsack, opened it, fumbled in it, pulled out of it something which he placed on the bed, put his shoes into one of his pockets, shut the whole thing up again, threw the knapsack on his shoulders, put on his cap, drew the visor down over his eyes, felt for his cudgel, went and placed it in the angle of the window; then returned to the bed, and resolutely seized the object which he had deposited there. It resembled a short bar of iron, pointed like a pike at one end. It would have been difficult to distinguish in that darkness for what employment that bit of iron could have been designed. Perhaps it was a lever; possibly it was a club.

In the daytime it would have been possible to recognize it as nothing more than a miner's candlestick. Convicts were, at that period, sometimes employed in quarrying stone from the lofty hills which environ Toulon, and it was not rare for them to have miners' tools at their command. These miners' candlesticks are of massive iron, terminated at the lower extremity by a point, by means of which they are stuck into the rock.

He took the candlestick in his right hand; holding his breath and trying to deaden the sound of his tread, he directed his steps to the door of the adjoining room, occupied by the Bishop, as we already know.

On arriving at this door, he found it ajar. The Bishop had not closed it.

CHAPTER XI

WHAT HE DOES

Jean Valjean listened. Not a sound.

He gave the door a push.

He pushed it gently with the tip of his finger, lightly, with the furtive and uneasy gentleness of a cat which is desirous of entering.

The door yielded to this pressure, and made an imperceptible and silent movement, which enlarged the opening a little.

He waited a moment; then gave the door a second and a bolder push.

It continued to yield in silence. The opening was now large enough to allow him to pass. But near the door there stood a little table, which formed an embarrassing angle with it, and barred the entrance.

Jean Valjean recognized the difficulty. It was necessary, at any cost, to enlarge the aperture still further.

He decided on his course of action, and gave the door a third push, more energetic than the two preceding. This time a badly oiled hinge suddenly emitted amid the silence a hoarse and prolonged cry.

Jean Valjean shuddered. The noise of the hinge rang in his ears with something of the piercing and formidable sound of the trump of the Day of Judgment.

In the fantastic exaggerations of the first moment he almost imagined that that hinge had just become animated, and had suddenly assumed a terrible life, and that it was barking like a dog to arouse every one, and warn and to wake those who were asleep. He halted, shuddering, bewildered, and fell back from the tips of his toes upon his heels. He heard the arteries in his temples beating like two forge hammers, and it seemed to him that his breath issued from his breast with the roar of the wind issuing from a cavern. It seemed impossible to him that the horrible clamor of that irritated hinge should not have disturbed the entire household, like the shock of an earthquake; the door, pushed by him, had taken the alarm, and had shouted; the old man would rise at once; the two old women would shriek out; people would come to their assistance; in less than a quarter of an hour the town would be in an uproar, and the gendarmerie on hand. For a moment he thought himself lost.

He remained where he was, petrified like the statue of salt, not daring to make a movement. Several minutes elapsed. The door had fallen wide open. He ventured to peep into the next room. Nothing had stirred there. He lent an ear. Nothing was moving in the house. The noise made by the rusty hinge had not awakened any one.

This first danger was past; but there still reigned a frightful tumult within him. Nevertheless, he did not retreat. Even when he had thought himself lost, he had not drawn back. His only thought now was to finish as soon as possible. He took a step and entered the room.

This room was in a state of perfect calm. Here and there vague and confused forms were distinguishable, which in the daylight were papers scattered on a table, open folios, volumes piled upon a stool, an armchair heaped with clothing, a prie-Dieu, and which at that hour were only shadowy corners and whitish spots. Jean Valjean advanced with precaution, taking care not to knock against the furniture. He could hear, at the extremity of the room, the even and tranquil breathing of the sleeping Bishop.

He suddenly came to a halt. He was near the bed. He had arrived there sooner than he had thought for.

Nature sometimes mingles her effects and her spectacles with our actions with sombre and intelligent appropriateness, as though she desired to make us reflect. For the last half-hour a large cloud had covered the heavens. At the moment when Jean Valjean paused in front of the bed, this cloud parted, as though on purpose, and a ray of light, traversing the long window, suddenly illuminated the Bishop's pale face. He was sleeping peacefully. He lay in his bed almost completely dressed, on account of the cold of the Basses-Alps, in a garment of brown wool, which covered his arms to the wrists. His head was thrown back on the pillow, in the careless attitude of repose; his hand, adorned with the pastoral ring, and whence had fallen so many good deeds and so many holy actions, was hanging over the edge of the bed. His whole face was illumined with a vague expression of satisfaction, of hope, and of felicity. It was more than a smile, and almost a radiance. He bore upon his brow the indescribable reflection of a light which was invisible. The soul of the just contemplates in sleep a mysterious heaven.

A reflection of that heaven rested on the Bishop.

It was, at the same time, a luminous transparency, for that heaven was within him. That heaven was his conscience.

At the moment when the ray of moonlight superposed itself, so to speak, upon that inward radiance, the sleeping Bishop seemed as in a glory. It remained, however, gentle and veiled in an ineffable half-light. That moon in the sky, that slumbering nature, that garden without a quiver, that house which was so calm, the hour, the moment, the silence, added some solemn and unspeakable quality to the venerable repose of this man, and enveloped in a sort of serene and majestic aureole that white hair, those closed eyes, that face in which all was hope and all was confidence, that head of an old man, and that slumber of an infant.

There was something almost divine in this man, who was thus august, without being himself aware of it.

Jean Valjean was in the shadow, and stood motionless, with his iron candlestick in his hand, frightened by this luminous old man. Never had he beheld anything like this. This confidence terrified him. The moral world has no grander spectacle than this: a troubled and uneasy conscience, which has arrived on the brink of an evil action, contemplating the slumber of the just.

That slumber in that isolation, and with a neighbor like himself, had about it something sublime, of which he was vaguely but imperiously conscious.

No one could have told what was passing within him, not even himself. In order to attempt to form an idea of it, it is necessary to think of the most violent of things in the presence of the most gentle. Even on his visage it would have been impossible to distinguish anything with certainty. It was a sort of haggard astonishment. He gazed at it, and that was all. But what was his thought? It would have been impossible to divine it. What was evident was, that he was touched and astounded. But what was the nature of this emotion?

His eye never quitted the old man. The only thing which was clearly to be inferred from his attitude and his physiognomy was a strange indecision. One would have said that he was hesitating between the two abysses,—the one in which one loses one's self and that in which one saves one's self. He seemed prepared to crush that skull or to kiss that hand.

At the expiration of a few minutes his left arm rose slowly towards his brow, and he took off his cap; then his arm fell back with the same deliberation, and Jean Valjean fell to meditating once more, his cap in his left hand, his club in his right hand, his hair bristling all over his savage head.

The Bishop continued to sleep in profound peace beneath that terrifying gaze.

The gleam of the moon rendered confusedly visible the crucifix over the chimney-piece, which seemed to be extending its arms to both of them, with a benediction for one and pardon for the other.

Suddenly Jean Valjean replaced his cap on his brow; then stepped rapidly past the bed, without glancing at the Bishop, straight to the cupboard, which he saw near the head; he raised his iron candlestick as though to force the lock; the key was there; he opened it; the first thing which presented itself to him was the basket of silverware; he seized it, traversed the chamber with long strides, without taking any precautions and without troubling himself about the noise, gained the door, re-entered the oratory, opened the window, seized his cudgel, bestrode the window-sill of the ground-floor, put the silver into his knapsack, threw away the basket, crossed the garden, leaped over the wall like a tiger, and fled.

CHAPTER XII

THE BISHOP WORKS

The next morning at sunrise Monseigneur Bienvenu was strolling in his garden. Madame Magloire ran up to him in utter consternation.

"Monseigneur, Monseigneur!" she exclaimed, "does your Grace know where the basket of silver is?"

"Yes," replied the Bishop.

"Jesus the Lord be blessed!" she resumed; "I did not know what had become of it."

The Bishop had just picked up the basket in a flower-bed. He presented it to Madame Magloire.

"Here it is."

"Well!" said she. "Nothing in it! And the silver?"

"Ah," returned the Bishop, "so it is the silver which troubles you? I don't know where it is."

"Great, good God! It is stolen! That man who was here last night has stolen it."

In a twinkling, with all the vivacity of an alert old woman, Madame Magloire had rushed to the oratory, entered the alcove, and returned to the Bishop. The Bishop had just bent down, and was sighing as he examined a plant of cochlearia des Guillons, which the basket had broken as it fell across the bed. He rose up at Madame Magloire's cry.

"Monseigneur, the man is gone! The silver has been stolen!"

As she uttered this exclamation, her eyes fell upon a corner of the garden, where traces of the wall having been scaled were visible. The coping of the wall had been torn away.

"Stay! yonder is the way he went. He jumped over into Cochefilet Lane. Ah, the abomination! He has stolen our silver!"

The Bishop remained silent for a moment; then he raised his grave eyes, and said gently to Madame Magloire:—

"And, in the first place, was that silver ours?"

Madame Magloire was speechless. Another silence ensued; then the Bishop went on:—

"Madame Magloire, I have for a long time detained that silver wrongfully. It belonged to the poor. Who was that man? A poor man, evidently."

"Alas! Jesus!" returned Madame Magloire. "It is not for my sake, nor for Mademoiselle's. It makes no difference to us. But it is for the sake of Monseigneur. What is Monseigneur to eat with now?"

The Bishop gazed at her with an air of amazement.

"Ah, come! Are there no such things as pewter forks and spoons?"

Madame Magloire shrugged her shoulders.

"Pewter has an odor."

"Iron forks and spoons, then."

Madame Magloire made an expressive grimace.

"Iron has a taste."

"Very well," said the Bishop; "wooden ones then."

A few moments later he was breakfasting at the very table at which Jean Valjean had sat on the previous evening. As he ate his breakfast, Monseigneur Welcome remarked gayly to his sister, who said nothing, and to Madame Magloire, who was grumbling under her breath, that one really does not need either fork or spoon, even of wood, in order to dip a bit of bread in a cup of milk.

"A pretty idea, truly," said Madame Magloire to herself, as she went and came, "to take in a man like that! and to lodge him close to one's self!

And how fortunate that he did nothing but steal! Ah, mon Dieu! it makes one shudder to think of it!"

As the brother and sister were about to rise from the table, there came a knock at the door.

"Come in," said the Bishop.

The door opened. A singular and violent group made its appearance on the threshold. Three men were holding a fourth man by the collar. The three men were gendarmes; the other was Jean Valjean.

A brigadier of gendarmes, who seemed to be in command of the group, was standing near the door. He entered and advanced to the Bishop, making a military salute.

"Monseigneur—" said he.

At this word, Jean Valjean, who was dejected and seemed overwhelmed, raised his head with an air of stupefaction.

"Monseigneur!" he murmured. "So he is not the cure?"

"Silence!" said the gendarme. "He is Monseigneur the Bishop."

In the meantime, Monseigneur Bienvenu had advanced as quickly as his great age permitted.

"Ah! here you are!" he exclaimed, looking at Jean Valjean. "I am glad to see you. Well, but how is this? I gave you the candlesticks too, which are of silver like the rest, and for which you can certainly get two hundred francs. Why did you not carry them away with your forks and spoons?"

Jean Valjean opened his eyes wide, and stared at the venerable Bishop with an expression which no human tongue can render any account of.

"Monseigneur," said the brigadier of gendarmes, "so what this man said is true, then? We came across him. He was walking like a man who is running away. We stopped him to look into the matter. He had this silver—"

"And he told you," interposed the Bishop with a smile, "that it had been given to him by a kind old fellow of a priest with whom he had passed the night? I see how the matter stands. And you have brought him back here? It is a mistake."

"In that case," replied the brigadier, "we can let him go?"

"Certainly," replied the Bishop.

The gendarmes released Jean Valjean, who recoiled.

"Is it true that I am to be released?" he said, in an almost inarticulate voice, and as though he were talking in his sleep.

"Yes, thou art released; dost thou not understand?" said one of the gendarmes.

"My friend," resumed the Bishop, "before you go, here are your candlesticks. Take them."

He stepped to the chimney-piece, took the two silver candlesticks, and brought them to Jean Valjean. The two women looked on without uttering a word, without a gesture, without a look which could disconcert the Bishop.

Jean Valjean was trembling in every limb. He took the two candlesticks mechanically, and with a bewildered air.

"Now," said the Bishop, "go in peace. By the way, when you return, my friend, it is not necessary to pass through the garden. You can always enter and depart through the street door. It is never fastened with anything but a latch, either by day or by night."

Then, turning to the gendarmes:—

"You may retire, gentlemen."

The gendarmes retired.

Jean Valjean was like a man on the point of fainting.

The Bishop drew near to him, and said in a low voice:—

"Do not forget, never forget, that you have promised to use this money in becoming an honest man."

Jean Valjean, who had no recollection of ever having promised anything, remained speechless. The Bishop had emphasized the words when he uttered them. He resumed with solemnity:—

"Jean Valjean, my brother, you no longer belong to evil, but to good. It is your soul that I buy from you; I withdraw it from black thoughts and the spirit of perdition, and I give it to God."

156

CHAPTER XIII

LITTLE GERVAIS

Jean Valjean left the town as though he were fleeing from it. He set out at a very hasty pace through the fields, taking whatever roads and paths presented themselves to him, without perceiving that he was incessantly retracing his steps. He wandered thus the whole morning, without having eaten anything and without feeling hungry. He was the prey of a throng of novel sensations. He was conscious of a sort of rage; he did not know against whom it was directed. He could not have told whether he was touched or humiliated. There came over him at moments a strange emotion which he resisted and to which he opposed the hardness acquired during the last twenty years of his life. This state of mind fatigued him. He perceived with dismay that the sort of frightful calm which the injustice of his misfortune had conferred upon him was giving way within him. He asked himself what would replace this. At times he would have actually preferred to be in prison with the gendarmes, and that things should not have happened in this way; it would have agitated him less. Although the season was tolerably far advanced, there were still a few late flowers in the hedge-rows here and there, whose odor as he passed through them in his march recalled to him memories of his childhood. These memories were almost intolerable to him, it was so long since they had recurred to him.

Unutterable thoughts assembled within him in this manner all day long.

As the sun declined to its setting, casting long shadows athwart the soil from every pebble, Jean Valjean sat down behind a bush upon a large ruddy plain, which was absolutely deserted. There was nothing on the horizon except the Alps. Not even the spire of a distant village. Jean Valjean might have been three leagues distant from D—A path which intersected the plain passed a few paces from the bush.

In the middle of this meditation, which would have contributed not a little to render his rags terrifying to any one who might have encountered him, a joyous sound became audible.

He turned his head and saw a little Savoyard, about ten years of age, coming up the path and singing, his hurdy-gurdy on his hip, and his marmot-box on his back,

One of those gay and gentle children, who go from land to land affording a view of their knees through the holes in their trousers.

Without stopping his song, the lad halted in his march from time to time, and played at knuckle-bones with some coins which he had in his hand—his whole fortune, probably.

Among this money there was one forty-sou piece.

The child halted beside the bush, without perceiving Jean Valjean, and tossed up his handful of sous, which, up to that time, he had caught with a good deal of adroitness on the back of his hand.

This time the forty-sou piece escaped him, and went rolling towards the brushwood until it reached Jean Valjean.

Jean Valjean set his foot upon it.

In the meantime, the child had looked after his coin and had caught sight of him.

He showed no astonishment, but walked straight up to the man.

The spot was absolutely solitary. As far as the eye could see there was not a person on the plain or on the path. The only sound was the tiny, feeble cries of a flock of birds of passage, which was traversing the heavens at an immense height. The child was standing with his back to the sun, which cast threads of gold in his hair and empurpled with its blood-red gleam the savage face of Jean Valjean.

"Sir," said the little Savoyard, with that childish confidence which is composed of ignorance and innocence, "my money."

"What is your name?" said Jean Valjean.

"Little Gervais, sir."

"Go away," said Jean Valjean.

"Sir," resumed the child, "give me back my money."

Jean Valjean dropped his head, and made no reply.

The child began again, "My money, sir."

Jean Valjean's eyes remained fixed on the earth.

"My piece of money!" cried the child, "my white piece! my silver!"

It seemed as though Jean Valjean did not hear him. The child grasped him by the collar of his blouse and shook him. At the same time he made an effort to displace the big iron-shod shoe which rested on his treasure.

"I want my piece of money! my piece of forty sous!"

The child wept. Jean Valjean raised his head. He still remained seated. His eyes were troubled. He gazed at the child, in a sort of amazement, then he stretched out his hand towards his cudgel and cried in a terrible voice, "Who's there?"

"I, sir," replied the child. "Little Gervais! I! Give me back my forty sous, if you please! Take your foot away, sir, if you please!"

Then irritated, though he was so small, and becoming almost menacing:—

"Come now, will you take your foot away? Take your foot away, or we'll see!"

"Ah! It's still you!" said Jean Valjean, and rising abruptly to his feet, his foot still resting on the silver piece, he added:—

"Will you take yourself off!"

The frightened child looked at him, then began to tremble from head to foot, and after a few moments of stupor he set out, running at the top of his speed, without daring to turn his neck or to utter a cry.

Nevertheless, lack of breath forced him to halt after a certain distance, and Jean Valjean heard him sobbing, in the midst of his own revery.

At the end of a few moments the child had disappeared.

The sun had set.

The shadows were descending around Jean Valjean. He had eaten nothing all day; it is probable that he was feverish.

He had remained standing and had not changed his attitude after the child's flight. The breath heaved his chest at long and irregular intervals. His gaze, fixed ten or twelve paces in front of him, seemed to be scrutinizing with profound attention the shape of an ancient fragment of blue earthenware which had fallen in the grass. All at once he shivered; he had just begun to feel the chill of evening.

He settled his cap more firmly on his brow, sought mechanically to cross and button his blouse, advanced a step and stopped to pick up his cudgel.

At that moment he caught sight of the forty-sou piece, which his foot had half ground into the earth, and which was shining among the pebbles. It was as though he had received a galvanic shock. "What is this?" he muttered between his teeth. He recoiled three paces, then halted, without being able to detach his gaze from the spot which his foot had trodden but an instant before, as though the thing which lay glittering there in the gloom had been an open eye riveted upon him.

At the expiration of a few moments he darted convulsively towards the silver coin, seized it, and straightened himself up again and began to gaze afar off over the plain, at the same time casting his eyes towards all points of the horizon, as he stood there erect and shivering, like a terrified wild animal which is seeking refuge.

He saw nothing. Night was falling, the plain was cold and vague, great banks of violet haze were rising in the gleam of the twilight.

He said, "Ah!" and set out rapidly in the direction in which the child had disappeared. After about thirty paces he paused, looked about him and saw nothing.

Then he shouted with all his might:—

"Little Gervais! Little Gervais!"

He paused and waited.

There was no reply.

The landscape was gloomy and deserted. He was encompassed by space. There was nothing around him but an obscurity in which his gaze was lost, and a silence which engulfed his voice.

An icy north wind was blowing, and imparted to things around him a sort of lugubrious life. The bushes shook their thin little arms with incredible fury. One would have said that they were threatening and pursuing some one.

He set out on his march again, then he began to run; and from time to time he halted and shouted into that solitude, with a voice which was the most formidable and the most disconsolate that it was possible to hear, "Little Gervais! Little Gervais!"

Assuredly, if the child had heard him, he would have been alarmed and would have taken good care not to show himself. But the child was no doubt already far away.

He encountered a priest on horseback. He stepped up to him and said:—

"Monsieur le Cure, have you seen a child pass?"

"No," said the priest.

"One named Little Gervais?"

"I have seen no one."

He drew two five-franc pieces from his money-bag and handed them to the priest.

"Monsieur le Cure, this is for your poor people. Monsieur le Cure, he was a little lad, about ten years old, with a marmot, I think, and a hurdy-gurdy. One of those Savoyards, you know?"

"I have not seen him."

"Little Gervais? There are no villages here? Can you tell me?"

"If he is like what you say, my friend, he is a little stranger. Such persons pass through these parts. We know nothing of them."

Jean Valjean seized two more coins of five francs each with violence, and gave them to the priest.

"For your poor," he said.

Then he added, wildly:—

"Monsieur l'Abbe, have me arrested. I am a thief."

The priest put spurs to his horse and fled in haste, much alarmed.

Jean Valjean set out on a run, in the direction which he had first taken.

In this way he traversed a tolerably long distance, gazing, calling, shouting, but he met no one. Two or three times he ran across the plain towards something which conveyed to him the effect of a human being reclining or crouching down; it turned out to be nothing but brushwood or rocks nearly on a level with the earth. At length, at a spot where three paths intersected each other, he stopped. The moon had risen. He sent his gaze into the distance and shouted for the last time, "Little Gervais! Little Gervais! Little Gervais!" His shout died away in the mist, without even awakening an echo. He murmured yet once more, "Little Gervais!" but in a feeble and almost inarticulate voice. It was his last effort; his legs gave way abruptly under him, as though an invisible power had suddenly overwhelmed him with the weight of his evil conscience; he fell exhausted, on a large stone, his fists clenched in his hair and his face on his knees, and he cried, "I am a wretch!"

Then his heart burst, and he began to cry. It was the first time that he had wept in nineteen years.

When Jean Valjean left the Bishop's house, he was, as we have seen, quite thrown out of everything that had been his thought hitherto. He could not yield to the evidence of what was going on within him. He hardened himself against the angelic action and the gentle words of the old man. "You have promised me to become an honest man. I buy your

162

soul. I take it away from the spirit of perversity; I give it to the good God."

This recurred to his mind unceasingly. To this celestial kindness he opposed pride, which is the fortress of evil within us. He was indistinctly conscious that the pardon of this priest was the greatest assault and the most formidable attack which had moved him yet; that his obduracy was finally settled if he resisted this clemency; that if he yielded, he should be obliged to renounce that hatred with which the actions of other men had filled his soul through so many years, and which pleased him; that this time it was necessary to conquer or to be conquered; and that a struggle, a colossal and final struggle, had been begun between his viciousness and the goodness of that man.

In the presence of these lights, he proceeded like a man who is intoxicated. As he walked thus with haggard eyes, did he have a distinct perception of what might result to him from his adventure at D—? Did he understand all those mysterious murmurs which warn or importune the spirit at certain moments of life? Did a voice whisper in his ear that he had just passed the solemn hour of his destiny; that there no longer remained a middle course for him; that if he were not henceforth the best of men, he would be the worst; that it behooved him now, so to speak, to mount higher than the Bishop, or fall lower than the convict; that if he wished to become good he must become an angel; that if he wished to remain evil, he must become a monster?

Here, again, some questions must be put, which we have already put to ourselves elsewhere: did he catch some shadow of all this in his thought, in a confused way? Misfortune certainly, as we have said, does form the education of the intelligence; nevertheless, it is doubtful whether Jean Valjean was in a condition to disentangle all that we have here indicated. If these ideas occurred to him, he but caught glimpses of, rather than saw them, and they only succeeded in throwing him into an unutterable and almost painful state of emotion. On emerging from that black and deformed thing which is called the galleys, the Bishop had hurt his soul, as too vivid a light would have hurt his eyes on emerging from the dark. The future life, the possible life which offered itself to him henceforth, all pure and radiant, filled him with tremors and anxiety. He no longer knew where he really was. Like an owl, who should suddenly see the sun rise, the convict had been dazzled and blinded, as it were, by virtue.

That which was certain, that which he did not doubt, was that he was no longer the same man, that everything about him was changed, that it was no longer in his power to make it as though the Bishop had not spoken to him and had not touched him.

In this state of mind he had encountered little Gervais, and had robbed him of his forty sous. Why? He certainly could not have explained it; was this the last effect and the supreme effort, as it were, of the evil thoughts which he had brought away from the galleys,—a remnant of impulse, a result of what is called in statics, acquired force? It was that, and it was also, perhaps, even less than that. Let us say it simply, it was not he who stole; it was not the man; it was the beast, who, by habit and instinct, had simply placed his foot upon that money, while the intelligence was struggling amid so many novel and hitherto unheard-of thoughts besetting it.

When intelligence re-awakened and beheld that action of the brute, Jean Valjean recoiled with anguish and uttered a cry of terror.

It was because,—strange phenomenon, and one which was possible only in the situation in which he found himself,—in stealing the money from that child, he had done a thing of which he was no longer capable.

However that may be, this last evil action had a decisive effect on him; it abruptly traversed that chaos which he bore in his mind, and dispersed it, placed on one side the thick obscurity, and on the other the light, and acted on his soul, in the state in which it then was, as certain chemical reagents act upon a troubled mixture by precipitating one element and clarifying the other.

164

First of all, even before examining himself and reflecting, all bewildered, like one who seeks to save himself, he tried to find the child in order to return his money to him; then, when he recognized the fact that this was impossible, he halted in despair. At the moment when he exclaimed "I am a wretch!" he had just perceived what he was, and he was already separated from himself to such a degree, that he seemed to himself to be no longer anything more than a phantom, and as if he had, there before him, in flesh and blood, the hideous galley-convict, Jean Valjean, cudgel in hand, his blouse on his hips, his knapsack filled with stolen objects on his back, with his resolute and gloomy visage, with his thoughts filled with abominable projects.

Excess of unhappiness had, as we have remarked, made him in some sort a visionary. This, then, was in the nature of a vision. He actually saw that Jean Valjean, that sinister face, before him. He had almost reached the point of asking himself who that man was, and he was horrified by him.

His brain was going through one of those violent and yet perfectly calm moments in which revery is so profound that it absorbs reality. One no longer beholds the object which one has before one, and one sees, as though apart from one's self, the figures which one has in one's own mind.

Thus he contemplated himself, so to speak, face to face, and at the same time, athwart this hallucination, he perceived in a mysterious depth a sort of light which he at first took for a torch. On scrutinizing this light which appeared to his conscience with more attention, he recognized the fact that it possessed a human form and that this torch was the Bishop.

His conscience weighed in turn these two men thus placed before it,—the Bishop and Jean Valjean. Nothing less than the first was required to soften the second. By one of those singular effects, which are peculiar to this sort of ecstasies, in proportion as his revery continued, as the Bishop grew great and resplendent in his eyes, so did Jean Valjean grow less and vanish. After a certain time he was no longer anything more than a shade. All at once he disappeared. The Bishop alone remained; he filled the whole soul of this wretched man with a magnificent radiance.

Jean Valjean wept for a long time. He wept burning tears, he sobbed with more weakness than a woman, with more fright than a child.

As he wept, daylight penetrated more and more clearly into his soul; an extraordinary light; a light at once ravishing and terrible. His past life, his first fault, his long expiation, his external brutishness, his internal hardness, his dismissal to liberty, rejoicing in manifold plans of vengeance, what had happened to him at the Bishop's, the last thing that he had done, that theft of forty sous from a child, a crime all the more cowardly, and all the more monstrous since it had come after the Bishop's pardon,—all this recurred to his mind and appeared clearly to him, but with a clearness which he had never hitherto witnessed. He examined his life, and it seemed horrible to him; his soul, and it seemed frightful to him. In the meantime a gentle light rested over this life and this soul. It seemed to him that he beheld Satan by the light of Paradise.

How many hours did he weep thus? What did he do after he had wept? Whither did he go! No one ever knew. The only thing which seems to be authenticated is that that same night the carrier who served Grenoble at that epoch, and who arrived at D—about three o'clock in the morning, saw, as he traversed the street in which the Bishop's residence was situated, a man in the attitude of prayer, kneeling on the pavement in the shadow, in front of the door of Monseigneur Welcome.

BOOK THIRD.

IN THE YEAR 1817

CHAPTER I

THE YEAR 1817

1817 is the year which Louis XVIII., with a certain royal assurance which was not wanting in pride, entitled the twenty-second of his reign. It is the year in which M. Bruguiere de Sorsum was celebrated. All the hairdressers' shops, hoping for powder and the return of the royal bird, were besmeared with azure and decked with fleurs-de-lys. It was the candid time at which Count Lynch sat every Sunday as church-warden in the church-warden's pew of Saint-Germain-des-Pres, in his costume of a peer of France, with his red ribbon and his long nose and the majesty of profile peculiar to a man who has performed a brilliant action. The brilliant action performed by M. Lynch was this: being mayor of Bordeaux, on the 12th of March, 1814, he had surrendered the city a little too promptly to M. the Duke d'Angouleme. Hence his peerage. In 1817 fashion swallowed up little boys of from four to six years of age in vast caps of morocco leather with ear-tabs resembling Esquimaux mitres. The French army was dressed in white, after the mode of the Austrian; the regiments were called legions; instead of numbers they bore the names of departments; Napoleon was at St. Helena; and since England refused him green cloth, he was having his old coats turned. In 1817 Pelligrini sang; Mademoiselle Bigottini danced; Potier reigned; Odry did not yet exist. Madame Saqui had succeeded to Forioso. There were still Prussians in France. M. Delalot was a personage. Legitimacy had just asserted itself by cutting off the hand, then the head, of Pleignier, of Carbonneau, and of Tolleron. The Prince de Talleyrand, grand chamberlain, and the Abbe Louis, appointed minister of finance, laughed as they looked at each other, with the laugh of the two augurs; both of them had celebrated, on the 14th of July, 1790, the mass of federation in the Champ de Mars; Talleyrand had said it as bishop, Louis had served it in the capacity of deacon. In 1817, in the side-alleys of this same Champ de Mars, two great cylinders of wood might have been seen lying in the rain, rotting amid the grass, painted blue, with traces of eagles and bees, from which the gilding was falling. These were the columns which two years before had upheld the Emperor's platform in the Champ de Mai. They were blackened here and there with the scorches of the bivouac of Austrians encamped near Gros-Caillou. Two or three of these columns had disappeared in these bivouac fires, and had warmed the large hands of the Imperial troops. The Field of May had this remarkable point: that it had been held in the month of June and in the Field of March (Mars). In this year, 1817, two things were popular: the Voltaire-Touquet and the snuff-box a la Charter. The most recent Parisian sensation was the crime of Dautun, who had thrown his brother's head into the fountain of the Flower-Market.

They had begun to feel anxious at the Naval Department, on account of the lack of news from that fatal frigate, The Medusa, which was destined to cover Chaumareix with infamy and Gericault with glory. Colonel Selves was going to Egypt to become Soliman-Pasha. The palace of Thermes, in the Rue de La Harpe, served as a shop for a cooper. On the platform of the octagonal tower of the Hotel de Cluny, the little shed of boards, which had served as an observatory to Messier, the naval astronomer under Louis XVI., was still to be seen. The Duchesse de Duras read to three or four friends her unpublished Ourika, in her boudoir furnished by X. in sky-blue satin. The N's were scratched off the Louvre. The bridge of Austerlitz had abdicated, and was entitled the bridge of the King's Garden [du Jardin du Roi], a double enigma, which disguised the bridge of Austerlitz and the Jardin des Plantes at one stroke. Louis XVIII., much preoccupied while annotating Horace with the corner of his finger-nail, heroes who have become emperors, and makers of wooden shoes who have become dauphins, had two anxieties,—Napoleon and Mathurin Bruneau. The French Academy had given for its prize subject, The Happiness procured through Study. M. Bellart was officially eloquent. In his shadow could be seen germinating that future advocate-general of Broe, dedicated to the sarcasms of Paul-Louis Courier. There was a false Chateaubriand, named Marchangy, in the interim, until there should be a false Marchangy, named d'Arlincourt. Claire d'Albe and Malek-Adel were masterpieces; Madame Cottin was proclaimed the chief writer of the epoch. The Institute had the academician, Napoleon Bonaparte, stricken from its list of members. A royal ordinance erected Angouleme into a naval school; for the Duc d'Angouleme, being lord high admiral, it was evident that the city of Angouleme had all the qualities of a seaport; otherwise the monarchical principle would have received a wound. In the Council of Ministers the question was agitated whether vignettes representing slack-rope performances, which adorned Franconi's advertising posters, and which attracted throngs of street urchins, should be tolerated. M. Paer, the author of Agnese, a good sort of fellow, with a square face and a wart on his cheek, directed the little private concerts of the Marquise de Sasenaye in the Rue Ville l'Eveque. All the young girls were singing the Hermit of Saint-Avelle, with words by Edmond Geraud. The Yellow Dwarf was transferred into Mirror. The Cafe Lemblin stood up for the Emperor, against the Cafe Valois, which upheld the Bourbons. The Duc de Berri, already surveyed from the shadow by Louvel, had just been married to a princess of Sicily. Madame de Stael had died a year previously. The body-guard hissed Mademoiselle Mars. The grand newspapers were all very small. Their form was restricted, but their liberty was great. The Constitutionnel was constitutional. La Minerve called Chateaubriand Chateaubriant. That t made the good middle-class people laugh heartily at the expense of the great writer. In journals which sold themselves, prostituted journalists, insulted the exiles of 1815. David had no longer any talent, Arnault had no longer any wit, Carnot was no longer honest, Soult had won no battles; it is true that Napoleon had no longer any genius. No one is ignorant of the fact that letters sent to an exile by post very rarely reached him, as the police made it their religious duty to intercept them. This is no new fact; Descartes complained of it in his exile. Now David, having, in a Belgian publication, shown some displeasure at not receiving letters which had been written to him, it struck the royalist journals as amusing; and they derided the prescribed man well on this occasion. What separated two men more than an abyss was to say, the regicides, or to say the voters; to say the enemies, or to say the allies; to say Napoleon, or to say Buonaparte. All sensible people were agreed that the era of revolution had been closed forever by King Louis XVIII., surnamed "The Immortal Author of the Charter." On the platform of the Pont-Neuf, the word Redivivus was carved on the pedestal that awaited the statue of Henry IV. M. Piet, in the Rue Therese, No. 4, was making the rough draft of his privy assembly to consolidate the monarchy. The leaders of the Right said at grave conjunctures, "We must write to Bacot." MM. Canuel, O'Mahoney, and De Chappedelaine were preparing the sketch, to some extent with Monsieur's approval, of what was to become later on "The Conspiracy of the Bord de l'Eau"— of the waterside. L'Epingle Noire was already plotting in his own quarter. Delaverderie was conferring with Trogoff. M. Decazes, who was liberal to a degree, reigned. Chateaubriand stood every morning at his window at No. 27 Rue Saint-Dominique, clad in footed trousers, and slippers, with a madras kerchief knotted over his gray hair, with his eyes fixed on a mirror, a complete set of dentist's instruments spread out before him, cleaning his teeth, which were charming, while he dictated The Monarchy according to the Charter to M. Pilorge, his secretary. Criticism, assuming an authoritative tone, preferred Lafon to Talma. M. de Feletez signed himself A.; M. Hoffmann signed himself Z. Charles Nodier wrote Therese Aubert. Divorce was abolished. Lyceums called themselves colleges. The collegians, decorated on the collar with a golden fleur-de-lys, fought each other apropos of the King of Rome. The counter-police of the chateau had denounced to her Royal Highness Madame, the portrait, everywhere exhibited, of M. the Duc d'Orleans, who made a better appearance in his uniform of a colonel-general of hussars than M. the Duc de Berri, in his uniform of colonel-general of dragoons—a serious inconvenience. The city of Paris was having the dome of the Invalides regilded at its own expense. Serious men asked themselves what M. de Trinquelague would do on such or such an occasion; M. Clausel de Montals differed on divers points from M. Clausel de Coussergues; M. de Salaberry was not satisfied. The comedian Picard, who belonged to the Academy, which the comedian Moliere had not been able to do, had The Two Philiberts played at the Odeon, upon whose pediment the removal of the letters still allowed THEATRE OF THE EMPRESS to be plainly read. People took part for or against Cugnet de Montarlot. Fabvier was factious; Bavoux was revolutionary. The Liberal, Pelicier, published an edition of Voltaire, with the following title: Works of Voltaire, of the French Academy. "That will attract purchasers," said the ingenious editor. The general opinion was that M. Charles Loyson would be the genius of the century; envy was beginning to gnaw at him—a sign of glory; and this verse was composed on him:—

"Even when Loyson steals, one feels that he has paws."

As Cardinal Fesch refused to resign, M. de Pins, Archbishop of Amasie, administered the diocese of Lyons. The quarrel over the valley of Dappes was begun between Switzerland and France by a memoir from Captain, afterwards General Dufour. Saint-Simon, ignored, was erecting his sublime dream. There was a celebrated Fourier at the Academy of Science, whom posterity has forgotten; and in some garret an obscure Fourier, whom the future will recall. Lord Byron was beginning to make his mark; a note to a poem by Millevoye introduced him to France in these terms: a certain Lord Baron. David d'Angers was trying to work in marble. The Abbe Caron was speaking, in terms of praise, to a private gathering of seminarists in the blind alley of Feuillantines, of an unknown priest, named Felicite-Robert, who, at a latter date, became Lamennais. A thing which smoked and clattered on the Seine with the noise of a swimming dog went and came beneath the windows of the Tuileries, from the Pont Royal to the Pont Louis XV.; it was a piece of mechanism which was not good for much; a sort of plaything, the idle dream of a dream-ridden inventor; an utopia—a steamboat. The Parisians stared indifferently at this useless thing. M. de Vaublanc, the reformer of the Institute by a coup d'etat, the distinguished author of numerous academicians, ordinances, and batches of members, after having created them, could not succeed in becoming one himself. The Faubourg Saint-Germain and the pavilion de Marsan wished to have M. Delaveau for prefect of police, on account of his piety. Dupuytren and Recamier entered into a quarrel in the amphitheatre of the School of Medicine, and threatened each other with their fists on the subject of the divinity of Jesus Christ. Cuvier, with one eye on Genesis and the other on nature, tried to please bigoted reaction by reconciling fossils with texts and by making mastodons flatter Moses.

M. Francois de Neufchateau, the praiseworthy cultivator of the memory of Parmentier, made a thousand efforts to have pomme de terre [potato] pronounced parmentiere, and succeeded therein not at all. The Abbe Gregoire, ex-bishop, ex-conventionary, ex-senator, had passed, in the royalist polemics, to the state of "Infamous Gregoire." The locution of which we have made use—passed to the state of—has been condemned as a neologism by M. Royer Collard. Under the third arch of the Pont de Jena, the new stone with which, the two years previously, the mining aperture made by Blucher to blow up the bridge had been stopped up, was still recognizable on account of its whiteness. Justice summoned to its bar a man who, on seeing the Comte d'Artois enter Notre Dame, had said aloud: "Sapristi! I regret the time when I saw Bonaparte and Talma enter the Bel Sauvage, arm in arm." A seditious utterance. Six months in prison. Traitors showed themselves unbuttoned; men who had gone over to the enemy on the eve of battle made no secret of their recompense, and strutted immodestly in the light of day, in the cynicism of riches and dignities; deserters from Ligny and Quatre-Bras, in the brazenness of their well-paid turpitude, exhibited their devotion to the monarchy in the most barefaced manner.

This is what floats up confusedly, pell-mell, for the year 1817, and is now forgotten. History neglects nearly all these particulars, and cannot do otherwise; the infinity would overwhelm it. Nevertheless, these details, which are wrongly called trivial,—there are no trivial facts in humanity, nor little leaves in vegetation,—are useful. It is of the physiognomy of the years that the physiognomy of the centuries is composed. In this year of 1817 four young Parisians arranged "a fine farce."

CHAPTER II

A DOUBLE QUARTETTE

These Parisians came, one from Toulouse, another from Limoges, the third from Cahors, and the fourth from Montauban; but they were students; and when one says student, one says Parisian: to study in Paris is to be born in Paris.

These young men were insignificant; every one has seen such faces; four specimens of humanity taken at random; neither good nor bad, neither wise nor ignorant, neither geniuses nor fools; handsome, with that charming April which is called twenty years. They were four Oscars; for, at that epoch, Arthurs did not yet exist. Burn for him the perfumes of Araby! exclaimed romance. Oscar advances. Oscar, I shall behold him! People had just emerged from Ossian; elegance was Scandinavian and Caledonian; the pure English style was only to prevail later, and the first of the Arthurs, Wellington, had but just won the battle of Waterloo.

These Oscars bore the names, one of Felix Tholomyes, of Toulouse; the second, Listolier, of Cahors; the next, Fameuil, of Limoges; the last, Blachevelle, of Montauban. Naturally, each of them had his mistress. Blachevelle loved Favourite, so named because she had been in England; Listolier adored Dahlia, who had taken for her nickname the name of a flower; Fameuil idolized Zephine, an abridgment of Josephine; Tholomyes had Fantine, called the Blonde, because of her beautiful, sunny hair.

Favourite, Dahlia, Zephine, and Fantine were four ravishing young women, perfumed and radiant, still a little like working-women, and not yet entirely divorced from their needles; somewhat disturbed by intrigues, but still retaining on their faces something of the serenity of toil, and in their souls that flower of honesty which survives the first fall in woman. One of the four was called the young, because she was the youngest of them, and one was called the old; the old one was twenty-three. Not to conceal anything, the three first were more experienced, more heedless, and more emancipated into the tumult of life than Fantine the Blonde, who was still in her first illusions.

Dahlia, Zephine, and especially Favourite, could not have said as much. There had already been more than one episode in their romance, though hardly begun; and the lover who had borne the name of Adolph in the first chapter had turned out to be Alphonse in the second, and Gustave in the third. Poverty and coquetry are two fatal counsellors; one scolds and the other flatters, and the beautiful daughters of the people have both of them whispering in their ear, each on its own side. These badly guarded souls listen. Hence the falls which they accomplish, and the stones which are thrown at them. They are overwhelmed with splendor of all that is immaculate and inaccessible. Alas! what if the Jungfrau were hungry?

Favourite having been in England, was admired by Dahlia and Zephine. She had had an establishment of her own very early in life. Her father was an old unmarried professor of mathematics, a brutal man and a braggart, who went out to give lessons in spite of his age. This professor, when he was a young man, had one day seen a chambermaid's gown catch on a fender; he had fallen in love in consequence of this accident. The result had been Favourite. She met her father from time to time, and he bowed to her. One morning an old woman with the air of a devotee, had entered her apartments, and had said to her, "You do not know me, Mamemoiselle?" "No." "I am your mother." Then the old woman opened the sideboard, and ate and drank, had a mattress which she owned brought in, and installed herself. This cross and pious old mother never spoke to Favourite, remained hours without uttering a word, breakfasted, dined, and supped for four, and went down to the porter's quarters for company, where she spoke ill of her daughter.

It was having rosy nails that were too pretty which had drawn Dahlia to Listolier, to others perhaps, to idleness. How could she make such nails work? She who wishes to remain virtuous must not have pity on her hands. As for Zephine, she had conquered Fameuil by her roguish and caressing little way of saying "Yes, sir."

The young men were comrades; the young girls were friends. Such loves are always accompanied by such friendships.

Goodness and philosophy are two distinct things; the proof of this is that, after making all due allowances for these little irregular households, Favourite, Zephine, and Dahlia were philosophical young women, while Fantine was a good girl.

Good! some one will exclaim; and Tholomyes? Solomon would reply that love forms a part of wisdom. We will confine ourselves to saying that the love of Fantine was a first love, a sole love, a faithful love.

She alone, of all the four, was not called "thou" by a single one of them.

Fantine was one of those beings who blossom, so to speak, from the dregs of the people. Though she had emerged from the most unfathomable depths of social shadow, she bore on her brow the sign of the anonymous and the unknown. She was born at M. sur M. Of what parents? Who can say? She had never known father or mother. She was called Fantine. Why Fantine? She had never borne any other name. At the epoch of her birth the Directory still existed. She had no family name; she had no family; no baptismal name; the Church no longer existed. She bore the name which pleased the first random passer-by, who had encountered her, when a very small child, running bare-legged in the street. She received the name as she received the water from the clouds upon her brow when it rained. She was called little Fantine. No one knew more than that. This human creature had entered life in just this way. At the age of ten, Fantine quitted the town and went to service with some farmers in the neighborhood. At fifteen she came to Paris "to seek her fortune." Fantine was beautiful, and remained pure as long as she could. She was a lovely blonde, with fine teeth. She had gold and pearls for her dowry; but her gold was on her head, and her pearls were in her mouth.

She worked for her living; then, still for the sake of her living,—for the heart, also, has its hunger,—she loved.

She loved Tholomyes.

An amour for him; passion for her. The streets of the Latin quarter, filled with throngs of students and grisettes, saw the beginning of their dream. Fantine had long evaded Tholomyes in the mazes of the hill of the Pantheon, where so many adventurers twine and untwine, but in such a way as constantly to encounter him again. There is a way of avoiding which resembles seeking. In short, the eclogue took place.

Blachevelle, Listolier, and Fameuil formed a sort of group of which Tholomyes was the head. It was he who possessed the wit.

Tholomyes was the antique old student; he was rich; he had an income of four thousand francs; four thousand francs! a splendid scandal on Mount Sainte-Genevieve. Tholomyes was a fast man of thirty, and badly preserved. He was wrinkled and toothless, and he had the beginning of a bald spot, of which he himself said with sadness, the skull at thirty, the knee at forty. His digestion was mediocre, and he had been attacked by a watering in one eye. But in proportion as his youth disappeared, gayety was kindled; he replaced his teeth with buffooneries, his hair with mirth, his health with irony, his weeping eye laughed incessantly. He was dilapidated but still in flower. His youth, which was packing up for departure long before its time, beat a retreat in good order, bursting with laughter, and no one saw anything but fire. He had had a piece rejected at the Vaudeville. He made a few verses now and then. In addition to this he doubted everything to the last degree, which is a vast force in the eyes of the weak. Being thus ironical and bald, he was the leader. Iron is an English word. Is it possible that irony is derived from it?

One day Tholomyes took the three others aside, with the gesture of an oracle, and said to them:—

"Fantine, Dahlia, Zephine, and Favourite have been teasing us for nearly a year to give them a surprise. We have promised them solemnly that we would. They are forever talking about it to us, to me in particular, just as the old women in Naples cry to Saint Januarius, 'Faccia gialluta, fa o miracolo, Yellow face, perform thy miracle,' so our beauties say to me incessantly, 'Tholomyes, when will you bring forth your surprise?' At the same time our parents keep writing to us. Pressure on both sides. The moment has arrived, it seems to me; let us discuss the question."

Thereupon, Tholomyes lowered his voice and articulated something so mirthful, that a vast and enthusiastic grin broke out upon the four mouths simultaneously, and Blachevelle exclaimed, "That is an idea."

A smoky tap-room presented itself; they entered, and the remainder of their confidential colloquy was lost in shadow.

The result of these shades was a dazzling pleasure party which took place on the following Sunday, the four young men inviting the four young girls.

CHAPTER III

FOUR AND FOUR

It is hard nowadays to picture to one's self what a pleasure-trip of students and grisettes to the country was like, forty-five years ago. The suburbs of Paris are no longer the same; the physiognomy of what may be called circumparisian life has changed completely in the last half-century; where there was the cuckoo, there is the railway car; where there was a tender-boat, there is now the steamboat; people speak of Fecamp nowadays as they spoke of Saint-Cloud in those days. The Paris of 1862 is a city which has France for its outskirts.

The four couples conscientiously went through with all the country follies possible at that time. The vacation was beginning, and it was a warm, bright, summer day. On the preceding day, Favourite, the only one who knew how to write, had written the following to Tholomyes in the name of the four: "It is a good hour to emerge from happiness." That is why they rose at five o'clock in the morning. Then they went to Saint-Cloud by the coach, looked at the dry cascade and exclaimed, "This must be very beautiful when there is water!" They breakfasted at the Tete-Noir, where Castaing had not yet been; they treated themselves to a game of ring-throwing under the quincunx of trees of the grand fountain; they ascended Diogenes' lantern, they gambled for macaroons at the roulette establishment of the Pont de Sevres, picked bouquets at Pateaux, bought reed-pipes at Neuilly, ate apple tarts everywhere, and were perfectly happy.

The young girls rustled and chatted like warblers escaped from their cage. It was a perfect delirium. From time to time they bestowed little taps on the young men. Matutinal intoxication of life! adorable years! the wings of the dragonfly quiver. Oh, whoever you may be, do you not remember? Have you rambled through the brushwood, holding aside the branches, on account of the charming head which is coming on behind you? Have you slid, laughing, down a slope all wet with rain, with a beloved woman holding your hand, and crying, "Ah, my new boots! what a state they are in!"

Let us say at once that that merry obstacle, a shower, was lacking in the case of this good-humored party, although Favourite had said as they set out, with a magisterial and maternal tone, "The slugs are crawling in the paths,—a sign of rain, children."

All four were madly pretty. A good old classic poet, then famous, a good fellow who had an Eleonore, M. le Chevalier de Labouisse, as he strolled that day beneath the chestnut-trees of Saint-Cloud, saw them pass about ten o'clock in the morning, and exclaimed, "There is one too many of them," as he thought of the Graces. Favourite, Blachevelle's friend, the one aged three and twenty, the old one, ran on in front under the great green boughs, jumped the ditches, stalked distractedly over bushes, and presided over this merry-making with the spirit of a young female faun. Zephine and Dahlia, whom chance had made beautiful in such a way that they set each off when they were together, and completed each other, never left each other, more from an instinct of coquetry than from friendship, and clinging to each other, they assumed English poses; the first keepsakes had just made their appearance, melancholy was dawning for women, as later on, Byronism dawned for men; and the hair of the tender sex began to droop dolefully. Zephine and Dahlia had their hair dressed in rolls. Listolier and Fameuil, who were engaged in discussing their professors, explained to Fantine the difference that existed between M. Delvincourt and M. Blondeau.

Blachevelle seemed to have been created expressly to carry Favourite's single-bordered, imitation India shawl of Ternaux's manufacture, on his arm on Sundays.

Tholomyes followed, dominating the group. He was very gay, but one felt the force of government in him; there was dictation in his joviality; his principal ornament was a pair of trousers of elephant-leg pattern of nankeen, with straps of braided copper wire; he carried a stout rattan worth two hundred francs in his hand, and, as he treated himself to everything, a strange thing called a cigar in his mouth. Nothing was sacred to him; he smoked.

"That Tholomyes is astounding!" said the others, with veneration. "What trousers! What energy!"

As for Fantine, she was a joy to behold. Her splendid teeth had evidently received an office from God,—laughter. She preferred to carry her little hat of sewed straw, with its long white strings, in her hand rather than on her head. Her thick blond hair, which was inclined to wave, and which easily uncoiled, and which it was necessary to fasten up incessantly, seemed made for the flight of Galatea under the willows. Her rosy lips babbled enchantingly. The corners of her mouth voluptuously turned up, as in the antique masks of Erigone, had an air of encouraging the audacious; but her long, shadowy lashes drooped discreetly over the jollity of the lower part of the face as though to call a halt. There was something indescribably harmonious and striking about her entire dress. She wore a gown of mauve barege, little reddish brown buskins, whose ribbons traced an X on her fine, white, open-worked stockings, and that sort of muslin spencer, a Marseilles invention, whose name, canezou, a corruption of the words quinze aout, pronounced after the fashion of the Canebiere, signifies fine weather, heat, and midday. The three others, less timid, as we have already said, wore low-necked dresses without disguise, which in summer, beneath flower-adorned hats, are very graceful and enticing; but by the side of these audacious outfits, blond Fantine's canezou, with its transparencies, its indiscretion, and its reticence, concealing and displaying at one and the same time, seemed an alluring godsend of decency, and the famous Court of Love, presided over by the Vicomtesse de Cette, with the sea-green eyes, would, perhaps, have awarded the prize for coquetry to this canezou, in the contest for the prize of modesty. The most ingenious is, at times, the wisest. This does happen.

Brilliant of face, delicate of profile, with eyes of a deep blue, heavy lids, feet arched and small, wrists and ankles admirably formed, a white skin which, here and there allowed the azure branching of the veins to be seen, joy, a cheek that was young and fresh, the robust throat of the Juno of AEgina, a strong and supple nape of the neck, shoulders modelled as though by Coustou, with a voluptuous dimple in the middle, visible through the muslin; a gayety cooled by dreaminess; sculptural and exquisite—such was Fantine; and beneath these feminine adornments and these ribbons one could divine a statue, and in that statue a soul.

Fantine was beautiful, without being too conscious of it. Those rare dreamers, mysterious priests of the beautiful who silently confront everything with perfection, would have caught a glimpse in this little working-woman, through the transparency of her Parisian grace, of the ancient sacred euphony. This daughter of the shadows was thoroughbred. She was beautiful in the two ways—style and rhythm. Style is the form of the ideal; rhythm is its movement.

We have said that Fantine was joy; she was also modesty.

To an observer who studied her attentively, that which breathed from her athwart all the intoxication of her age, the season, and her love affair, was an invincible expression of reserve and modesty. She remained a little astonished. This chaste astonishment is the shade of difference which separates Psyche from Venus. Fantine had the long, white, fine fingers of the vestal virgin who stirs the ashes of the sacred fire with a golden pin. Although she would have refused nothing to Tholomyes, as we shall have more than ample opportunity to see, her face in repose was supremely virginal; a sort of serious and almost austere dignity suddenly overwhelmed her at certain times, and there was nothing more singular and disturbing than to see gayety become so suddenly extinct there, and meditation succeed to cheerfulness without any transition state. This sudden and sometimes severely accentuated gravity resembled the disdain of a goddess. Her brow, her nose, her chin, presented that equilibrium of outline which is quite distinct from equilibrium of proportion, and from which harmony of countenance results; in the very characteristic interval which separates the base of the nose from the upper lip, she had that imperceptible and charming fold, a mysterious sign of chastity, which makes Barberousse fall in love with a Diana found in the treasures of Iconia.

Love is a fault; so be it. Fantine was innocence floating high over fault.

CHAPTER IV

THOLOMYES IS SO MERRY THAT HE SINGS A SPANISH DITTY

That day was composed of dawn, from one end to the other. All nature seemed to be having a holiday, and to be laughing. The flower-beds of Saint-Cloud perfumed the air; the breath of the Seine rustled the leaves vaguely; the branches gesticulated in the wind, bees pillaged the jasmines; a whole bohemia of butterflies swooped down upon the yarrow, the clover, and the sterile oats; in the august park of the King of France there was a pack of vagabonds, the birds.

The four merry couples, mingled with the sun, the fields, the flowers, the trees, were resplendent.

And in this community of Paradise, talking, singing, running, dancing, chasing butterflies, plucking convolvulus, wetting their pink, open-work stockings in the tall grass, fresh, wild, without malice, all received, to some extent, the kisses of all, with the exception of Fantine, who was hedged about with that vague resistance of hers composed of dreaminess and wildness, and who was in love. "You always have a queer look about you," said Favourite to her.

Such things are joys. These passages of happy couples are a profound appeal to life and nature, and make a caress and light spring forth from everything. There was once a fairy who created the fields and forests expressly for those in love,—in that eternal hedge-school of lovers, which is forever beginning anew, and which will last as long as there are hedges and scholars. Hence the popularity of spring among thinkers. The patrician and the knife-grinder, the duke and the peer, the limb of the law, the courtiers and townspeople, as they used to say in olden times, all are subjects of this fairy. They laugh and hunt, and there is in the air the brilliance of an apotheosis—what a transfiguration effected by love! Notaries' clerks are gods. And the little cries, the pursuits through the grass, the waists embraced on the fly, those jargons which are melodies, those adorations which burst forth in the manner of pronouncing a syllable, those cherries torn from one mouth by another,—all this blazes forth and takes its place among the celestial glories. Beautiful women waste themselves sweetly. They think that this will never come to an end. Philosophers, poets, painters, observe these ecstasies and know not what to make of it, so greatly are they dazzled by it. The departure for Cythera! exclaims Watteau; Lancret, the painter of plebeians, contemplates his bourgeois, who have flitted away into the azure sky; Diderot stretches out his arms to all these love idyls, and d'Urfe mingles druids with them.

After breakfast the four couples went to what was then called the King's Square to see a newly arrived plant from India, whose name escapes our memory at this moment, and which, at that epoch, was attracting all Paris to Saint-Cloud. It was an odd and charming shrub with a long stem, whose numerous branches, bristling and leafless and as fine as threads, were covered with a million tiny white rosettes; this gave the shrub the air of a head of hair studded with flowers. There was always an admiring crowd about it.

After viewing the shrub, Tholomyes exclaimed, "I offer you asses!" and having agreed upon a price with the owner of the asses, they returned by way of Vanvres and Issy. At Issy an incident occurred. The truly national park, at that time owned by Bourguin the contractor, happened to be wide open. They passed the gates, visited the manikin anchorite in his grotto, tried the mysterious little effects of the famous cabinet of mirrors, the wanton trap worthy of a satyr become a millionaire or of Turcaret metamorphosed into a Priapus. They had stoutly shaken the swing attached to the two chestnut-trees celebrated by the Abbe de Bernis. As he swung these beauties, one after the other, producing folds in the fluttering skirts which Greuze would have found to his taste, amid peals of laughter, the Toulousan Tholomyes, who was somewhat of a Spaniard, Toulouse being the cousin of Tolosa, sang, to a melancholy chant, the old ballad gallega, probably inspired by some lovely maid dashing in full flight upon a rope between two trees:—

"Soy de Badajoz,	"Badajoz is my home,
Amor me llama,	And Love is my name;
Toda mi alma,	To my eyes in flame,
Es en mi ojos,	All my soul doth come;
Porque ensenas,	For instruction meet
A tuas piernas.	I receive at thy feet"

Fantine alone refused to swing.

"I don't like to have people put on airs like that," muttered Favourite, with a good deal of acrimony.

After leaving the asses there was a fresh delight; they crossed the Seine in a boat, and proceeding from Passy on foot they reached the barrier of l'Etoile. They had been up since five o'clock that morning, as the reader will remember; but bah! there is no such thing as fatigue on Sunday, said Favourite; on Sunday fatigue does not work.

About three o'clock the four couples, frightened at their happiness, were sliding down the Russian mountains, a singular edifice which then occupied the heights of Beaujon, and whose undulating line was visible above the trees of the Champs Elysees.

From time to time Favourite exclaimed:—

"And the surprise? I claim the surprise."

"Patience," replied Tholomyes.

188

CHAPTER V

AT BOMBARDA'S

The Russian mountains having been exhausted, they began to think about dinner; and the radiant party of eight, somewhat weary at last, became stranded in Bombarda's public house, a branch establishment which had been set up in the Champs-Elysees by that famous restaurant-keeper, Bombarda, whose sign could then be seen in the Rue de Rivoli, near Delorme Alley.

A large but ugly room, with an alcove and a bed at the end (they had been obliged to put up with this accommodation in view of the Sunday crowd); two windows whence they could survey beyond the elms, the quay and the river; a magnificent August sunlight lightly touching the panes; two tables; upon one of them a triumphant mountain of bouquets, mingled with the hats of men and women; at the other the four couples seated round a merry confusion of platters, dishes, glasses, and bottles; jugs of beer mingled with flasks of wine; very little order on the table, some disorder beneath it;

> "They made beneath the table
> A noise, a clatter of the feet that was abominable,"

says Moliere.

This was the state which the shepherd idyl, begun at five o'clock in the morning, had reached at half-past four in the afternoon. The sun was setting; their appetites were satisfied.

The Champs-Elysees, filled with sunshine and with people, were nothing but light and dust, the two things of which glory is composed. The horses of Marly, those neighing marbles, were prancing in a cloud of gold. Carriages were going and coming. A squadron of magnificent body-guards, with their clarions at their head, were descending the Avenue de Neuilly; the white flag, showing faintly rosy in the setting sun, floated over the dome of the Tuileries. The Place de la Concorde, which had become the Place Louis XV. once more, was choked with happy promenaders. Many wore the silver fleur-de-lys suspended from the white-watered ribbon, which had not yet wholly disappeared from button-holes in the year 1817. Here and there choruses of little girls threw to the winds, amid the passersby, who formed into circles and applauded, the then celebrated Bourbon air, which was destined to strike the Hundred Days with lightning, and which had for its refrain:—

"Rendez-nous notre pere de Gand,
    Rendez-nous notre pere."

"Give us back our father from Ghent,
    Give us back our father."

Groups of dwellers in the suburbs, in Sunday array, sometimes even decorated with the fleur-de-lys, like the bourgeois, scattered over the large square and the Marigny square, were playing at rings and revolving on the wooden horses; others were engaged in drinking; some journeyman printers had on paper caps; their laughter was audible. Every thing was radiant. It was a time of undisputed peace and profound royalist security; it was the epoch when a special and private report of Chief of Police Angeles to the King, on the subject of the suburbs of Paris, terminated with these lines:—

190

"Taking all things into consideration, Sire, there is nothing to be feared from these people. They are as heedless and as indolent as cats. The populace is restless in the provinces; it is not in Paris. These are very pretty men, Sire. It would take all of two of them to make one of your grenadiers. There is nothing to be feared on the part of the populace of Paris the capital. It is remarkable that the stature of this population should have diminished in the last fifty years; and the populace of the suburbs is still more puny than at the time of the Revolution. It is not dangerous. In short, it is an amiable rabble."

Prefects of the police do not deem it possible that a cat can transform itself into a lion; that does happen, however, and in that lies the miracle wrought by the populace of Paris. Moreover, the cat so despised by Count Anglès possessed the esteem of the republics of old. In their eyes it was liberty incarnate; and as though to serve as pendant to the Minerva Aptera of the Piraeus, there stood on the public square in Corinth the colossal bronze figure of a cat. The ingenuous police of the Restoration beheld the populace of Paris in too "rose-colored" a light; it is not so much of "an amiable rabble" as it is thought. The Parisian is to the Frenchman what the Athenian was to the Greek: no one sleeps more soundly than he, no one is more frankly frivolous and lazy than he, no one can better assume the air of forgetfulness; let him not be trusted nevertheless; he is ready for any sort of cool deed; but when there is glory at the end of it, he is worthy of admiration in every sort of fury. Give him a pike, he will produce the 10th of August; give him a gun, you will have Austerlitz. He is Napoleon's stay and Danton's resource. Is it a question of country, he enlists; is it a question of liberty, he tears up the pavements. Beware! his hair filled with wrath, is epic; his blouse drapes itself like the folds of a chlamys. Take care! he will make of the first Rue Grenetat which comes to hand Caudine Forks. When the hour strikes, this man of the faubourgs will grow in stature; this little man will arise, and his gaze will be terrible, and his breath will become a tempest, and there will issue forth from that slender chest enough wind to disarrange the folds of the Alps. It is, thanks to the suburban man of Paris, that the Revolution, mixed with arms, conquers Europe. He sings; it is his delight. Proportion his song to his nature, and you will see! As long as he has for refrain nothing but la Carmagnole, he only overthrows Louis XVI.; make him sing the Marseillaise, and he will free the world.

This note jotted down on the margin of Angles' report, we will return to our four couples. The dinner, as we have said, was drawing to its close.

CHAPTER VI

A CHAPTER IN WHICH THEY ADORE EACH OTHER

Chat at table, the chat of love; it is as impossible to reproduce one as the other; the chat of love is a cloud; the chat at table is smoke.

Fameuil and Dahlia were humming. Tholomyes was drinking. Zephine was laughing, Fantine smiling, Listolier blowing a wooden trumpet which he had purchased at Saint-Cloud.

Favourite gazed tenderly at Blachevelle and said:—

"Blachevelle, I adore you."

This called forth a question from Blachevelle:—

"What would you do, Favourite, if I were to cease to love you?"

"I!" cried Favourite. "Ah! Do not say that even in jest! If you were to cease to love me, I would spring after you, I would scratch you, I should rend you, I would throw you into the water, I would have you arrested."

Blachevelle smiled with the voluptuous self-conceit of a man who is tickled in his self-love. Favourite resumed:—

"Yes, I would scream to the police! Ah! I should not restrain myself, not at all! Rabble!"

Blachevelle threw himself back in his chair, in an ecstasy, and closed both eyes proudly.

Dahlia, as she ate, said in a low voice to Favourite, amid the uproar:—

"So you really idolize him deeply, that Blachevelle of yours?"

"I? I detest him," replied Favourite in the same tone, seizing her fork again. "He is avaricious. I love the little fellow opposite me in my house. He is very nice, that young man; do you know him? One can see that he is an actor by profession. I love actors. As soon as he comes in, his mother says to him: 'Ah! mon Dieu! my peace of mind is gone. There he goes with his shouting. But, my dear, you are splitting my head!' So he goes up to rat-ridden garrets, to black holes, as high as he can mount, and there he sets to singing, declaiming, how do I know what? so that he can be heard down stairs! He earns twenty sous a day at an attorney's by penning quibbles. He is the son of a former precentor of Saint-Jacques-du-Haut-Pas. Ah! he is very nice. He idolizes me so, that one day when he saw me making batter for some pancakes, he said to me: 'Mamselle, make your gloves into fritters, and I will eat them.' It is only artists who can say such things as that. Ah! he is very nice. I am in a fair way to go out of my head over that little fellow. Never mind; I tell Blachevelle that I adore him—how I lie! Hey! How I do lie!"

Favourite paused, and then went on:—

"I am sad, you see, Dahlia. It has done nothing but rain all summer; the wind irritates me; the wind does not abate. Blachevelle is very stingy; there are hardly any green peas in the market; one does not know what to eat. I have the spleen, as the English say, butter is so dear! and then you see it is horrible, here we are dining in a room with a bed in it, and that disgusts me with life."

CHAPTER VII

THE WISDOM OF THOLOMYES

In the meantime, while some sang, the rest talked together tumultuously all at once; it was no longer anything but noise. Tholomyes intervened.

"Let us not talk at random nor too fast," he exclaimed. "Let us reflect, if we wish to be brilliant. Too much improvisation empties the mind in a stupid way. Running beer gathers no froth. No haste, gentlemen. Let us mingle majesty with the feast. Let us eat with meditation; let us make haste slowly. Let us not hurry. Consider the springtime; if it makes haste, it is done for; that is to say, it gets frozen. Excess of zeal ruins peach-trees and apricot-trees. Excess of zeal kills the grace and the mirth of good dinners. No zeal, gentlemen! Grimod de la Reyniere agrees with Talleyrand."

A hollow sound of rebellion rumbled through the group.

"Leave us in peace, Tholomyes," said Blachevelle.

"Down with the tyrant!" said Fameuil.

"Bombarda, Bombance, and Bambochel!" cried Listolier.

"Sunday exists," resumed Fameuil.

"We are sober," added Listolier.

"Tholomyes," remarked Blachevelle, "contemplate my calmness [mon calme]."

"You are the Marquis of that," retorted Tholomyes.

This mediocre play upon words produced the effect of a stone in a pool. The Marquis de Montcalm was at that time a celebrated royalist. All the frogs held their peace.

"Friends," cried Tholomyes, with the accent of a man who had recovered his empire, "Come to yourselves. This pun which has fallen from the skies must not be received with too much stupor. Everything which falls in that way is not necessarily worthy of enthusiasm and respect. The pun is the dung of the mind which soars. The jest falls, no matter where; and the mind after producing a piece of stupidity plunges into the azure depths. A whitish speck flattened against the rock does not prevent the condor from soaring aloft. Far be it from me to insult the pun! I honor it in proportion to its merits; nothing more. All the most august, the most sublime, the most charming of humanity, and perhaps outside of humanity, have made puns. Jesus Christ made a pun on St. Peter, Moses on Isaac, AEschylus on Polynices, Cleopatra on Octavius. And observe that Cleopatra's pun preceded the battle of Actium, and that had it not been for it, no one would have remembered the city of Toryne, a Greek name which signifies a ladle. That once conceded, I return to my exhortation. I repeat, brothers, I repeat, no zeal, no hubbub, no excess; even in witticisms, gayety, jollities, or plays on words. Listen to me. I have the prudence of Amphiaraus and the baldness of Caesar. There must be a limit, even to rebuses. Est modus in rebus.

"There must be a limit, even to dinners. You are fond of apple turnovers, ladies; do not indulge in them to excess. Even in the matter of turnovers, good sense and art are requisite. Gluttony chastises the glutton, Gula punit Gulax. Indigestion is charged by the good God with preaching morality to stomachs. And remember this: each one of our passions, even love, has a stomach which must not be filled too full. In all things the word finis must be written in good season; self-control must be exercised when the matter becomes urgent; the bolt must be drawn on appetite; one must set one's own fantasy to the violin, and carry one's self to the post. The sage is the man who knows how, at a given moment, to effect his own arrest. Have some confidence in me, for I have succeeded to some extent in my study of the law, according to the verdict of my examinations, for I know the difference between the question put and the question pending, for I have sustained a thesis in Latin upon the manner in which torture was administered at Rome at the epoch when Munatius Demens was quaestor of the Parricide; because I am going to be a doctor, apparently it does not follow that it is absolutely necessary that I should be an imbecile. I recommend you to moderation in your desires. It is true that my name is Felix Tholomyes; I speak well. Happy is he who, when the hour strikes, takes a heroic resolve, and abdicates like Sylla or Origenes."

Favourite listened with profound attention.

"Felix," said she, "what a pretty word! I love that name. It is Latin; it means prosper."

Tholomyes went on:—

"Quirites, gentlemen, caballeros, my friends. Do you wish never to feel the prick, to do without the nuptial bed, and to brave love? Nothing more simple. Here is the receipt: lemonade, excessive exercise, hard labor; work yourself to death, drag blocks, sleep not, hold vigil, gorge yourself with nitrous beverages, and potions of nymphaeas; drink emulsions of poppies and agnus castus; season this with a strict diet, starve yourself, and add thereto cold baths, girdles of herbs, the application of a plate of lead, lotions made with the subacetate of lead, and fomentations of oxycrat."

"I prefer a woman," said Listolier.

"Woman," resumed Tholomyes; "distrust her. Woe to him who yields himself to the unstable heart of woman! Woman is perfidious and disingenuous. She detests the serpent from professional jealousy. The serpent is the shop over the way."

"Tholomyes!" cried Blachevelle, "you are drunk!"

"Pardieu," said Tholomyes.

"Then be gay," resumed Blachevelle.

"I agree to that," responded Tholomyes.

And, refilling his glass, he rose.

"Glory to wine! Nunc te, Bacche, canam! Pardon me ladies; that is Spanish. And the proof of it, senoras, is this: like people, like cask. The arrobe of Castile contains sixteen litres; the cantaro of Alicante, twelve; the almude of the Canaries, twenty-five; the cuartin of the Balearic Isles, twenty-six; the boot of Tzar Peter, thirty. Long live that Tzar who was great, and long live his boot, which was still greater! Ladies, take the advice of a friend; make a mistake in your neighbor if you see fit. The property of love is to err. A love affair is not made to crouch down and brutalize itself like an English serving-maid who has callouses on her knees from scrubbing. It is not made for that; it errs gayly, our gentle love. It has been said, error is human; I say, error is love. Ladies, I idolize you all. O Zephine, O Josephine, face more than irregular, you would be charming were you not all askew. You have the air of a pretty face upon which some one has sat down by mistake. As for Favourite, O nymphs and muses! one day when Blachevelle was crossing the gutter in the Rue Guerin-Boisseau, he espied a beautiful girl with white stockings well drawn up, which displayed her legs. This prologue pleased him, and Blachevelle fell in love. The one he loved was Favourite. O Favourite, thou hast Ionian lips. There was a Greek painter named Euphorion, who was surnamed the painter of the lips. That Greek alone would have been worthy to paint thy mouth. Listen! before thee, there was never a creature worthy of the name. Thou wert made to receive the apple like Venus, or to eat it like Eve; beauty begins with thee. I have just referred to Eve; it is thou who hast created her. Thou deservest the letters-patent of the beautiful woman. O Favourite, I cease to address you as 'thou,' because I pass from poetry to prose. You were speaking of my name a little while ago. That touched me; but let us, whoever we may be, distrust names. They may delude us. I am called Felix, and I am not happy. Words are liars. Let us not blindly accept the indications which they afford us. It would be a mistake to write to Liege[2] for corks, and to Pau for gloves. Miss Dahlia, were I in your place, I would call myself Rosa. A flower should smell sweet, and woman should have wit. I say nothing of Fantine; she is a dreamer, a musing, thoughtful, pensive person; she is a phantom possessed of the form of a nymph and the modesty of a nun, who has strayed into the life of a grisette, but who takes refuge in illusions, and who sings and prays and gazes into the azure without very well knowing what she sees or what she is doing, and who, with her eyes fixed on heaven, wanders in a garden where there are more birds than are in existence. O Fantine, know this: I, Tholomyes, I am all illusion; but she does not even hear me, that blond maid of Chimeras! as for the rest, everything about her is freshness, suavity, youth, sweet morning light. O Fantine, maid worthy of being called Marguerite or Pearl, you are a woman from the beauteous Orient. Ladies, a second piece of advice: do not marry; marriage is a graft; it takes well or ill; avoid that risk. But bah! what am I saying? I am wasting my words. Girls are incurable on the subject of marriage, and all that we wise men can say will not prevent the waistcoat-makers and the shoe-stitchers from dreaming of husbands studded with diamonds. Well, so be it; but, my beauties, remember this, you eat too much sugar. You have but one fault, O woman, and that is nibbling sugar. O nibbling sex, your pretty little white teeth adore sugar. Now, heed me well, sugar is a salt. All salts are withering. Sugar is the most desiccating of all salts; it sucks the liquids of the blood through the veins; hence the coagulation, and then the solidification of the blood; hence tubercles in the lungs, hence death. That is why diabetes borders on consumption. Then, do not crunch sugar, and you will live. I turn to the men: gentlemen, make conquest, rob each other of your well-beloved without remorse. Chassez across. In love there are no friends. Everywhere where there is a pretty woman hostility is open. No quarter, war to the death! a pretty woman is a casus belli; a pretty woman is flagrant misdemeanor. All the invasions of history have been determined by petticoats. Woman is man's right. Romulus carried off the Sabines; William carried off the Saxon women; Caesar carried off the Roman women. The man who is not loved soars like a vulture over the mistresses of other men; and for my own part, to all those unfortunate men who are widowers, I throw the sublime

199

proclamation of Bonaparte to the army of Italy: "Soldiers, you are in need of everything; the enemy has it."

2 Liege: a cork-tree. Pau: a jest on peau, skin.

Tholomyes paused.

"Take breath, Tholomyes," said Blachevelle.

At the same moment Blachevelle, supported by Listolier and Fameuil, struck up to a plaintive air, one of those studio songs composed of the first words which come to hand, rhymed richly and not at all, as destitute of sense as the gesture of the tree and the sound of the wind, which have their birth in the vapor of pipes, and are dissipated and take their flight with them. This is the couplet by which the group replied to Tholomyes' harangue:—

"The father turkey-cocks so grave
Some money to an agent gave,
That master good Clermont-Tonnerre
Might be made pope on Saint Johns' day fair.
But this good Clermont could not be
Made pope, because no priest was he;
And then their agent, whose wrath burned,
With all their money back returned."

This was not calculated to calm Tholomyes' improvisation; he emptied his glass, filled, refilled it, and began again:—

"Down with wisdom! Forget all that I have said. Let us be neither prudes nor prudent men nor prudhommes. I propose a toast to mirth; be merry. Let us complete our course of law by folly and eating! Indigestion and the digest. Let Justinian be the male, and Feasting, the female! Joy in the depths! Live, O creation! The world is a great diamond. I am happy.

The birds are astonishing. What a festival everywhere! The nightingale is a gratuitous Elleviou. Summer, I salute thee! O Luxembourg! O Georgics of the Rue Madame, and of the Allee de l'Observatoire! O pensive infantry soldiers! O all those charming nurses who, while they guard the children, amuse themselves! The pampas of America would please me if I had not the arcades of the Odeon. My soul flits away into the virgin forests and to the savannas. All is beautiful. The flies buzz in the sun. The sun has sneezed out the humming bird. Embrace me, Fantine!"

He made a mistake and embraced Favourite.

CHAPTER VIII

THE DEATH OF A HORSE

"The dinners are better at Edon's than at Bombarda's," exclaimed Zephine.

"I prefer Bombarda to Edon," declared Blachevelle. "There is more luxury. It is more Asiatic. Look at the room downstairs; there are mirrors [glaces] on the walls."

"I prefer them [glaces, ices] on my plate," said Favourite.

Blachevelle persisted:—

"Look at the knives. The handles are of silver at Bombarda's and of bone at Edon's. Now, silver is more valuable than bone."

"Except for those who have a silver chin," observed Tholomyes.

He was looking at the dome of the Invalides, which was visible from Bombarda's windows.

A pause ensued.

"Tholomyes," exclaimed Fameuil, "Listolier and I were having a discussion just now."

"A discussion is a good thing," replied Tholomyes; "a quarrel is better."

"We were disputing about philosophy."

"Well?"

"Which do you prefer, Descartes or Spinoza?"

"Desaugiers," said Tholomyes.

This decree pronounced, he took a drink, and went on:—

"I consent to live. All is not at an end on earth since we can still talk nonsense. For that I return thanks to the immortal gods. We lie. One lies, but one laughs. One affirms, but one doubts. The unexpected bursts forth from the syllogism. That is fine. There are still human beings here below who know how to open and close the surprise box of the paradox merrily. This, ladies, which you are drinking with so tranquil an air is Madeira wine, you must know, from the vineyard of Coural das Freiras, which is three hundred and seventeen fathoms above the level of the sea. Attention while you drink! three hundred and seventeen fathoms! and Monsieur Bombarda, the magnificent eating-house keeper, gives you those three hundred and seventeen fathoms for four francs and fifty centimes."

Again Fameuil interrupted him:—

"Tholomyes, your opinions fix the law. Who is your favorite author?"

"Ber—"

"Quin?"

"No; Choux."

And Tholomyes continued:—

"Honor to Bombarda! He would equal Munophis of Elephanta if he could but get me an Indian dancing-girl, and Thygelion of Chaeronea if he could bring me a Greek courtesan; for, oh, ladies! there were Bombardas in Greece and in Egypt. Apuleius tells us of them. Alas! always the same, and nothing new; nothing more unpublished by the creator in creation! Nil sub sole novum, says Solomon; amor omnibus idem, says Virgil; and Carabine mounts with Carabin into the bark at Saint-Cloud, as Aspasia embarked with Pericles upon the fleet at Samos. One last word. Do you know what Aspasia was, ladies? Although she lived at an epoch when women had, as yet, no soul, she was a soul; a soul of a rosy and purple hue, more ardent hued than fire, fresher than the dawn. Aspasia was a creature in whom two extremes of womanhood met; she was the goddess prostitute; Socrates plus Manon Lescaut. Aspasia was created in case a mistress should be needed for Prometheus."

Tholomyes, once started, would have found some difficulty in stopping, had not a horse fallen down upon the quay just at that moment. The shock caused the cart and the orator to come to a dead halt. It was a Beauceron mare, old and thin, and one fit for the knacker, which was dragging a very heavy cart. On arriving in front of Bombarda's, the worn-out, exhausted beast had refused to proceed any further. This incident attracted a crowd. Hardly had the cursing and indignant carter had time to utter with proper energy the sacramental word, Matin (the jade), backed up with a pitiless cut of the whip, when the jade fell, never to rise again. On hearing the hubbub made by the passersby, Tholomyes' merry auditors turned their heads, and Tholomyes took advantage of the opportunity to bring his allocution to a close with this melancholy strophe:—

> "Elle etait de ce monde ou coucous et carrosses[3]
>> Ont le meme destin;
> Et, rosse, elle a vecu ce que vivant les rosses,
>> L'espace d'un matin!"

3 She belonged to that circle where cuckoos and carriages share the same fate; and a jade herself, she lived, as jades live, for the space of a morning (or jade).

"Poor horse!" sighed Fantine.

And Dahlia exclaimed:—

"There is Fantine on the point of crying over horses. How can one be such a pitiful fool as that!"

At that moment Favourite, folding her arms and throwing her head back, looked resolutely at Tholomyes and said:—

"Come, now! the surprise?"

"Exactly. The moment has arrived," replied Tholomyes. "Gentlemen, the hour for giving these ladies a surprise has struck. Wait for us a moment, ladies."

"It begins with a kiss," said Blachevelle.

"On the brow," added Tholomyes.

Each gravely bestowed a kiss on his mistress's brow; then all four filed out through the door, with their fingers on their lips.

Favourite clapped her hands on their departure.

"It is beginning to be amusing already," said she.

"Don't be too long," murmured Fantine; "we are waiting for you."

CHAPTER IX

A MERRY END TO MIRTH

When the young girls were left alone, they leaned two by two on the window-sills, chatting, craning out their heads, and talking from one window to the other.

They saw the young men emerge from the Cafe Bombarda arm in arm. The latter turned round, made signs to them, smiled, and disappeared in that dusty Sunday throng which makes a weekly invasion into the Champs-Elysees.

"Don't be long!" cried Fantine.

"What are they going to bring us?" said Zephine.

"It will certainly be something pretty," said Dahlia.

"For my part," said Favourite, "I want it to be of gold."

Their attention was soon distracted by the movements on the shore of the lake, which they could see through the branches of the large trees, and which diverted them greatly.

It was the hour for the departure of the mail-coaches and diligences. Nearly all the stage-coaches for the south and west passed through the Champs-Elysees. The majority followed the quay and went through the Passy Barrier. From moment to moment, some huge vehicle, painted yellow and black, heavily loaded, noisily harnessed, rendered shapeless by trunks, tarpaulins, and valises, full of heads which immediately disappeared, rushed through the crowd with all the sparks of a forge, with dust for smoke, and an air of fury, grinding the pavements, changing all the paving-stones into steels. This uproar delighted the young girls. Favourite exclaimed:—

"What a row! One would say that it was a pile of chains flying away."

It chanced that one of these vehicles, which they could only see with difficulty through the thick elms, halted for a moment, then set out again at a gallop. This surprised Fantine.

"That's odd!" said she. "I thought the diligence never stopped."

Favourite shrugged her shoulders.

"This Fantine is surprising. I am coming to take a look at her out of curiosity. She is dazzled by the simplest things. Suppose a case: I am a traveller; I say to the diligence, 'I will go on in advance; you shall pick me up on the quay as you pass.' The diligence passes, sees me, halts, and takes me. That is done every day. You do not know life, my dear."

In this manner a certain time elapsed. All at once Favourite made a movement, like a person who is just waking up.

"Well," said she, "and the surprise?"

"Yes, by the way," joined in Dahlia, "the famous surprise?"

"They are a very long time about it!" said Fantine.

As Fantine concluded this sigh, the waiter who had served them at dinner entered. He held in his hand something which resembled a letter.

"What is that?" demanded Favourite.

The waiter replied:—

"It is a paper that those gentlemen left for these ladies."

"Why did you not bring it at once?"

"Because," said the waiter, "the gentlemen ordered me not to deliver it to the ladies for an hour."

Favourite snatched the paper from the waiter's hand. It was, in fact, a letter.

"Stop!" said she; "there is no address; but this is what is written on it—"

"THIS IS THE SURPRISE."

She tore the letter open hastily, opened it, and read [she knew how to read]:—

"OUR BELOVED:—

"You must know that we have parents. Parents—you do not know much about such things. They are called fathers and mothers by the civil code, which is puerile and honest. Now, these parents groan, these old folks implore us, these good men and these good women call us prodigal sons; they desire our return, and offer to kill calves for us. Being virtuous, we obey them. At the hour when you read this, five fiery horses will be bearing us to our papas and mammas. We are pulling up our stakes, as Bossuet says. We are going; we are gone. We flee in the arms of Lafitte and on the wings of Caillard. The Toulouse diligence tears us from the abyss, and the abyss is you, O our little beauties! We return to society, to duty, to respectability, at full trot, at the rate of three leagues an hour. It is necessary for the good of the country that we should be, like the rest of the world, prefects, fathers of families, rural police, and councillors of state. Venerate us. We are sacrificing ourselves. Mourn for us in haste, and replace us with speed. If this letter lacerates you, do the same by it. Adieu.

"For the space of nearly two years we have made you happy. We bear you no grudge for that.

"Signed:

BLACHEVELLE.
FAMUEIL.
LISTOLIER.
FELIX THOLOMYES.

"Postscriptum. The dinner is paid for."

The four young women looked at each other.

Favourite was the first to break the silence.

"Well!" she exclaimed, "it's a very pretty farce, all the same."

"It is very droll," said Zephine.

"That must have been Blachevelle's idea," resumed Favourite. "It makes me in love with him. No sooner is he gone than he is loved. This is an adventure, indeed."

"No," said Dahlia; "it was one of Tholomyes' ideas. That is evident."

"In that case," retorted Favourite, "death to Blachevelle, and long live Tholomyes!"

"Long live Tholomyes!" exclaimed Dahlia and Zephine.

And they burst out laughing.

Fantine laughed with the rest.

An hour later, when she had returned to her room, she wept. It was her first love affair, as we have said; she had given herself to this Tholomyes as to a husband, and the poor girl had a child.

BOOK FOURTH.

TO CONFIDE IS SOMETIMES TO DELIVER INTO A PERSON'S POWER

CHAPTER I

ONE MOTHER MEETS ANOTHER MOTHER

There was, at Montfermeil, near Paris, during the first quarter of this century, a sort of cook-shop which no longer exists. This cook-shop was kept by some people named Thenardier, husband and wife. It was situated in Boulanger Lane. Over the door there was a board nailed flat against the wall. Upon this board was painted something which resembled a man carrying another man on his back, the latter wearing the big gilt epaulettes of a general, with large silver stars; red spots represented blood; the rest of the picture consisted of smoke, and probably represented a battle. Below ran this inscription: AT THE SIGN OF SERGEANT OF WATERLOO (Au Sargent de Waterloo).

Nothing is more common than a cart or a truck at the door of a hostelry. Nevertheless, the vehicle, or, to speak more accurately, the fragment of a vehicle, which encumbered the street in front of the cook-shop of the Sergeant of Waterloo, one evening in the spring of 1818, would certainly have attracted, by its mass, the attention of any painter who had passed that way.

It was the fore-carriage of one of those trucks which are used in wooded tracts of country, and which serve to transport thick planks and the trunks of trees. This fore-carriage was composed of a massive iron axle-tree with a pivot, into which was fitted a heavy shaft, and which was supported by two huge wheels. The whole thing was compact, overwhelming, and misshapen. It seemed like the gun-carriage of an enormous cannon. The ruts of the road had bestowed on the wheels, the fellies, the hub, the axle, and the shaft, a layer of mud, a hideous yellowish daubing hue, tolerably like that with which people are fond of ornamenting cathedrals. The wood was disappearing under mud, and the iron beneath rust. Under the axle-tree hung, like drapery, a huge chain, worthy of some Goliath of a convict. This chain suggested, not the beams, which it was its office to transport, but the mastodons and mammoths which it might have served to harness; it had the air of the galleys, but of cyclopean and superhuman galleys, and it seemed to have been detached from some monster. Homer would have bound Polyphemus with it, and Shakespeare, Caliban.

Why was that fore-carriage of a truck in that place in the street? In the first place, to encumber the street; next, in order that it might finish the process of rusting. There is a throng of institutions in the old social order, which one comes across in this fashion as one walks about outdoors, and which have no other reasons for existence than the above.

The centre of the chain swung very near the ground in the middle, and in the loop, as in the rope of a swing, there were seated and grouped, on that particular evening, in exquisite interlacement, two little girls; one about two years and a half old, the other, eighteen months; the younger in the arms of the other. A handkerchief, cleverly knotted about them, prevented their falling out. A mother had caught sight of that frightful chain, and had said, "Come! there's a plaything for my children."

The two children, who were dressed prettily and with some elegance, were radiant with pleasure; one would have said that they were two roses amid old iron; their eyes were a triumph; their fresh cheeks were full of laughter. One had chestnut hair; the other, brown. Their innocent faces were two delighted surprises; a blossoming shrub which grew near wafted to the passers-by perfumes which seemed to emanate from them; the child of eighteen months displayed her pretty little bare stomach with the chaste indecency of childhood. Above and around these two delicate heads, all made of happiness and steeped in light, the gigantic fore-carriage, black with rust, almost terrible, all entangled in curves and wild angles, rose in a vault, like the entrance of a cavern. A few paces apart, crouching down upon the threshold of the hostelry, the mother, not a very prepossessing woman, by the way, though touching at that moment, was swinging the two children by means of a long cord, watching them carefully, for fear of accidents, with that animal and celestial expression which is peculiar to maternity. At every backward and forward swing the hideous links emitted a strident sound, which resembled a cry of rage; the little girls were in ecstasies; the setting sun mingled in this joy, and nothing could be more charming than this caprice of chance which had made of a chain of Titans the swing of cherubim.

As she rocked her little ones, the mother hummed in a discordant voice a romance then celebrated:—

"It must be, said a warrior."

Her song, and the contemplation of her daughters, prevented her hearing and seeing what was going on in the street.

In the meantime, some one had approached her, as she was beginning the first couplet of the romance, and suddenly she heard a voice saying very near her ear:—

"You have two beautiful children there, Madame."

"To the fair and tender Imogene—"

replied the mother, continuing her romance; then she turned her head.

A woman stood before her, a few paces distant. This woman also had a child, which she carried in her arms.

She was carrying, in addition, a large carpet-bag, which seemed very heavy.

This woman's child was one of the most divine creatures that it is possible to behold. It was a girl, two or three years of age. She could have entered into competition with the two other little ones, so far as the coquetry of her dress was concerned; she wore a cap of fine linen, ribbons on her bodice, and Valenciennes lace on her cap. The folds of her skirt were raised so as to permit a view of her white, firm, and dimpled leg. She was admirably rosy and healthy. The little beauty inspired a desire to take a bite from the apples of her cheeks. Of her eyes nothing could be known, except that they must be very large, and that they had magnificent lashes. She was asleep.

She slept with that slumber of absolute confidence peculiar to her age. The arms of mothers are made of tenderness; in them children sleep profoundly.

As for the mother, her appearance was sad and poverty-stricken. She was dressed like a working-woman who is inclined to turn into a peasant again. She was young. Was she handsome? Perhaps; but in that attire it was not apparent. Her hair, a golden lock of which had escaped, seemed very thick, but was severely concealed beneath an ugly, tight, close, nun-like cap, tied under the chin. A smile displays beautiful teeth when one has them; but she did not smile. Her eyes did not seem to have been dry for a very long time. She was pale; she had a very weary and rather sickly appearance. She gazed upon her daughter asleep in her arms with the air peculiar to a mother who has nursed her own child. A large blue handkerchief, such as the Invalides use, was folded into a fichu, and concealed her figure clumsily. Her hands were sunburnt and all dotted with freckles, her forefinger was hardened and lacerated with the needle; she wore a cloak of coarse brown woollen stuff, a linen gown, and coarse shoes. It was Fantine.

It was Fantine, but difficult to recognize. Nevertheless, on scrutinizing her attentively, it was evident that she still retained her beauty. A melancholy fold, which resembled the beginning of irony, wrinkled her right cheek. As for her toilette, that aerial toilette of muslin and ribbons, which seemed made of mirth, of folly, and of music, full of bells, and perfumed with lilacs had vanished like that beautiful and dazzling hoarfrost which is mistaken for diamonds in the sunlight; it melts and leaves the branch quite black.

Ten months had elapsed since the "pretty farce."

What had taken place during those ten months? It can be divined.

After abandonment, straightened circumstances. Fantine had immediately lost sight of Favourite, Zephine and Dahlia; the bond once broken on the side of the men, it was loosed between the women; they would have been greatly astonished had any one told them a fortnight later, that they had been friends; there no longer existed any reason for such a thing. Fantine had remained alone. The father of her child gone,—alas! such ruptures are irrevocable,—she found herself absolutely isolated, minus the habit of work and plus the taste for pleasure. Drawn away by her liaison with Tholomyes to disdain the pretty trade which she knew, she had neglected to keep her market open; it was now closed to her. She had no resource. Fantine barely knew how to read, and did not know how to write; in her childhood she had only been taught to sign her name; she had a public letter-writer indite an epistle to Tholomyes, then a second, then a third. Tholomyes replied to none of them. Fantine heard the gossips say, as they looked at her child: "Who takes those children seriously! One only shrugs one's shoulders over such children!" Then she thought of Tholomyes, who had shrugged his shoulders over his child, and who did not take that innocent being seriously; and her heart grew gloomy toward that man. But what was she to do? She no longer knew to whom to apply. She had committed a fault, but the foundation of her nature, as will be remembered, was modesty and virtue. She was vaguely conscious that she was on the verge of falling into distress, and of gliding into a worse state. Courage was necessary; she possessed it, and held herself firm. The idea of returning to her native town of M. sur M. occurred to her. There, some one might possibly know her and give her work; yes, but it would be necessary to conceal her fault. In a confused way she perceived the necessity of a separation which would be more painful than the first one. Her heart contracted, but she took her resolution. Fantine, as we shall see, had the fierce bravery of life. She had already valiantly renounced finery, had dressed herself in linen, and had put all her silks, all her ornaments, all her ribbons, and all her laces on her daughter, the only vanity which was left to her, and a holy one it was. She sold all that she had, which produced for her two hundred francs; her little debts paid, she had only about eighty francs left. At the age of twenty-two, on a beautiful spring morning, she quitted Paris, bearing her child on her back. Any one who had seen these two pass would have had pity on them. This woman had, in all the world, nothing but her child, and the child had, in all the world, no one but this woman. Fantine had nursed her child, and this had tired her chest, and she coughed a little.

We shall have no further occasion to speak of M. Felix Tholomyes. Let us confine ourselves to saying, that, twenty years later, under King Louis Philippe, he was a great provincial lawyer, wealthy and influential, a wise elector, and a very severe juryman; he was still a man of pleasure.

Towards the middle of the day, after having, from time to time, for the sake of resting herself, travelled, for three or four sous a league, in what was then known as the Petites Voitures des Environs de Paris, the "little suburban coach service," Fantine found herself at Montfermeil, in the alley Boulanger.

As she passed the Thenardier hostelry, the two little girls, blissful in the monster swing, had dazzled her in a manner, and she had halted in front of that vision of joy.

Charms exist. These two little girls were a charm to this mother.

She gazed at them in much emotion. The presence of angels is an announcement of Paradise. She thought that, above this inn, she beheld the mysterious HERE of Providence. These two little creatures were evidently happy. She gazed at them, she admired them, in such emotion that at the moment when their mother was recovering her breath between two couplets of her song, she could not refrain from addressing to her the remark which we have just read:—

"You have two pretty children, Madame."

218

The most ferocious creatures are disarmed by caresses bestowed on their young.

The mother raised her head and thanked her, and bade the wayfarer sit down on the bench at the door, she herself being seated on the threshold. The two women began to chat.

"My name is Madame Thenardier," said the mother of the two little girls. "We keep this inn."

Then, her mind still running on her romance, she resumed humming between her teeth:—

> "It must be so; I am a knight,
> And I am off to Palestine."

This Madame Thenardier was a sandy-complexioned woman, thin and angular—the type of the soldier's wife in all its unpleasantness; and what was odd, with a languishing air, which she owed to her perusal of romances. She was a simpering, but masculine creature. Old romances produce that effect when rubbed against the imagination of cook-shop woman. She was still young; she was barely thirty. If this crouching woman had stood upright, her lofty stature and her frame of a perambulating colossus suitable for fairs, might have frightened the traveller at the outset, troubled her confidence, and disturbed what caused what we have to relate to vanish. A person who is seated instead of standing erect—destinies hang upon such a thing as that.

The traveller told her story, with slight modifications.

That she was a working-woman; that her husband was dead; that her work in Paris had failed her, and that she was on her way to seek it elsewhere, in her own native parts; that she had left Paris that morning on foot; that, as she was carrying her child, and felt fatigued, she had got into the Villemomble coach when she met it; that from Villemomble she had come to Montfermeil on foot; that the little one had walked a little, but not much, because she was so young, and that she had been obliged to take her up, and the jewel had fallen asleep.

At this word she bestowed on her daughter a passionate kiss, which woke her. The child opened her eyes, great blue eyes like her mother's, and looked at—what? Nothing; with that serious and sometimes severe air of little children, which is a mystery of their luminous innocence in the presence of our twilight of virtue. One would say that they feel themselves to be angels, and that they know us to be men. Then the child began to laugh; and although the mother held fast to her, she slipped to the ground with the unconquerable energy of a little being which wished to run. All at once she caught sight of the two others in the swing, stopped short, and put out her tongue, in sign of admiration.

Mother Thenardier released her daughters, made them descend from the swing, and said:—

"Now amuse yourselves, all three of you."

Children become acquainted quickly at that age, and at the expiration of a minute the little Thenardiers were playing with the new-comer at making holes in the ground, which was an immense pleasure.

The new-comer was very gay; the goodness of the mother is written in the gayety of the child; she had seized a scrap of wood which served her for a shovel, and energetically dug a cavity big enough for a fly. The grave-digger's business becomes a subject for laughter when performed by a child.

The two women pursued their chat.

"What is your little one's name?"

"Cosette."

For Cosette, read Euphrasie. The child's name was Euphrasie. But out of Euphrasie the mother had made Cosette by that sweet and graceful instinct of mothers and of the populace which changes Josepha into Pepita, and Francoise into Sillette. It is a sort of derivative which disarranges and disconcerts the whole science of etymologists. We have known a grandmother who succeeded in turning Theodore into Gnon.

220

"How old is she?"

"She is going on three."

"That is the age of my eldest."

In the meantime, the three little girls were grouped in an attitude of profound anxiety and blissfulness; an event had happened; a big worm had emerged from the ground, and they were afraid; and they were in ecstasies over it.

Their radiant brows touched each other; one would have said that there were three heads in one aureole.

"How easily children get acquainted at once!" exclaimed Mother Thenardier; "one would swear that they were three sisters!"

This remark was probably the spark which the other mother had been waiting for. She seized the Thenardier's hand, looked at her fixedly, and said:—

"Will you keep my child for me?"

The Thenardier made one of those movements of surprise which signify neither assent nor refusal.

Cosette's mother continued:—

"You see, I cannot take my daughter to the country. My work will not permit it. With a child one can find no situation. People are ridiculous in the country. It was the good God who caused me to pass your inn. When I caught sight of your little ones, so pretty, so clean, and so happy, it overwhelmed me. I said: 'Here is a good mother. That is just the thing; that will make three sisters.' And then, it will not be long before I return. Will you keep my child for me?"

"I must see about it," replied the Thenardier.

"I will give you six francs a month."

Here a man's voice called from the depths of the cook-shop:—

"Not for less than seven francs. And six months paid in advance."

"Six times seven makes forty-two," said the Thenardier.

"I will give it," said the mother.

"And fifteen francs in addition for preliminary expenses," added the man's voice.

"Total, fifty-seven francs," said Madame Thenardier. And she hummed vaguely, with these figures:—

"It must be, said a warrior."

"I will pay it," said the mother. "I have eighty francs. I shall have enough left to reach the country, by travelling on foot. I shall earn money there, and as soon as I have a little I will return for my darling."

The man's voice resumed:—

"The little one has an outfit?"

"That is my husband," said the Thenardier.

"Of course she has an outfit, the poor treasure.—I understood perfectly that it was your husband.—And a beautiful outfit, too! a senseless outfit, everything by the dozen, and silk gowns like a lady. It is here, in my carpet-bag."

"You must hand it over," struck in the man's voice again.

"Of course I shall give it to you," said the mother. "It would be very queer if I were to leave my daughter quite naked!"

The master's face appeared.

"That's good," said he.

The bargain was concluded. The mother passed the night at the inn, gave up her money and left her child, fastened her carpet-bag once more, now reduced in volume by the removal of the outfit, and light henceforth and set out on the following morning, intending to return soon. People arrange such departures tranquilly; but they are despairs!

A neighbor of the Thenardiers met this mother as she was setting out, and came back with the remark:—

"I have just seen a woman crying in the street so that it was enough to rend your heart."

When Cosette's mother had taken her departure, the man said to the woman:—

"That will serve to pay my note for one hundred and ten francs which falls due tomorrow; I lacked fifty francs. Do you know that I should have had a bailiff and a protest after me? You played the mouse-trap nicely with your young ones."

"Without suspecting it," said the woman.

CHAPTER II

FIRST SKETCH OF TWO UNPREPOSSESSING FIGURES

The mouse which had been caught was a pitiful specimen; but the cat rejoices even over a lean mouse.

Who were these Thenardiers?

Let us say a word or two of them now. We will complete the sketch later on.

These beings belonged to that bastard class composed of coarse people who have been successful, and of intelligent people who have descended in the scale, which is between the class called "middle" and the class denominated as "inferior," and which combines some of the defects of the second with nearly all the vices of the first, without possessing the generous impulse of the workingman nor the honest order of the bourgeois.

They were of those dwarfed natures which, if a dull fire chances to warm them up, easily become monstrous. There was in the woman a substratum of the brute, and in the man the material for a blackguard. Both were susceptible, in the highest degree, of the sort of hideous progress which is accomplished in the direction of evil. There exist crab-like souls which are continually retreating towards the darkness, retrograding in life rather than advancing, employing experience to augment their deformity, growing incessantly worse, and becoming more and more impregnated with an ever-augmenting blackness. This man and woman possessed such souls.

Thenardier, in particular, was troublesome for a physiognomist. One can only look at some men to distrust them; for one feels that they are dark in both directions. They are uneasy in the rear and threatening in front. There is something of the unknown about them. One can no more answer for what they have done than for what they will do. The shadow which they bear in their glance denounces them. From merely hearing them utter a word or seeing them make a gesture, one obtains a glimpse of sombre secrets in their past and of sombre mysteries in their future.

This Thenardier, if he himself was to be believed, had been a soldier—a sergeant, he said. He had probably been through the campaign of 1815, and had even conducted himself with tolerable valor, it would seem. We shall see later on how much truth there was in this. The sign of his hostelry was in allusion to one of his feats of arms. He had painted it himself; for he knew how to do a little of everything, and badly.

It was at the epoch when the ancient classical romance which, after having been Clelie, was no longer anything but Lodoiska, still noble, but ever more and more vulgar, having fallen from Mademoiselle de Scuderi to Madame Bournon-Malarme, and from Madame de Lafayette to Madame Barthelemy-Hadot, was setting the loving hearts of the portresses of Paris aflame, and even ravaging the suburbs to some extent. Madame Thenardier was just intelligent enough to read this sort of books. She lived on them. In them she drowned what brains she possessed. This had given her, when very young, and even a little later, a sort of pensive attitude towards her husband, a scamp of a certain depth, a ruffian lettered to the extent of the grammar, coarse and fine at one and the same time, but, so far as sentimentalism was concerned, given to the perusal of Pigault-Lebrun, and "in what concerns the sex," as he said in his jargon—a downright, unmitigated lout. His wife was twelve or fifteen years younger than he was. Later on, when her hair, arranged in a romantically drooping fashion, began to grow gray, when the Magaera began to be developed from the Pamela, the female Thenardier was nothing but a coarse, vicious woman, who had dabbled in stupid romances. Now, one cannot read nonsense with impunity. The result was that her eldest daughter was named Eponine; as for the younger, the poor little thing came near being called Gulnare; I know not to what diversion, effected by a romance of Ducray-Dumenil, she owed the fact that she merely bore the name of Azelma.

However, we will remark by the way, everything was not ridiculous and superficial in that curious epoch to which we are alluding, and which may be designated as the anarchy of baptismal names. By the side of this romantic element which we have just indicated there is the social symptom. It is not rare for the neatherd's boy nowadays to bear the name of Arthur, Alfred, or Alphonse, and for the vicomte—if there are still any vicomtes—to be called Thomas, Pierre, or Jacques. This displacement, which places the "elegant" name on the plebeian and the rustic name on the aristocrat, is nothing else than an eddy of equality. The irresistible penetration of the new inspiration is there as everywhere else. Beneath this apparent discord there is a great and a profound thing,—the French Revolution.

CHAPTER III

THE LARK

It is not all in all sufficient to be wicked in order to prosper. The cook-shop was in a bad way.

Thanks to the traveller's fifty-seven francs, Thenardier had been able to avoid a protest and to honor his signature. On the following month they were again in need of money. The woman took Cosette's outfit to Paris, and pawned it at the pawnbroker's for sixty francs. As soon as that sum was spent, the Thenardiers grew accustomed to look on the little girl merely as a child whom they were caring for out of charity; and they treated her accordingly. As she had no longer any clothes, they dressed her in the cast-off petticoats and chemises of the Thenardier brats; that is to say, in rags. They fed her on what all the rest had left—a little better than the dog, a little worse than the cat. Moreover, the cat and the dog were her habitual table-companions; Cosette ate with them under the table, from a wooden bowl similar to theirs.

The mother, who had established herself, as we shall see later on, at M. sur M., wrote, or, more correctly, caused to be written, a letter every month, that she might have news of her child. The Thenardiers replied invariably, "Cosette is doing wonderfully well."

At the expiration of the first six months the mother sent seven francs for the seventh month, and continued her remittances with tolerable regularity from month to month. The year was not completed when

Thenardier said: "A fine favor she is doing us, in sooth! What does she expect us to do with her seven francs?" and he wrote to demand twelve francs. The mother, whom they had persuaded into the belief that her child was happy, "and was coming on well," submitted, and forwarded the twelve francs.

Certain natures cannot love on the one hand without hating on the other. Mother Thenardier loved her two daughters passionately, which caused her to hate the stranger.

It is sad to think that the love of a mother can possess villainous aspects. Little as was the space occupied by Cosette, it seemed to her as though it were taken from her own, and that that little child diminished the air which her daughters breathed. This woman, like many women of her sort, had a load of caresses and a burden of blows and injuries to dispense each day. If she had not had Cosette, it is certain that her daughters, idolized as they were, would have received the whole of it; but the stranger did them the service to divert the blows to herself. Her daughters received nothing but caresses. Cosette could not make a motion which did not draw down upon her head a heavy shower of violent blows and unmerited chastisement. The sweet, feeble being, who should not have understood anything of this world or of God, incessantly punished, scolded, ill-used, beaten, and seeing beside her two little creatures like herself, who lived in a ray of dawn!

Madame Thenardier was vicious with Cosette. Eponine and Azelma were vicious. Children at that age are only copies of their mother. The size is smaller; that is all.

A year passed; then another.

People in the village said:—

"Those Thenardiers are good people. They are not rich, and yet they are bringing up a poor child who was abandoned on their hands!"

They thought that Cosette's mother had forgotten her.

In the meanwhile, Thenardier, having learned, it is impossible to say by what obscure means, that the child was probably a bastard, and that the mother could not acknowledge it, exacted fifteen francs a month, saying that "the creature" was growing and "eating," and threatening to send her away. "Let her not bother me," he exclaimed, "or I'll fire her brat right into the middle of her secrets. I must have an increase." The mother paid the fifteen francs.

From year to year the child grew, and so did her wretchedness.

As long as Cosette was little, she was the scape-goat of the two other children; as soon as she began to develop a little, that is to say, before she was even five years old, she became the servant of the household.

Five years old! the reader will say; that is not probable. Alas! it is true. Social suffering begins at all ages. Have we not recently seen the trial of a man named Dumollard, an orphan turned bandit, who, from the age of five, as the official documents state, being alone in the world, "worked for his living and stole"?

Cosette was made to run on errands, to sweep the rooms, the courtyard, the street, to wash the dishes, to even carry burdens. The Thenardiers considered themselves all the more authorized to behave in this manner, since the mother, who was still at M. sur M., had become irregular in her payments. Some months she was in arrears.

If this mother had returned to Montfermeil at the end of these three years, she would not have recognized her child. Cosette, so pretty and rosy on her arrival in that house, was now thin and pale. She had an indescribably uneasy look. "The sly creature," said the Thenardiers.

Injustice had made her peevish, and misery had made her ugly. Nothing remained to her except her beautiful eyes, which inspired pain, because, large as they were, it seemed as though one beheld in them a still larger amount of sadness.

It was a heart-breaking thing to see this poor child, not yet six years old, shivering in the winter in her old rags of linen, full of holes, sweeping the street before daylight, with an enormous broom in her tiny red hands, and a tear in her great eyes.

She was called the Lark in the neighborhood. The populace, who are fond of these figures of speech, had taken a fancy to bestow this name on this trembling, frightened, and shivering little creature, no bigger than a bird, who was awake every morning before any one else in the house or the village, and was always in the street or the fields before daybreak.

Only the little lark never sang.

BOOK FIFTH.

THE DESCENT.

CHAPTER I

THE HISTORY OF A PROGRESS IN BLACK GLASS TRINKETS

And in the meantime, what had become of that mother who according to the people at Montfermeil, seemed to have abandoned her child? Where was she? What was she doing?

After leaving her little Cosette with the Thenardiers, she had continued her journey, and had reached M. sur M.

This, it will be remembered, was in 1818.

Fantine had quitted her province ten years before. M. sur M. had changed its aspect. While Fantine had been slowly descending from wretchedness to wretchedness, her native town had prospered.

About two years previously one of those industrial facts which are the grand events of small districts had taken place.

This detail is important, and we regard it as useful to develop it at length; we should almost say, to underline it.

From time immemorial, M. sur M. had had for its special industry the imitation of English jet and the black glass trinkets of Germany. This industry had always vegetated, on account of the high price of the raw material, which reacted on the manufacture. At the moment when Fantine returned to M. sur M., an unheard-of transformation had taken place in the production of "black goods." Towards the close of 1815 a man, a stranger, had established himself in the town, and had been inspired with the idea of substituting, in this manufacture, gum-lac for resin, and, for bracelets in particular, slides of sheet-iron simply laid together, for slides of soldered sheet-iron.

This very small change had effected a revolution.

This very small change had, in fact, prodigiously reduced the cost of the raw material, which had rendered it possible in the first place, to raise the price of manufacture, a benefit to the country; in the second place, to improve the workmanship, an advantage to the consumer; in the third place, to sell at a lower price, while trebling the profit, which was a benefit to the manufacturer.

Thus three results ensued from one idea.

In less than three years the inventor of this process had become rich, which is good, and had made every one about him rich, which is better. He was a stranger in the Department. Of his origin, nothing was known; of the beginning of his career, very little. It was rumored that he had come to town with very little money, a few hundred francs at the most.

It was from this slender capital, enlisted in the service of an ingenious idea, developed by method and thought, that he had drawn his own fortune, and the fortune of the whole countryside.

On his arrival at M. sur M. he had only the garments, the appearance, and the language of a workingman.

It appears that on the very day when he made his obscure entry into the little town of M. sur M., just at nightfall, on a December evening, knapsack on back and thorn club in hand, a large fire had broken out in the town-hall. This man had rushed into the flames and saved, at the risk of his own life, two children who belonged to the captain of the gendarmerie; this is why they had forgotten to ask him for his passport. Afterwards they had learned his name. He was called Father Madeleine.

CHAPTER II

MADELEINE

He was a man about fifty years of age, who had a preoccupied air, and who was good. That was all that could be said about him.

Thanks to the rapid progress of the industry which he had so admirably re-constructed, M. sur M. had become a rather important centre of trade. Spain, which consumes a good deal of black jet, made enormous purchases there each year. M. sur M. almost rivalled London and Berlin in this branch of commerce. Father Madeleine's profits were such, that at the end of the second year he was able to erect a large factory, in which there were two vast workrooms, one for the men, and the other for women. Any one who was hungry could present himself there, and was sure of finding employment and bread. Father Madeleine required of the men good will, of the women pure morals, and of all, probity. He had separated the work-rooms in order to separate the sexes, and so that the women and girls might remain discreet. On this point he was inflexible. It was the only thing in which he was in a manner intolerant. He was all the more firmly set on this severity, since M. sur M., being a garrison town, opportunities for corruption abounded. However, his coming had been a boon, and his presence was a godsend. Before Father Madeleine's arrival, everything had languished in the country; now everything lived with a healthy life of toil. A strong circulation warmed everything and penetrated everywhere. Slack seasons and wretchedness were unknown.

There was no pocket so obscure that it had not a little money in it; no dwelling so lowly that there was not some little joy within it.

Father Madeleine gave employment to every one. He exacted but one thing: Be an honest man. Be an honest woman.

As we have said, in the midst of this activity of which he was the cause and the pivot, Father Madeleine made his fortune; but a singular thing in a simple man of business, it did not seem as though that were his chief care. He appeared to be thinking much of others, and little of himself. In 1820 he was known to have a sum of six hundred and thirty thousand francs lodged in his name with Laffitte; but before reserving these six hundred and thirty thousand francs, he had spent more than a million for the town and its poor.

The hospital was badly endowed; he founded six beds there. M. sur M. is divided into the upper and the lower town. The lower town, in which he lived, had but one school, a miserable hovel, which was falling to ruin: he constructed two, one for girls, the other for boys. He allotted a salary from his own funds to the two instructors, a salary twice as large as their meagre official salary, and one day he said to some one who expressed surprise, "The two prime functionaries of the state are the nurse and the schoolmaster." He created at his own expense an infant school, a thing then almost unknown in France, and a fund for aiding old and infirm workmen. As his factory was a centre, a new quarter, in which there were a good many indigent families, rose rapidly around him; he established there a free dispensary.

At first, when they watched his beginnings, the good souls said, "He's a jolly fellow who means to get rich." When they saw him enriching the country before he enriched himself, the good souls said, "He is an ambitious man." This seemed all the more probable since the man was religious, and even practised his religion to a certain degree, a thing which was very favorably viewed at that epoch. He went regularly to low mass every Sunday. The local deputy, who nosed out all rivalry everywhere, soon began to grow uneasy over this religion. This deputy had been a member of the legislative body of the Empire, and shared the religious ideas of a father of the Oratoire, known under the name of Fouche, Duc d'Otrante, whose creature and friend he had been. He indulged in gentle raillery at God with closed doors. But when he beheld the wealthy manufacturer Madeleine going to low mass at seven o'clock, he perceived in him a possible candidate, and resolved to outdo him; he took a Jesuit confessor, and went to high mass and to vespers. Ambition was at that time, in the direct acceptation of the word, a race to the steeple. The poor profited by this terror as well as the good God, for the honorable deputy also founded two beds in the hospital, which made twelve.

Nevertheless, in 1819 a rumor one morning circulated through the town to the effect that, on the representations of the prefect and in consideration of the services rendered by him to the country, Father Madeleine was to be appointed by the King, mayor of M. sur M. Those who had pronounced this new-comer to be "an ambitious fellow," seized with delight on this opportunity which all men desire, to exclaim, "There! what did we say!" All M. sur M. was in an uproar. The rumor was well founded. Several days later the appointment appeared in the Moniteur. On the following day Father Madeleine refused.

In this same year of 1819 the products of the new process invented by Madeleine figured in the industrial exhibition; when the jury made their report, the King appointed the inventor a chevalier of the Legion of Honor. A fresh excitement in the little town. Well, so it was the cross that he wanted! Father Madeleine refused the cross.

Decidedly this man was an enigma. The good souls got out of their predicament by saying, "After all, he is some sort of an adventurer."

We have seen that the country owed much to him; the poor owed him everything; he was so useful and he was so gentle that people had been obliged to honor and respect him. His workmen, in particular, adored him, and he endured this adoration with a sort of melancholy gravity. When he was known to be rich, "people in society" bowed to him, and he received invitations in the town; he was called, in town, Monsieur

Madeleine; his workmen and the children continued to call him Father Madeleine, and that was what was most adapted to make him smile. In proportion as he mounted, throve, invitations rained down upon him. "Society" claimed him for its own. The prim little drawing-rooms on M. sur M., which, of course, had at first been closed to the artisan, opened both leaves of their folding-doors to the millionnaire. They made a thousand advances to him. He refused.

This time the good gossips had no trouble. "He is an ignorant man, of no education. No one knows where he came from. He would not know how to behave in society. It has not been absolutely proved that he knows how to read."

When they saw him making money, they said, "He is a man of business." When they saw him scattering his money about, they said, "He is an ambitious man." When he was seen to decline honors, they said, "He is an adventurer." When they saw him repulse society, they said, "He is a brute."

In 1820, five years after his arrival in M. sur M., the services which he had rendered to the district were so dazzling, the opinion of the whole country round about was so unanimous, that the King again appointed him mayor of the town. He again declined; but the prefect resisted his refusal, all the notabilities of the place came to implore him, the people in the street besought him; the urging was so vigorous that he ended by accepting. It was noticed that the thing which seemed chiefly to bring him to a decision was the almost irritated apostrophe addressed to him by an old woman of the people, who called to him from her threshold, in an angry way: "A good mayor is a useful thing. Is he drawing back before the good which he can do?"

This was the third phase of his ascent. Father Madeleine had become Monsieur Madeleine. Monsieur Madeleine became Monsieur le Maire.

CHAPTER III

SUMS DEPOSITED WITH LAFFITTE

On the other hand, he remained as simple as on the first day. He had gray hair, a serious eye, the sunburned complexion of a laborer, the thoughtful visage of a philosopher. He habitually wore a hat with a wide brim, and a long coat of coarse cloth, buttoned to the chin. He fulfilled his duties as mayor; but, with that exception, he lived in solitude. He spoke to but few people. He avoided polite attentions; he escaped quickly; he smiled to relieve himself of the necessity of talking; he gave, in order to get rid of the necessity for smiling, The women said of him, "What a good-natured bear!" His pleasure consisted in strolling in the fields.

He always took his meals alone, with an open book before him, which he read. He had a well-selected little library. He loved books; books are cold but safe friends. In proportion as leisure came to him with fortune, he seemed to take advantage of it to cultivate his mind. It had been observed that, ever since his arrival at M. sur M. his language had grown more polished, more choice, and more gentle with every passing year. He liked to carry a gun with him on his strolls, but he rarely made use of it. When he did happen to do so, his shooting was something so infallible as to inspire terror. He never killed an inoffensive animal. He never shot at a little bird.

Although he was no longer young, it was thought that he was still prodigiously strong. He offered his assistance to any one who was in need of it, lifted a horse, released a wheel clogged in the mud, or stopped a runaway bull by the horns. He always had his pockets full of money when he went out; but they were empty on his return. When he passed through a village, the ragged brats ran joyously after him, and surrounded him like a swarm of gnats.

It was thought that he must, in the past, have lived a country life, since he knew all sorts of useful secrets, which he taught to the peasants. He taught them how to destroy scurf on wheat, by sprinkling it and the granary and inundating the cracks in the floor with a solution of common salt; and how to chase away weevils by hanging up orviot in bloom everywhere, on the walls and the ceilings, among the grass and in the houses.

He had "recipes" for exterminating from a field, blight, tares, foxtail, and all parasitic growths which destroy the wheat. He defended a rabbit warren against rats, simply by the odor of a guinea-pig which he placed in it.

One day he saw some country people busily engaged in pulling up nettles; he examined the plants, which were uprooted and already dried, and said: "They are dead. Nevertheless, it would be a good thing to know how to make use of them. When the nettle is young, the leaf makes an excellent vegetable; when it is older, it has filaments and fibres like hemp and flax. Nettle cloth is as good as linen cloth. Chopped up, nettles are good for poultry; pounded, they are good for horned cattle. The seed of the nettle, mixed with fodder, gives gloss to the hair of animals; the root, mixed with salt, produces a beautiful yellow coloring-matter. Moreover, it is an excellent hay, which can be cut twice. And what is required for the nettle? A little soil, no care, no culture. Only the seed falls as it is ripe, and it is difficult to collect it. That is all. With the exercise of a little care, the nettle could be made useful; it is neglected and it becomes hurtful. It is exterminated. How many men resemble the nettle!" He added, after a pause: "Remember this, my friends: there are no such things as bad plants or bad men. There are only bad cultivators."

240

The children loved him because he knew how to make charming little trifles of straw and cocoanuts.

When he saw the door of a church hung in black, he entered: he sought out funerals as other men seek christenings. Widowhood and the grief of others attracted him, because of his great gentleness; he mingled with the friends clad in mourning, with families dressed in black, with the priests groaning around a coffin. He seemed to like to give to his thoughts for text these funereal psalmodies filled with the vision of the other world. With his eyes fixed on heaven, he listened with a sort of aspiration towards all the mysteries of the infinite, those sad voices which sing on the verge of the obscure abyss of death.

He performed a multitude of good actions, concealing his agency in them as a man conceals himself because of evil actions. He penetrated houses privately, at night; he ascended staircases furtively. A poor wretch on returning to his attic would find that his door had been opened, sometimes even forced, during his absence. The poor man made a clamor over it: some malefactor had been there! He entered, and the first thing he beheld was a piece of gold lying forgotten on some piece of furniture. The "malefactor" who had been there was Father Madeleine.

He was affable and sad. The people said: "There is a rich man who has not a haughty air. There is a happy man who has not a contented air."

Some people maintained that he was a mysterious person, and that no one ever entered his chamber, which was a regular anchorite's cell, furnished with winged hour-glasses and enlivened by cross-bones and skulls of dead men! This was much talked of, so that one of the elegant and malicious young women of M. sur M. came to him one day, and asked: "Monsieur le Maire, pray show us your chamber. It is said to be a grotto." He smiled, and introduced them instantly into this "grotto." They were well punished for their curiosity. The room was very simply furnished in mahogany, which was rather ugly, like all furniture of that sort, and hung with paper worth twelve sous. They could see nothing remarkable about it, except two candlesticks of antique pattern which stood on the chimney-piece and appeared to be silver, "for they were hall-marked," an observation full of the type of wit of petty towns.

Nevertheless, people continued to say that no one ever got into the room, and that it was a hermit's cave, a mysterious retreat, a hole, a tomb.

It was also whispered about that he had "immense" sums deposited with Laffitte, with this peculiar feature, that they were always at his immediate disposal, so that, it was added, M. Madeleine could make his appearance at Laffitte's any morning, sign a receipt, and carry off his two or three millions in ten minutes. In reality, "these two or three millions" were reducible, as we have said, to six hundred and thirty or forty thousand francs.

CHAPTER IV

M. MADELEINE IN MOURNING

At the beginning of 1820 the newspapers announced the death of M. Myriel, Bishop of D—, surnamed "Monseigneur Bienvenu," who had died in the odor of sanctity at the age of eighty-two.

The Bishop of D—to supply here a detail which the papers omitted— had been blind for many years before his death, and content to be blind, as his sister was beside him.

Let us remark by the way, that to be blind and to be loved, is, in fact, one of the most strangely exquisite forms of happiness upon this earth, where nothing is complete. To have continually at one's side a woman, a daughter, a sister, a charming being, who is there because you need her and because she cannot do without you; to know that we are indispensable to a person who is necessary to us; to be able to incessantly measure one's affection by the amount of her presence which she bestows on us, and to say to ourselves, "Since she consecrates the whole of her time to me, it is because I possess the whole of her heart"; to behold her thought in lieu of her face; to be able to verify the fidelity of one being amid the eclipse of the world; to regard the rustle of a gown as the sound of wings; to hear her come and go, retire, speak, return, sing, and to think that one is the centre of these steps, of this speech; to manifest at each instant one's personal attraction; to feel one's self all the more powerful because of one's infirmity; to become in one's obscurity, and through one's obscurity, the star around which this angel gravitates,—few felicities equal this. The supreme happiness of life consists in the conviction that one is loved; loved for one's own sake—let us say rather, loved in spite of one's self; this conviction the blind man possesses. To be served in distress is to be caressed. Does he lack anything? No. One does not lose the sight when one has love. And what love! A love wholly constituted of virtue! There is no blindness where there is certainty. Soul seeks soul, gropingly, and finds it. And this soul, found and tested, is a woman. A hand sustains you; it is hers: a mouth lightly touches your brow; it is her mouth: you hear a breath very near you; it is hers. To have everything of her, from her worship to her pity, never to be left, to have that sweet weakness aiding you, to lean upon that immovable reed, to touch Providence with one's hands, and to be able to take it in one's arms,—God made tangible,—what bliss! The heart, that obscure, celestial flower, undergoes a mysterious blossoming. One would not exchange that shadow for all brightness! The angel soul is there, uninterruptedly there; if she departs, it is but to return again; she vanishes like a dream, and reappears like reality. One feels warmth approaching, and behold! she is there. One overflows with serenity, with gayety, with ecstasy; one is a radiance amid the night. And there are a thousand little cares. Nothings, which are enormous in that void. The most ineffable accents of the feminine voice employed to lull you, and supplying the vanished universe to you. One is caressed with the soul. One sees nothing, but one feels that one is adored. It is a paradise of shadows.

It was from this paradise that Monseigneur Welcome had passed to the other.

The announcement of his death was reprinted by the local journal of M. sur M. On the following day, M. Madeleine appeared clad wholly in black, and with crape on his hat.

This mourning was noticed in the town, and commented on. It seemed to throw a light on M. Madeleine's origin. It was concluded that some relationship existed between him and the venerable Bishop. "He has gone into mourning for the Bishop of D—" said the drawing-rooms;

this raised M. Madeleine's credit greatly, and procured for him, instantly and at one blow, a certain consideration in the noble world of M. sur M. The microscopic Faubourg Saint-Germain of the place meditated raising the quarantine against M. Madeleine, the probable relative of a bishop. M. Madeleine perceived the advancement which he had obtained, by the more numerous courtesies of the old women and the more plentiful smiles of the young ones. One evening, a ruler in that petty great world, who was curious by right of seniority, ventured to ask him, "M. le Maire is doubtless a cousin of the late Bishop of D—?"

He said, "No, Madame."

"But," resumed the dowager, "you are wearing mourning for him."

He replied, "It is because I was a servant in his family in my youth."

Another thing which was remarked, was, that every time that he encountered in the town a young Savoyard who was roaming about the country and seeking chimneys to sweep, the mayor had him summoned, inquired his name, and gave him money. The little Savoyards told each other about it: a great many of them passed that way.

CHAPTER V

VAGUE FLASHES ON THE HORIZON

Little by little, and in the course of time, all this opposition subsided. There had at first been exercised against M. Madeleine, in virtue of a sort of law which all those who rise must submit to, blackening and calumnies; then they grew to be nothing more than ill-nature, then merely malicious remarks, then even this entirely disappeared; respect became complete, unanimous, cordial, and towards 1821 the moment arrived when the word "Monsieur le Maire" was pronounced at M. sur M. with almost the same accent as "Monseigneur the Bishop" had been pronounced in D— in 1815. People came from a distance of ten leagues around to consult M. Madeleine. He put an end to differences, he prevented lawsuits, he reconciled enemies. Every one took him for the judge, and with good reason. It seemed as though he had for a soul the book of the natural law. It was like an epidemic of veneration, which in the course of six or seven years gradually took possession of the whole district.

One single man in the town, in the arrondissement, absolutely escaped this contagion, and, whatever Father Madeleine did, remained his opponent as though a sort of incorruptible and imperturbable instinct kept him on the alert and uneasy. It seems, in fact, as though there existed in certain men a veritable bestial instinct, though pure and upright, like all instincts, which creates antipathies and sympathies, which fatally separates one nature from another nature, which does not hesitate, which feels no disquiet, which does not hold its peace, and which never belies itself, clear in its obscurity, infallible, imperious, intractable, stubborn to all counsels of the intelligence and to all the dissolvents of reason, and which, in whatever manner destinies are arranged, secretly warns the man-dog of the presence of the man-cat, and the man-fox of the presence of the man-lion.

It frequently happened that when M. Madeleine was passing along a street, calm, affectionate, surrounded by the blessings of all, a man of lofty stature, clad in an iron-gray frock-coat, armed with a heavy cane, and wearing a battered hat, turned round abruptly behind him, and followed him with his eyes until he disappeared, with folded arms and a slow shake of the head, and his upper lip raised in company with his lower to his nose, a sort of significant grimace which might be translated by: "What is that man, after all? I certainly have seen him somewhere. In any case, I am not his dupe."

This person, grave with a gravity which was almost menacing, was one of those men who, even when only seen by a rapid glimpse, arrest the spectator's attention.

His name was Javert, and he belonged to the police.

At M. sur M. he exercised the unpleasant but useful functions of an inspector. He had not seen Madeleine's beginnings. Javert owed the post which he occupied to the protection of M. Chabouillet, the secretary of the Minister of State, Comte Angeles, then prefect of police at Paris. When Javert arrived at M. sur M. the fortune of the great manufacturer was already made, and Father Madeleine had become Monsieur Madeleine.

Certain police officers have a peculiar physiognomy, which is complicated with an air of baseness mingled with an air of authority. Javert possessed this physiognomy minus the baseness.

It is our conviction that if souls were visible to the eyes, we should be able to see distinctly that strange thing that each one individual of the human race corresponds to some one of the species of the animal creation; and we could easily recognize this truth, hardly perceived by the thinker, that from the oyster to the eagle, from the pig to the tiger, all animals exist in man, and that each one of them is in a man. Sometimes even several of them at a time.

Animals are nothing else than the figures of our virtues and our vices, straying before our eyes, the visible phantoms of our souls. God shows them to us in order to induce us to reflect. Only since animals are mere shadows, God has not made them capable of education in the full sense of the word; what is the use? On the contrary, our souls being realities and having a goal which is appropriate to them, God has bestowed on them intelligence; that is to say, the possibility of education. Social education, when well done, can always draw from a soul, of whatever sort it may be, the utility which it contains.

This, be it said, is of course from the restricted point of view of the terrestrial life which is apparent, and without prejudging the profound question of the anterior or ulterior personality of the beings which are not man. The visible *I* in nowise authorizes the thinker to deny the latent *I*. Having made this reservation, let us pass on.

Now, if the reader will admit, for a moment, with us, that in every man there is one of the animal species of creation, it will be easy for us to say what there was in Police Officer Javert.

The peasants of Asturias are convinced that in every litter of wolves there is one dog, which is killed by the mother because, otherwise, as he grew up, he would devour the other little ones.

Give to this dog-son of a wolf a human face, and the result will be Javert.

Javert had been born in prison, of a fortune-teller, whose husband was in the galleys. As he grew up, he thought that he was outside the pale of society, and he despaired of ever re-entering it. He observed that society unpardoningly excludes two classes of men,—those who attack it and those who guard it; he had no choice except between these two classes; at the same time, he was conscious of an indescribable foundation of rigidity, regularity, and probity, complicated with an inexpressible hatred

248

for the race of bohemians whence he was sprung. He entered the police; he succeeded there. At forty years of age he was an inspector.

During his youth he had been employed in the convict establishments of the South.

Before proceeding further, let us come to an understanding as to the words, "human face," which we have just applied to Javert.

The human face of Javert consisted of a flat nose, with two deep nostrils, towards which enormous whiskers ascended on his cheeks. One felt ill at ease when he saw these two forests and these two caverns for the first time. When Javert laughed,—and his laugh was rare and terrible,—his thin lips parted and revealed to view not only his teeth, but his gums, and around his nose there formed a flattened and savage fold, as on the muzzle of a wild beast. Javert, serious, was a watchdog; when he laughed, he was a tiger. As for the rest, he had very little skull and a great deal of jaw; his hair concealed his forehead and fell over his eyebrows; between his eyes there was a permanent, central frown, like an imprint of wrath; his gaze was obscure; his mouth pursed up and terrible; his air that of ferocious command.

This man was composed of two very simple and two very good sentiments, comparatively; but he rendered them almost bad, by dint of exaggerating them,—respect for authority, hatred of rebellion; and in his eyes, murder, robbery, all crimes, are only forms of rebellion. He enveloped in a blind and profound faith every one who had a function in the state, from the prime minister to the rural policeman. He covered with scorn, aversion, and disgust every one who had once crossed the legal threshold of evil. He was absolute, and admitted no exceptions. On the one hand, he said, "The functionary can make no mistake; the magistrate is never the wrong." On the other hand, he said, "These men are irremediably lost. Nothing good can come from them." He fully shared the opinion of those extreme minds which attribute to human law I know not what power of making, or, if the reader will have it so, of authenticating, demons, and who place a Styx at the base of society. He was stoical, serious, austere; a melancholy dreamer, humble and haughty, like fanatics. His glance was like a gimlet, cold and piercing. His whole life hung on these two words: watchfulness and supervision. He had introduced a straight line into what is the most crooked thing in the world; he possessed the conscience of his usefulness, the religion of his functions, and he was a spy as other men are priests. Woe to the man who fell into his hands! He would have arrested his own father, if the latter had escaped from the galleys, and would have denounced his mother, if she had broken her ban. And he would have done it with that sort of inward satisfaction which is conferred by virtue. And, withal, a life of privation, isolation, abnegation, chastity, with never a diversion. It was implacable duty; the police understood, as the Spartans understood Sparta, a pitiless lying in wait, a ferocious honesty, a marble informer, Brutus in Vidocq.

Javert's whole person was expressive of the man who spies and who withdraws himself from observation. The mystical school of Joseph de Maistre, which at that epoch seasoned with lofty cosmogony those things which were called the ultra newspapers, would not have failed to declare that Javert was a symbol. His brow was not visible; it disappeared beneath his hat: his eyes were not visible, since they were lost under his eyebrows: his chin was not visible, for it was plunged in his cravat: his hands were not visible; they were drawn up in his sleeves: and his cane was not visible; he carried it under his coat. But when the occasion presented itself, there was suddenly seen to emerge from all this shadow, as from an ambuscade, a narrow and angular forehead, a baleful glance, a threatening chin, enormous hands, and a monstrous cudgel.

In his leisure moments, which were far from frequent, he read, although he hated books; this caused him to be not wholly illiterate. This could be recognized by some emphasis in his speech.

As we have said, he had no vices. When he was pleased with himself, he permitted himself a pinch of snuff. Therein lay his connection with humanity.

The reader will have no difficulty in understanding that Javert was the terror of that whole class which the annual statistics of the Ministry of Justice designates under the rubric, Vagrants. The name of Javert routed them by its mere utterance; the face of Javert petrified them at sight.

Such was this formidable man.

Javert was like an eye constantly fixed on M. Madeleine. An eye full of suspicion and conjecture. M. Madeleine had finally perceived the fact; but it seemed to be of no importance to him. He did not even put a question to Javert; he neither sought nor avoided him; he bore that embarrassing and almost oppressive gaze without appearing to notice it. He treated Javert with ease and courtesy, as he did all the rest of the world.

It was divined, from some words which escaped Javert, that he had secretly investigated, with that curiosity which belongs to the race, and into which there enters as much instinct as will, all the anterior traces which Father Madeleine might have left elsewhere. He seemed to know, and he sometimes said in covert words, that some one had gleaned certain information in a certain district about a family which had disappeared. Once he chanced to say, as he was talking to himself, "I think I have him!" Then he remained pensive for three days, and uttered not a word. It seemed that the thread which he thought he held had broken.

Moreover, and this furnishes the necessary corrective for the too absolute sense which certain words might present, there can be nothing really infallible in a human creature, and the peculiarity of instinct is that it can become confused, thrown off the track, and defeated. Otherwise, it would be superior to intelligence, and the beast would be found to be provided with a better light than man.

Javert was evidently somewhat disconcerted by the perfect naturalness and tranquillity of M. Madeleine.

One day, nevertheless, his strange manner appeared to produce an impression on M. Madeleine. It was on the following occasion.

CHAPTER VI

FATHER FAUCHELEVENT

One morning M. Madeleine was passing through an unpaved alley of M. sur M.; he heard a noise, and saw a group some distance away. He approached. An old man named Father Fauchelevent had just fallen beneath his cart, his horse having tumbled down.

This Fauchelevent was one of the few enemies whom M. Madeleine had at that time. When Madeleine arrived in the neighborhood, Fauchelevent, an ex-notary and a peasant who was almost educated, had a business which was beginning to be in a bad way. Fauchelevent had seen this simple workman grow rich, while he, a lawyer, was being ruined. This had filled him with jealousy, and he had done all he could, on every occasion, to injure Madeleine. Then bankruptcy had come; and as the old man had nothing left but a cart and a horse, and neither family nor children, he had turned carter.

The horse had two broken legs and could not rise. The old man was caught in the wheels. The fall had been so unlucky that the whole weight of the vehicle rested on his breast. The cart was quite heavily laden. Father Fauchelevent was rattling in the throat in the most lamentable manner. They had tried, but in vain, to drag him out. An unmethodical effort, aid awkwardly given, a wrong shake, might kill him. It was impossible to disengage him otherwise than by lifting the vehicle off of him. Javert, who had come up at the moment of the accident, had sent for a jack-screw.

M. Madeleine arrived. People stood aside respectfully.

"Help!" cried old Fauchelevent. "Who will be good and save the old man?"

M. Madeleine turned towards those present:—

"Is there a jack-screw to be had?"

"One has been sent for," answered the peasant.

"How long will it take to get it?"

"They have gone for the nearest, to Flachot's place, where there is a farrier; but it makes no difference; it will take a good quarter of an hour."

"A quarter of an hour!" exclaimed Madeleine.

It had rained on the preceding night; the soil was soaked.

The cart was sinking deeper into the earth every moment, and crushing the old carter's breast more and more. It was evident that his ribs would be broken in five minutes more.

"It is impossible to wait another quarter of an hour," said Madeleine to the peasants, who were staring at him.

"We must!"

"But it will be too late then! Don't you see that the cart is sinking?"

"Well!"

"Listen," resumed Madeleine; "there is still room enough under the cart to allow a man to crawl beneath it and raise it with his back. Only half a minute, and the poor man can be taken out. Is there any one here who has stout loins and heart? There are five louis d'or to be earned!"

Not a man in the group stirred.

"Ten louis," said Madeleine.

The persons present dropped their eyes. One of them muttered: "A man would need to be devilish strong. And then he runs the risk of getting crushed!"

"Come," began Madeleine again, "twenty louis."

The same silence.

"It is not the will which is lacking," said a voice.

M. Madeleine turned round, and recognized Javert. He had not noticed him on his arrival.

Javert went on:—

"It is strength. One would have to be a terrible man to do such a thing as lift a cart like that on his back."

Then, gazing fixedly at M. Madeleine, he went on, emphasizing every word that he uttered:—

"Monsieur Madeleine, I have never known but one man capable of doing what you ask."

Madeleine shuddered.

Javert added, with an air of indifference, but without removing his eyes from Madeleine:—

"He was a convict."

"Ah!" said Madeleine.

"In the galleys at Toulon."

Madeleine turned pale.

Meanwhile, the cart continued to sink slowly. Father Fauchelevent rattled in the throat, and shrieked:—

"I am strangling! My ribs are breaking! a screw! something! Ah!"

Madeleine glanced about him.

"Is there, then, no one who wishes to earn twenty louis and save the life of this poor old man?"

No one stirred. Javert resumed:—

"I have never known but one man who could take the place of a screw, and he was that convict."

"Ah! It is crushing me!" cried the old man.

Madeleine raised his head, met Javert's falcon eye still fixed upon him, looked at the motionless peasants, and smiled sadly. Then, without saying a word, he fell on his knees, and before the crowd had even had time to utter a cry, he was underneath the vehicle.

A terrible moment of expectation and silence ensued.

They beheld Madeleine, almost flat on his stomach beneath that terrible weight, make two vain efforts to bring his knees and his elbows together. They shouted to him, "Father Madeleine, come out!" Old Fauchelevent himself said to him, "Monsieur Madeleine, go away! You see that I am fated to die! Leave me! You will get yourself crushed also!" Madeleine made no reply.

All the spectators were panting. The wheels had continued to sink, and it had become almost impossible for Madeleine to make his way from under the vehicle.

Suddenly the enormous mass was seen to quiver, the cart rose slowly, the wheels half emerged from the ruts. They heard a stifled voice crying, "Make haste! Help!" It was Madeleine, who had just made a final effort.

They rushed forwards. The devotion of a single man had given force and courage to all. The cart was raised by twenty arms. Old Fauchelevent was saved.

Madeleine rose. He was pale, though dripping with perspiration. His clothes were torn and covered with mud. All wept. The old man kissed his knees and called him the good God. As for him, he bore upon his countenance an indescribable expression of happy and celestial suffering, and he fixed his tranquil eye on Javert, who was still staring at him.

CHAPTER VII

FAUCHELEVENT BECOMES A GARDENER IN PARIS

Fauchelevent had dislocated his kneepan in his fall. Father Madeleine had him conveyed to an infirmary which he had established for his workmen in the factory building itself, and which was served by two sisters of charity. On the following morning the old man found a thousand-franc bank-note on his night-stand, with these words in Father Madeleine's writing: "I purchase your horse and cart." The cart was broken, and the horse was dead. Fauchelevent recovered, but his knee remained stiff. M. Madeleine, on the recommendation of the sisters of charity and of his priest, got the good man a place as gardener in a female convent in the Rue Saint-Antoine in Paris.

Some time afterwards, M. Madeleine was appointed mayor. The first time that Javert beheld M. Madeleine clothed in the scarf which gave him authority over the town, he felt the sort of shudder which a watch-dog might experience on smelling a wolf in his master's clothes. From that time forth he avoided him as much as he possibly could. When the requirements of the service imperatively demanded it, and he could not do otherwise than meet the mayor, he addressed him with profound respect.

This prosperity created at M. sur M. by Father Madeleine had, besides the visible signs which we have mentioned, another symptom which was none the less significant for not being visible. This never deceives. When the population suffers, when work is lacking, when there is no commerce, the tax-payer resists imposts through penury, he exhausts and oversteps his respite, and the state expends a great deal of money in the charges for compelling and collection. When work is abundant, when the country is rich and happy, the taxes are paid easily and cost the state nothing. It may be said, that there is one infallible thermometer of the public misery and riches,—the cost of collecting the taxes. In the course of seven years the expense of collecting the taxes had diminished three-fourths in the arrondissement of M. sur M., and this led to this arrondissement being frequently cited from all the rest by M. de Villele, then Minister of Finance.

Such was the condition of the country when Fantine returned thither. No one remembered her. Fortunately, the door of M. Madeleine's factory was like the face of a friend. She presented herself there, and was admitted to the women's workroom. The trade was entirely new to Fantine; she could not be very skilful at it, and she therefore earned but little by her day's work; but it was sufficient; the problem was solved; she was earning her living.

CHAPTER VIII

MADAME VICTURNIEN EXPENDS THIRTY FRANCS ON MORALITY

When Fantine saw that she was making her living, she felt joyful for a moment. To live honestly by her own labor, what mercy from heaven! The taste for work had really returned to her. She bought a looking-glass, took pleasure in surveying in it her youth, her beautiful hair, her fine teeth; she forgot many things; she thought only of Cosette and of the possible future, and was almost happy. She hired a little room and furnished on credit on the strength of her future work—a lingering trace of her improvident ways. As she was not able to say that she was married she took good care, as we have seen, not to mention her little girl.

At first, as the reader has seen, she paid the Thenardiers promptly. As she only knew how to sign her name, she was obliged to write through a public letter-writer.

She wrote often, and this was noticed. It began to be said in an undertone, in the women's workroom, that Fantine "wrote letters" and that "she had ways about her."

There is no one for spying on people's actions like those who are not concerned in them. Why does that gentleman never come except at nightfall? Why does Mr. So-and-So never hang his key on its nail on Tuesday? Why does he always take the narrow streets? Why does Madame always descend from her hackney-coach before reaching her house? Why does she send out to purchase six sheets of note paper, when she has a "whole stationer's shop full of it?" etc. There exist beings who, for the sake of obtaining the key to these enigmas, which are, moreover, of no consequence whatever to them, spend more money, waste more time, take more trouble, than would be required for ten good actions, and that gratuitously, for their own pleasure, without receiving any other payment for their curiosity than curiosity. They will follow up such and such a man or woman for whole days; they will do sentry duty for hours at a time on the corners of the streets, under alley-way doors at night, in cold and rain; they will bribe errand-porters, they will make the drivers of hackney-coaches and lackeys tipsy, buy a waiting-maid, suborn a porter. Why? For no reason. A pure passion for seeing, knowing, and penetrating into things. A pure itch for talking. And often these secrets once known, these mysteries made public, these enigmas illuminated by the light of day, bring on catastrophies, duels, failures, the ruin of families, and broken lives, to the great joy of those who have "found out everything," without any interest in the matter, and by pure instinct. A sad thing.

Certain persons are malicious solely through a necessity for talking. Their conversation, the chat of the drawing-room, gossip of the anteroom, is like those chimneys which consume wood rapidly; they need a great amount of combustibles; and their combustibles are furnished by their neighbors.

So Fantine was watched.

In addition, many a one was jealous of her golden hair and of her white teeth.

It was remarked that in the workroom she often turned aside, in the midst of the rest, to wipe away a tear. These were the moments when she was thinking of her child; perhaps, also, of the man whom she had loved.

Breaking the gloomy bonds of the past is a mournful task.

It was observed that she wrote twice a month at least, and that she paid the carriage on the letter. They managed to obtain the address: Monsieur, Monsieur Thenardier, inn-keeper at Montfermeil. The public writer, a good old man who could not fill his stomach with red wine without emptying his pocket of secrets, was made to talk in the wine-shop. In short, it was discovered that Fantine had a child. "She must be a pretty sort of a woman." An old gossip was found, who made the trip to Montfermeil, talked to the Thenardiers, and said on her return: "For my five and thirty francs I have freed my mind. I have seen the child."

The gossip who did this thing was a gorgon named Madame Victurnien, the guardian and door-keeper of every one's virtue. Madame Victurnien was fifty-six, and re-enforced the mask of ugliness with the mask of age. A quavering voice, a whimsical mind. This old dame had once been young—astonishing fact! In her youth, in '93, she had married a monk who had fled from his cloister in a red cap, and passed from the Bernardines to the Jacobins. She was dry, rough, peevish, sharp, captious, almost venomous; all this in memory of her monk, whose widow she was, and who had ruled over her masterfully and bent her to his will. She was a nettle in which the rustle of the cassock was visible. At the Restoration she had turned bigot, and that with so much energy that the priests had forgiven her her monk. She had a small property, which she bequeathed with much ostentation to a religious community. She was in high favor at the episcopal palace of Arras. So this Madame Victurnien went to Montfermeil, and returned with the remark, "I have seen the child."

All this took time. Fantine had been at the factory for more than a year, when, one morning, the superintendent of the workroom handed her fifty francs from the mayor, told her that she was no longer employed in the shop, and requested her, in the mayor's name, to leave the neighborhood.

This was the very month when the Thenardiers, after having demanded twelve francs instead of six, had just exacted fifteen francs instead of twelve.

Fantine was overwhelmed. She could not leave the neighborhood; she was in debt for her rent and furniture. Fifty francs was not sufficient to cancel this debt. She stammered a few supplicating words. The superintendent ordered her to leave the shop on the instant. Besides, Fantine was only a moderately good workwoman. Overcome with shame, even more than with despair, she quitted the shop, and returned to her room. So her fault was now known to every one.

She no longer felt strong enough to say a word. She was advised to see the mayor; she did not dare. The mayor had given her fifty francs because he was good, and had dismissed her because he was just. She bowed before the decision.

CHAPTER IX

MADAME VICTURNIEN'S SUCCESS

So the monk's widow was good for something.

But M. Madeleine had heard nothing of all this. Life is full of just such combinations of events. M. Madeleine was in the habit of almost never entering the women's workroom.

At the head of this room he had placed an elderly spinster, whom the priest had provided for him, and he had full confidence in this superintendent,—a truly respectable person, firm, equitable, upright, full of the charity which consists in giving, but not having in the same degree that charity which consists in understanding and in forgiving. M. Madeleine relied wholly on her. The best men are often obliged to delegate their authority. It was with this full power, and the conviction that she was doing right, that the superintendent had instituted the suit, judged, condemned, and executed Fantine.

As regards the fifty francs, she had given them from a fund which M. Madeleine had intrusted to her for charitable purposes, and for giving assistance to the workwomen, and of which she rendered no account.

Fantine tried to obtain a situation as a servant in the neighborhood; she went from house to house. No one would have her. She could not leave town. The second-hand dealer, to whom she was in debt for her furniture—and what furniture!—said to her, "If you leave, I will have you arrested as a thief." The householder, whom she owed for her rent, said to her, "You are young and pretty; you can pay." She divided the fifty francs between the landlord and the furniture-dealer, returned to the latter three-quarters of his goods, kept only necessaries, and found herself without work, without a trade, with nothing but her bed, and still about fifty francs in debt.

She began to make coarse shirts for soldiers of the garrison, and earned twelve sous a day. Her daughter cost her ten. It was at this point that she began to pay the Thenardiers irregularly.

However, the old woman who lighted her candle for her when she returned at night, taught her the art of living in misery. Back of living on little, there is the living on nothing. These are the two chambers; the first is dark, the second is black.

Fantine learned how to live without fire entirely in the winter; how to give up a bird which eats a half a farthing's worth of millet every two days; how to make a coverlet of one's petticoat, and a petticoat of one's coverlet; how to save one's candle, by taking one's meals by the light of the opposite window. No one knows all that certain feeble creatures, who have grown old in privation and honesty, can get out of a sou. It ends by being a talent. Fantine acquired this sublime talent, and regained a little courage.

At this epoch she said to a neighbor, "Bah! I say to myself, by only sleeping five hours, and working all the rest of the time at my sewing, I shall always manage to nearly earn my bread. And, then, when one is sad, one eats less. Well, sufferings, uneasiness, a little bread on one hand, trouble on the other,—all this will support me."

It would have been a great happiness to have her little girl with her in this distress. She thought of having her come. But what then! Make her share her own destitution! And then, she was in debt to the Thenardiers! How could she pay them? And the journey! How pay for that?

The old woman who had given her lessons in what may be called the life of indigence, was a sainted spinster named Marguerite, who was pious with a true piety, poor and charitable towards the poor, and even towards the rich, knowing how to write just sufficiently to sign herself Marguerite, and believing in God, which is science.

There are many such virtuous people in this lower world; some day they will be in the world above. This life has a morrow.

At first, Fantine had been so ashamed that she had not dared to go out.

When she was in the street, she divined that people turned round behind her, and pointed at her; every one stared at her and no one greeted her; the cold and bitter scorn of the passers-by penetrated her very flesh and soul like a north wind.

It seems as though an unfortunate woman were utterly bare beneath the sarcasm and the curiosity of all in small towns. In Paris, at least, no one knows you, and this obscurity is a garment. Oh! how she would have liked to betake herself to Paris! Impossible!

She was obliged to accustom herself to disrepute, as she had accustomed herself to indigence. Gradually she decided on her course. At the expiration of two or three months she shook off her shame, and began to go about as though there were nothing the matter. "It is all the same to me," she said.

She went and came, bearing her head well up, with a bitter smile, and was conscious that she was becoming brazen-faced.

Madame Victurnien sometimes saw her passing, from her window, noticed the distress of "that creature" who, "thanks to her," had been "put back in her proper place," and congratulated herself. The happiness of the evil-minded is black.

Excess of toil wore out Fantine, and the little dry cough which troubled her increased. She sometimes said to her neighbor, Marguerite, "Just feel how hot my hands are!"

Nevertheless, when she combed her beautiful hair in the morning with an old broken comb, and it flowed about her like floss silk, she experienced a moment of happy coquetry.

CHAPTER X

RESULT OF THE SUCCESS

She had been dismissed towards the end of the winter; the summer passed, but winter came again. Short days, less work. Winter: no warmth, no light, no noonday, the evening joining on to the morning, fogs, twilight; the window is gray; it is impossible to see clearly at it. The sky is but a vent-hole. The whole day is a cavern. The sun has the air of a beggar. A frightful season! Winter changes the water of heaven and the heart of man into a stone. Her creditors harrassed her.

Fantine earned too little. Her debts had increased. The Thenardiers, who were not promptly paid, wrote to her constantly letters whose contents drove her to despair, and whose carriage ruined her. One day they wrote to her that her little Cosette was entirely naked in that cold weather, that she needed a woollen skirt, and that her mother must send at least ten francs for this. She received the letter, and crushed it in her hands all day long. That evening she went into a barber's shop at the corner of the street, and pulled out her comb. Her admirable golden hair fell to her knees.

"What splendid hair!" exclaimed the barber.

"How much will you give me for it?" said she.

"Ten francs."

"Cut it off."

She purchased a knitted petticoat and sent it to the Thenardiers. This petticoat made the Thenardiers furious. It was the money that they wanted. They gave the petticoat to Eponine. The poor Lark continued to shiver.

Fantine thought: "My child is no longer cold. I have clothed her with my hair." She put on little round caps which concealed her shorn head, and in which she was still pretty.

Dark thoughts held possession of Fantine's heart.

When she saw that she could no longer dress her hair, she began to hate every one about her. She had long shared the universal veneration for Father Madeleine; yet, by dint of repeating to herself that it was he who had discharged her, that he was the cause of her unhappiness, she came to hate him also, and most of all. When she passed the factory in working hours, when the workpeople were at the door, she affected to laugh and sing.

An old workwoman who once saw her laughing and singing in this fashion said, "There's a girl who will come to a bad end."

She took a lover, the first who offered, a man whom she did not love, out of bravado and with rage in her heart. He was a miserable scamp, a sort of mendicant musician, a lazy beggar, who beat her, and who abandoned her as she had taken him, in disgust.

She adored her child.

The lower she descended, the darker everything grew about her, the more radiant shone that little angel at the bottom of her heart. She said, "When I get rich, I will have my Cosette with me;" and she laughed. Her cough did not leave her, and she had sweats on her back.

One day she received from the Thenardiers a letter couched in the following terms: "Cosette is ill with a malady which is going the rounds of the neighborhood. A miliary fever, they call it. Expensive drugs are required. This is ruining us, and we can no longer pay for them. If you do not send us forty francs before the week is out, the little one will be dead."

She burst out laughing, and said to her old neighbor: "Ah! they are good! Forty francs! the idea! That makes two napoleons! Where do they think I am to get them? These peasants are stupid, truly."

266

Nevertheless she went to a dormer window in the staircase and read the letter once more. Then she descended the stairs and emerged, running and leaping and still laughing.

Some one met her and said to her, "What makes you so gay?"

She replied: "A fine piece of stupidity that some country people have written to me. They demand forty francs of me. So much for you, you peasants!"

As she crossed the square, she saw a great many people collected around a carriage of eccentric shape, upon the top of which stood a man dressed in red, who was holding forth. He was a quack dentist on his rounds, who was offering to the public full sets of teeth, opiates, powders and elixirs.

Fantine mingled in the group, and began to laugh with the rest at the harangue, which contained slang for the populace and jargon for respectable people. The tooth-puller espied the lovely, laughing girl, and suddenly exclaimed: "You have beautiful teeth, you girl there, who are laughing; if you want to sell me your palettes, I will give you a gold napoleon apiece for them."

"What are my palettes?" asked Fantine.

"The palettes," replied the dental professor, "are the front teeth, the two upper ones."

"How horrible!" exclaimed Fantine.

"Two napoleons!" grumbled a toothless old woman who was present. "Here's a lucky girl!"

Fantine fled and stopped her ears that she might not hear the hoarse voice of the man shouting to her: "Reflect, my beauty! two napoleons; they may prove of service. If your heart bids you, come this evening to the inn of the Tillac d'Argent; you will find me there."

Fantine returned home. She was furious, and related the occurrence to her good neighbor Marguerite: "Can you understand such a thing? Is he not an abominable man? How can they allow such people to go about the country! Pull out my two front teeth! Why, I should be horrible! My hair will grow again, but my teeth! Ah! what a monster of a man! I should prefer to throw myself head first on the pavement from the fifth story! He told me that he should be at the Tillac d'Argent this evening."

"And what did he offer?" asked Marguerite.

"Two napoleons."

"That makes forty francs."

"Yes," said Fantine; "that makes forty francs."

She remained thoughtful, and began her work. At the expiration of a quarter of an hour she left her sewing and went to read the Thenardiers' letter once more on the staircase.

On her return, she said to Marguerite, who was at work beside her:—

"What is a miliary fever? Do you know?"

"Yes," answered the old spinster; "it is a disease."

"Does it require many drugs?"

"Oh! terrible drugs."

"How does one get it?"

"It is a malady that one gets without knowing how."

"Then it attacks children?"

"Children in particular."

"Do people die of it?"

"They may," said Marguerite.

Fantine left the room and went to read her letter once more on the staircase.

That evening she went out, and was seen to turn her steps in the direction of the Rue de Paris, where the inns are situated.

The next morning, when Marguerite entered Fantine's room before daylight,—for they always worked together, and in this manner used only one candle for the two,—she found Fantine seated on her bed, pale and frozen. She had not lain down. Her cap had fallen on her knees. Her candle had burned all night, and was almost entirely consumed. Marguerite halted on the threshold, petrified at this tremendous wastefulness, and exclaimed:—

"Lord! the candle is all burned out! Something has happened."

Then she looked at Fantine, who turned toward her her head bereft of its hair.

Fantine had grown ten years older since the preceding night.

"Jesus!" said Marguerite, "what is the matter with you, Fantine?"

"Nothing," replied Fantine. "Quite the contrary. My child will not die of that frightful malady, for lack of succor. I am content."

So saying, she pointed out to the spinster two napoleons which were glittering on the table.

"Ah! Jesus God!" cried Marguerite. "Why, it is a fortune! Where did you get those louis d'or?"

"I got them," replied Fantine.

At the same time she smiled. The candle illuminated her countenance. It was a bloody smile. A reddish saliva soiled the corners of her lips, and she had a black hole in her mouth.

The two teeth had been extracted.

She sent the forty francs to Montfermeil.

After all it was a ruse of the Thenardiers to obtain money. Cosette was not ill.

Fantine threw her mirror out of the window. She had long since quitted her cell on the second floor for an attic with only a latch to fasten it, next the roof; one of those attics whose extremity forms an angle with the floor, and knocks you on the head every instant. The poor occupant can reach the end of his chamber as he can the end of his destiny, only by bending over more and more.

She had no longer a bed; a rag which she called her coverlet, a mattress on the floor, and a seatless chair still remained. A little rosebush which she had, had dried up, forgotten, in one corner. In the other corner was a butter-pot to hold water, which froze in winter, and in which the various levels of the water remained long marked by these circles of ice. She had lost her shame; she lost her coquetry. A final sign. She went out, with dirty caps. Whether from lack of time or from indifference, she no longer mended her linen. As the heels wore out, she dragged her stockings down into her shoes. This was evident from the perpendicular wrinkles. She patched her bodice, which was old and worn out, with scraps of calico which tore at the slightest movement. The people to whom she was indebted made "scenes" and gave her no peace. She found them in the street, she found them again on her staircase. She passed many a night weeping and thinking. Her eyes were very bright, and she felt a steady pain in her shoulder towards the top of the left shoulder-blade. She coughed a great deal. She deeply hated Father Madeleine, but made no complaint. She sewed seventeen hours a day; but a contractor for the work of prisons, who made the prisoners work at a discount, suddenly made prices fall, which reduced the daily earnings of working-women to nine sous. Seventeen hours of toil, and nine sous a day! Her creditors were more pitiless than ever. The second-hand dealer, who had taken back nearly all his furniture, said to her incessantly, "When will you pay me, you hussy?" What did they want of her, good God! She felt that she was being hunted, and something of the wild beast developed in her. About the same time, Thenardier wrote to her that he had waited with decidedly too much amiability and that he must have a hundred francs at once; otherwise he would turn little Cosette out of doors, convalescent as she was from her heavy illness, into the cold and the streets, and that she might do what she liked with herself, and die if she chose. "A hundred francs," thought Fantine. "But in what trade can one earn a hundred sous a day?"

"Come!" said she, "let us sell what is left."

The unfortunate girl became a woman of the town.

CHAPTER XI

CHRISTUS NOS LIBERAVIT

What is this history of Fantine? It is society purchasing a slave.

From whom? From misery.

From hunger, cold, isolation, destitution. A dolorous bargain. A soul for a morsel of bread. Misery offers; society accepts.

The sacred law of Jesus Christ governs our civilization, but it does not, as yet, permeate it; it is said that slavery has disappeared from European civilization. This is a mistake. It still exists; but it weighs only upon the woman, and it is called prostitution.

It weighs upon the woman, that is to say, upon grace, weakness, beauty, maternity. This is not one of the least of man's disgraces.

At the point in this melancholy drama which we have now reached, nothing is left to Fantine of that which she had formerly been.

She has become marble in becoming mire. Whoever touches her feels cold. She passes; she endures you; she ignores you; she is the severe and dishonored figure. Life and the social order have said their last word for her. All has happened to her that will happen to her. She has felt everything, borne everything, experienced everything, suffered everything, lost everything, mourned everything. She is resigned, with that resignation which resembles indifference, as death resembles sleep. She no longer avoids anything. Let all the clouds fall upon her, and all the ocean sweep over her! What matters it to her? She is a sponge that is soaked.

At least, she believes it to be so; but it is an error to imagine that fate can be exhausted, and that one has reached the bottom of anything whatever.

Alas! What are all these fates, driven on pell-mell? Whither are they going? Why are they thus?

He who knows that sees the whole of the shadow.

He is alone. His name is God.

CHAPTER XII

M. BAMATABOIS'S INACTIVITY

There is in all small towns, and there was at M. sur M. in particular, a class of young men who nibble away an income of fifteen hundred francs with the same air with which their prototypes devour two hundred thousand francs a year in Paris. These are beings of the great neuter species: impotent men, parasites, cyphers, who have a little land, a little folly, a little wit; who would be rustics in a drawing-room, and who think themselves gentlemen in the dram-shop; who say, "My fields, my peasants, my woods"; who hiss actresses at the theatre to prove that they are persons of taste; quarrel with the officers of the garrison to prove that they are men of war; hunt, smoke, yawn, drink, smell of tobacco, play billiards, stare at travellers as they descend from the diligence, live at the cafe, dine at the inn, have a dog which eats the bones under the table, and a mistress who eats the dishes on the table; who stick at a sou, exaggerate the fashions, admire tragedy, despise women, wear out their old boots, copy London through Paris, and Paris through the medium of Pont-A-Mousson, grow old as dullards, never work, serve no use, and do no great harm.

M. Felix Tholomyes, had he remained in his own province and never beheld Paris, would have been one of these men.

If they were richer, one would say, "They are dandies;" if they were poorer, one would say, "They are idlers." They are simply men without employment. Among these unemployed there are bores, the bored, dreamers, and some knaves.

At that period a dandy was composed of a tall collar, a big cravat, a watch with trinkets, three vests of different colors, worn one on top of the other—the red and blue inside; of a short-waisted olive coat, with a codfish tail, a double row of silver buttons set close to each other and running up to the shoulder; and a pair of trousers of a lighter shade of olive, ornamented on the two seams with an indefinite, but always uneven, number of lines, varying from one to eleven—a limit which was never exceeded. Add to this, high shoes with little irons on the heels, a tall hat with a narrow brim, hair worn in a tuft, an enormous cane, and conversation set off by puns of Potier. Over all, spurs and a mustache. At that epoch mustaches indicated the bourgeois, and spurs the pedestrian.

The provincial dandy wore the longest of spurs and the fiercest of mustaches.

It was the period of the conflict of the republics of South America with the King of Spain, of Bolivar against Morillo. Narrow-brimmed hats were royalist, and were called morillos; liberals wore hats with wide brims, which were called bolivars.

Eight or ten months, then, after that which is related in the preceding pages, towards the first of January, 1823, on a snowy evening, one of these dandies, one of these unemployed, a "right thinker," for he wore a morillo, and was, moreover, warmly enveloped in one of those large cloaks which completed the fashionable costume in cold weather, was amusing himself by tormenting a creature who was prowling about in a ball-dress, with neck uncovered and flowers in her hair, in front of the officers' cafe. This dandy was smoking, for he was decidedly fashionable.

Each time that the woman passed in front of him, he bestowed on her, together with a puff from his cigar, some apostrophe which he considered witty and mirthful, such as, "How ugly you are!—Will you get out of my sight?—You have no teeth!" etc., etc. This gentleman was known as M. Bamatabois. The woman, a melancholy, decorated spectre which went and came through the snow, made him no reply, did not even glance at him, and nevertheless continued her promenade in silence, and with a sombre regularity, which brought her every five minutes within reach of this sarcasm, like the condemned soldier who returns under the rods. The small effect which he produced no doubt piqued the lounger; and taking advantage of a moment when her back was turned, he crept up behind her with the gait of a wolf, and stifling his laugh, bent down, picked up a handful of snow from the pavement, and thrust it abruptly into her back, between her bare shoulders. The woman uttered a roar, whirled round, gave a leap like a panther, and hurled herself upon the man, burying her nails in his face, with the most frightful words which could fall from the guard-room into the gutter. These insults, poured forth in a voice roughened by brandy, did, indeed, proceed in hideous wise from a mouth which lacked its two front teeth. It was Fantine.

At the noise thus produced, the officers ran out in throngs from the cafe, passers-by collected, and a large and merry circle, hooting and applauding, was formed around this whirlwind composed of two beings, whom there was some difficulty in recognizing as a man and a woman: the man struggling, his hat on the ground; the woman striking out with feet and fists, bareheaded, howling, minus hair and teeth, livid with wrath, horrible.

Suddenly a man of lofty stature emerged vivaciously from the crowd, seized the woman by her satin bodice, which was covered with mud, and said to her, "Follow me!"

The woman raised her head; her furious voice suddenly died away. Her eyes were glassy; she turned pale instead of livid, and she trembled with a quiver of terror. She had recognized Javert.

The dandy took advantage of the incident to make his escape.

CHAPTER XIII

THE SOLUTION OF SOME QUESTIONS CONNECTED WITH THE MUNICIPAL POLICE

Javert thrust aside the spectators, broke the circle, and set out with long strides towards the police station, which is situated at the extremity of the square, dragging the wretched woman after him. She yielded mechanically. Neither he nor she uttered a word. The cloud of spectators followed, jesting, in a paroxysm of delight. Supreme misery an occasion for obscenity.

On arriving at the police station, which was a low room, warmed by a stove, with a glazed and grated door opening on the street, and guarded by a detachment, Javert opened the door, entered with Fantine, and shut the door behind him, to the great disappointment of the curious, who raised themselves on tiptoe, and craned their necks in front of the thick glass of the station-house, in their effort to see. Curiosity is a sort of gluttony. To see is to devour.

On entering, Fantine fell down in a corner, motionless and mute, crouching down like a terrified dog.

The sergeant of the guard brought a lighted candle to the table. Javert seated himself, drew a sheet of stamped paper from his pocket, and began to write.

This class of women is consigned by our laws entirely to the discretion of the police. The latter do what they please, punish them, as seems good to them, and confiscate at their will those two sorry things which they entitle their industry and their liberty. Javert was impassive; his grave face betrayed no emotion whatever. Nevertheless, he was seriously and deeply preoccupied. It was one of those moments when he was exercising without control, but subject to all the scruples of a severe conscience, his redoubtable discretionary power. At that moment he was conscious that his police agent's stool was a tribunal. He was entering judgment. He judged and condemned. He summoned all the ideas which could possibly exist in his mind, around the great thing which he was doing. The more he examined the deed of this woman, the more shocked he felt. It was evident that he had just witnessed the commission of a crime. He had just beheld, yonder, in the street, society, in the person of a freeholder and an elector, insulted and attacked by a creature who was outside all pales. A prostitute had made an attempt on the life of a citizen. He had seen that, he, Javert. He wrote in silence.

When he had finished he signed the paper, folded it, and said to the sergeant of the guard, as he handed it to him, "Take three men and conduct this creature to jail."

Then, turning to Fantine, "You are to have six months of it." The unhappy woman shuddered.

"Six months! six months of prison!" she exclaimed. "Six months in which to earn seven sous a day! But what will become of Cosette? My daughter! my daughter! But I still owe the Thenardiers over a hundred francs; do you know that, Monsieur Inspector?"

She dragged herself across the damp floor, among the muddy boots of all those men, without rising, with clasped hands, and taking great strides on her knees.

"Monsieur Javert," said she, "I beseech your mercy. I assure you that I was not in the wrong. If you had seen the beginning, you would have seen. I swear to you by the good God that I was not to blame! That gentleman, the bourgeois, whom I do not know, put snow in my back. Has any one the right to put snow down our backs when we are walking along peaceably, and doing no harm to any one? I am rather ill, as you see.

And then, he had been saying impertinent things to me for a long time: 'You are ugly! you have no teeth!' I know well that I have no longer those teeth. I did nothing; I said to myself, 'The gentleman is amusing himself.' I was honest with him; I did not speak to him. It was at that moment that he put the snow down my back. Monsieur Javert, good Monsieur Inspector! is there not some person here who saw it and can tell you that this is quite true? Perhaps I did wrong to get angry. You know that one is not master of one's self at the first moment. One gives way to vivacity; and then, when some one puts something cold down your back just when you are not expecting it! I did wrong to spoil that gentleman's hat. Why did he go away? I would ask his pardon. Oh, my God! It makes no difference to me whether I ask his pardon. Do me the favor today, for this once, Monsieur Javert. Hold! you do not know that in prison one can earn only seven sous a day; it is not the government's fault, but seven sous is one's earnings; and just fancy, I must pay one hundred francs, or my little girl will be sent to me. Oh, my God! I cannot have her with me. What I do is so vile! Oh, my Cosette! Oh, my little angel of the Holy Virgin! what will become of her, poor creature? I will tell you: it is the Thenardiers, inn-keepers, peasants; and such people are unreasonable. They want money. Don't put me in prison! You see, there is a little girl who will be turned out into the street to get along as best she may, in the very heart of the winter; and you must have pity on such a being, my good Monsieur Javert. If she were older, she might earn her living; but it cannot be done at that age. I am not a bad woman at bottom. It is not cowardliness and gluttony that have made me what I am. If I have drunk brandy, it was out of misery. I do not love it; but it benumbs the senses. When I was happy, it was only necessary to glance into my closets, and it would have been evident that I was not a coquettish and untidy woman. I had linen, a great deal of linen. Have pity on me, Monsieur Javert!"

She spoke thus, rent in twain, shaken with sobs, blinded with tears, her neck bare, wringing her hands, and coughing with a dry, short cough, stammering softly with a voice of agony. Great sorrow is a divine and terrible ray, which transfigures the unhappy. At that moment Fantine had become beautiful once more. From time to time she paused, and tenderly kissed the police agent's coat. She would have softened a heart of granite; but a heart of wood cannot be softened.

"Come!" said Javert, "I have heard you out. Have you entirely finished? You will get six months. Now march! The Eternal Father in person could do nothing more."

At these solemn words, "the Eternal Father in person could do nothing more," she understood that her fate was sealed. She sank down, murmuring, "Mercy!"

Javert turned his back.

The soldiers seized her by the arms.

A few moments earlier a man had entered, but no one had paid any heed to him. He shut the door, leaned his back against it, and listened to Fantine's despairing supplications.

At the instant when the soldiers laid their hands upon the unfortunate woman, who would not rise, he emerged from the shadow, and said:—

"One moment, if you please."

Javert raised his eyes and recognized M. Madeleine. He removed his hat, and, saluting him with a sort of aggrieved awkwardness:—

"Excuse me, Mr. Mayor—"

The words "Mr. Mayor" produced a curious effect upon Fantine. She rose to her feet with one bound, like a spectre springing from the earth, thrust aside the soldiers with both arms, walked straight up to M. Madeleine before any one could prevent her, and gazing intently at him, with a bewildered air, she cried:—

"Ah! so it is you who are M. le Maire!"

Then she burst into a laugh, and spit in his face.

M. Madeleine wiped his face, and said:—

"Inspector Javert, set this woman at liberty."

Javert felt that he was on the verge of going mad. He experienced at that moment, blow upon blow and almost simultaneously, the most violent emotions which he had ever undergone in all his life. To see a woman of the town spit in the mayor's face was a thing so monstrous that, in his most daring flights of fancy, he would have regarded it as a sacrilege to believe it possible. On the other hand, at the very bottom of his thought, he made a hideous comparison as to what this woman was, and as to what this mayor might be; and then he, with horror, caught a glimpse of I know not what simple explanation of this prodigious attack. But when he beheld that mayor, that magistrate, calmly wipe his face and say, "Set this woman at liberty," he underwent a sort of intoxication of amazement; thought and word failed him equally; the sum total of possible astonishment had been exceeded in his case. He remained mute.

The words had produced no less strange an effect on Fantine. She raised her bare arm, and clung to the damper of the stove, like a person who is reeling. Nevertheless, she glanced about her, and began to speak in a low voice, as though talking to herself:—

"At liberty! I am to be allowed to go! I am not to go to prison for six months! Who said that? It is not possible that any one could have said that. I did not hear aright. It cannot have been that monster of a mayor! Was it you, my good Monsieur Javert, who said that I was to be set free? Oh, see here! I will tell you about it, and you will let me go. That monster of a mayor, that old blackguard of a mayor, is the cause of all. Just imagine, Monsieur Javert, he turned me out! all because of a pack of rascally women, who gossip in the workroom. If that is not a horror, what is? To dismiss a poor girl who is doing her work honestly! Then I could no longer earn enough, and all this misery followed. In the first place, there is one improvement which these gentlemen of the police ought to make, and that is, to prevent prison contractors from wronging poor people. I will explain it to you, you see: you are earning twelve sous at shirt-making, the price falls to nine sous; and it is not enough to live on. Then one has to become whatever one can. As for me, I had my little Cosette, and I was actually forced to become a bad woman. Now you understand how it is that that blackguard of a mayor caused all the mischief. After that I stamped on that gentleman's hat in front of the officers' café; but he had spoiled my whole dress with snow. We women have but one silk dress for evening wear. You see that I did not do wrong deliberately—truly, Monsieur Javert; and everywhere I behold women who are far more wicked than I, and who are much happier. O Monsieur Javert! it was you who gave orders that I am to be set free, was it not? Make inquiries, speak to my landlord; I am paying my rent now; they will tell you that I am perfectly honest. Ah! my God! I beg your pardon; I have unintentionally touched the damper of the stove, and it has made it smoke."

M. Madeleine listened to her with profound attention. While she was speaking, he fumbled in his waistcoat, drew out his purse and opened it. It was empty. He put it back in his pocket. He said to Fantine, "How much did you say that you owed?"

Fantine, who was looking at Javert only, turned towards him:—

"Was I speaking to you?"

Then, addressing the soldiers:—

"Say, you fellows, did you see how I spit in his face? Ah! you old wretch of a mayor, you came here to frighten me, but I'm not afraid of you. I am afraid of Monsieur Javert. I am afraid of my good Monsieur Javert!"

So saying, she turned to the inspector again:—

"And yet, you see, Mr. Inspector, it is necessary to be just. I understand that you are just, Mr. Inspector; in fact, it is perfectly simple: a man amuses himself by putting snow down a woman's back, and that makes the officers laugh; one must divert themselves in some way; and we—well, we are here for them to amuse themselves with, of course! And then, you, you come; you are certainly obliged to preserve order, you lead off the woman who is in the wrong; but on reflection, since you are a good man, you say that I am to be set at liberty; it is for the sake of the little one, for six months in prison would prevent my supporting my child. 'Only, don't do it again, you hussy!' Oh! I won't do it again, Monsieur

Javert! They may do whatever they please to me now; I will not stir. But today, you see, I cried because it hurt me. I was not expecting that snow from the gentleman at all; and then as I told you, I am not well; I have a cough; I seem to have a burning ball in my stomach, and the doctor tells me, 'Take care of yourself.' Here, feel, give me your hand; don't be afraid—it is here."

She no longer wept, her voice was caressing; she placed Javert's coarse hand on her delicate, white throat and looked smilingly at him.

All at once she rapidly adjusted her disordered garments, dropped the folds of her skirt, which had been pushed up as she dragged herself along, almost to the height of her knee, and stepped towards the door, saying to the soldiers in a low voice, and with a friendly nod:—

"Children, Monsieur l'Inspecteur has said that I am to be released, and I am going."

She laid her hand on the latch of the door. One step more and she would be in the street.

Javert up to that moment had remained erect, motionless, with his eyes fixed on the ground, cast athwart this scene like some displaced statue, which is waiting to be put away somewhere.

The sound of the latch roused him. He raised his head with an expression of sovereign authority, an expression all the more alarming in proportion as the authority rests on a low level, ferocious in the wild beast, atrocious in the man of no estate.

"Sergeant!" he cried, "don't you see that that jade is walking off! Who bade you let her go?"

"I," said Madeleine.

Fantine trembled at the sound of Javert's voice, and let go of the latch as a thief relinquishes the article which he has stolen. At the sound of Madeleine's voice she turned around, and from that moment forth she uttered no word, nor dared so much as to breathe freely, but her glance strayed from Madeleine to Javert, and from Javert to Madeleine in turn, according to which was speaking.

It was evident that Javert must have been exasperated beyond measure before he would permit himself to apostrophize the sergeant as he had done, after the mayor's suggestion that Fantine should be set at liberty. Had he reached the point of forgetting the mayor's presence? Had he finally declared to himself that it was impossible that any "authority" should have given such an order, and that the mayor must certainly have said one thing by mistake for another, without intending it? Or, in view of the enormities of which he had been a witness for the past two hours, did he say to himself, that it was necessary to recur to supreme resolutions, that it was indispensable that the small should be made great, that the police spy should transform himself into a magistrate, that the policeman should become a dispenser of justice, and that, in this prodigious extremity, order, law, morality, government, society in its entirety, was personified in him, Javert?

However that may be, when M. Madeleine uttered that word, *I*, as we have just heard, Police Inspector Javert was seen to turn toward the mayor, pale, cold, with blue lips, and a look of despair, his whole body agitated by an imperceptible quiver and an unprecedented occurrence, and say to him, with downcast eyes but a firm voice:—

"Mr. Mayor, that cannot be."

"Why not?" said M. Madeleine.

"This miserable woman has insulted a citizen."

"Inspector Javert," replied the mayor, in a calm and conciliating tone, "listen. You are an honest man, and I feel no hesitation in explaining matters to you. Here is the true state of the case: I was passing through the square just as you were leading this woman away; there were still groups of people standing about, and I made inquiries and learned everything; it was the townsman who was in the wrong and who should have been arrested by properly conducted police."

Javert retorted:—

"This wretch has just insulted Monsieur le Maire."

"That concerns me," said M. Madeleine. "My own insult belongs to me, I think. I can do what I please about it."

"I beg Monsieur le Maire's pardon. The insult is not to him but to the law."

"Inspector Javert," replied M. Madeleine, "the highest law is conscience. I have heard this woman; I know what I am doing."

"And I, Mr. Mayor, do not know what I see."

"Then content yourself with obeying."

"I am obeying my duty. My duty demands that this woman shall serve six months in prison."

M. Madeleine replied gently:—

"Heed this well; she will not serve a single day."

At this decisive word, Javert ventured to fix a searching look on the mayor and to say, but in a tone of voice that was still profoundly respectful:—

"I am sorry to oppose Monsieur le Maire; it is for the first time in my life, but he will permit me to remark that I am within the bounds of my authority. I confine myself, since Monsieur le Maire desires it, to the question of the gentleman. I was present. This woman flung herself on Monsieur Bamatabnois, who is an elector and the proprietor of that handsome house with a balcony, which forms the corner of the esplanade, three stories high and entirely of cut stone. Such things as there are in the world! In any case, Monsieur le Maire, this is a question of police regulations in the streets, and concerns me, and I shall detain this woman Fantine."

Then M. Madeleine folded his arms, and said in a severe voice which no one in the town had heard hitherto:—

"The matter to which you refer is one connected with the municipal police. According to the terms of articles nine, eleven, fifteen, and sixty-six of the code of criminal examination, I am the judge. I order that this woman shall be set at liberty."

Javert ventured to make a final effort.

"But, Mr. Mayor—"

"I refer you to article eighty-one of the law of the 13th of December, 1799, in regard to arbitrary detention."

"Monsieur le Maire, permit me—"

"Not another word."

"But—"

"Leave the room," said M. Madeleine.

Javert received the blow erect, full in the face, in his breast, like a Russian soldier. He bowed to the very earth before the mayor and left the room.

Fantine stood aside from the door and stared at him in amazement as he passed.

Nevertheless, she also was the prey to a strange confusion. She had just seen herself a subject of dispute between two opposing powers. She had seen two men who held in their hands her liberty, her life, her soul, her child, in combat before her very eyes; one of these men was drawing her towards darkness, the other was leading her back towards the light. In this conflict, viewed through the exaggerations of terror, these two men had appeared to her like two giants; the one spoke like her demon, the other like her good angel. The angel had conquered the demon, and, strange to say, that which made her shudder from head to foot was the fact that this angel, this liberator, was the very man whom she abhorred, that mayor whom she had so long regarded as the author of all her woes, that Madeleine! And at the very moment when she had insulted him in so hideous a fashion, he had saved her! Had she, then, been mistaken? Must she change her whole soul? She did not know; she trembled. She listened in bewilderment, she looked on in affright, and at every word uttered by M. Madeleine she felt the frightful shades of hatred crumble and melt within her, and something warm and ineffable, indescribable, which was both joy, confidence and love, dawn in her heart.

When Javert had taken his departure, M. Madeleine turned to her and said to her in a deliberate voice, like a serious man who does not wish to weep and who finds some difficulty in speaking:—

"I have heard you. I knew nothing about what you have mentioned. I believe that it is true, and I feel that it is true. I was even ignorant of the fact that you had left my shop. Why did you not apply to me? But here; I will pay your debts, I will send for your child, or you shall go to her. You shall live here, in Paris, or where you please. I undertake the care of your child and yourself. You shall not work any longer if you do not like. I will give all the money you require. You shall be honest and happy once more. And listen! I declare to you that if all is as you say,—and I do not doubt it,—you have never ceased to be virtuous and holy in the sight of God. Oh! poor woman."

This was more than Fantine could bear. To have Cosette! To leave this life of infamy. To live free, rich, happy, respectable with Cosette; to see all these realities of paradise blossom of a sudden in the midst of her misery. She stared stupidly at this man who was talking to her, and could only give vent to two or three sobs, "Oh! Oh! Oh!"

Her limbs gave way beneath her, she knelt in front of M. Madeleine, and before he could prevent her he felt her grasp his hand and press her lips to it.

Then she fainted.

BOOK SIXTH.

JAVERT

CHAPTER I

THE BEGINNING OF REPOSE

M. Madeleine had Fantine removed to that infirmary which he had established in his own house. He confided her to the sisters, who put her to bed. A burning fever had come on. She passed a part of the night in delirium and raving. At length, however, she fell asleep.

On the morrow, towards midday, Fantine awoke. She heard some one breathing close to her bed; she drew aside the curtain and saw M. Madeleine standing there and looking at something over her head. His gaze was full of pity, anguish, and supplication. She followed its direction, and saw that it was fixed on a crucifix which was nailed to the wall.

Thenceforth, M. Madeleine was transfigured in Fantine's eyes. He seemed to her to be clothed in light. He was absorbed in a sort of prayer. She gazed at him for a long time without daring to interrupt him. At last she said timidly:—

"What are you doing?"

M. Madeleine had been there for an hour. He had been waiting for Fantine to awake. He took her hand, felt of her pulse, and replied:—

"How do you feel?"

"Well, I have slept," she replied; "I think that I am better, It is nothing."

He answered, responding to the first question which she had put to him as though he had just heard it:—

"I was praying to the martyr there on high."

And he added in his own mind, "For the martyr here below."

M. Madeleine had passed the night and the morning in making inquiries. He knew all now. He knew Fantine's history in all its heart-rending details. He went on:—

"You have suffered much, poor mother. Oh! do not complain; you now have the dowry of the elect. It is thus that men are transformed into angels. It is not their fault they do not know how to go to work otherwise. You see this hell from which you have just emerged is the first form of heaven. It was necessary to begin there."

He sighed deeply. But she smiled on him with that sublime smile in which two teeth were lacking.

That same night, Javert wrote a letter. The next morning be posted it himself at the office of M. sur M. It was addressed to Paris, and the superscription ran: To Monsieur Chabouillet, Secretary of Monsieur le Prefet of Police. As the affair in the station-house had been bruited about, the post-mistress and some other persons who saw the letter before it was sent off, and who recognized Javert's handwriting on the cover, thought that he was sending in his resignation.

M. Madeleine made haste to write to the Thenardiers. Fantine owed them one hundred and twenty francs. He sent them three hundred francs, telling them to pay themselves from that sum, and to fetch the child instantly to M. sur M., where her sick mother required her presence.

This dazzled Thenardier. "The devil!" said the man to his wife; "don't let's allow the child to go. This lark is going to turn into a milch cow. I see through it. Some ninny has taken a fancy to the mother."

He replied with a very well drawn-up bill for five hundred and some odd francs. In this memorandum two indisputable items figured up over three hundred francs,—one for the doctor, the other for the apothecary who had attended and physicked Eponine and Azelma through two long illnesses. Cosette, as we have already said, had not been ill. It was only a question of a trifling substitution of names. At the foot of the memorandum Thenardier wrote, Received on account, three hundred francs.

M. Madeleine immediately sent three hundred francs more, and wrote, "Make haste to bring Cosette."

"Christi!" said Thenardier, "let's not give up the child."

In the meantime, Fantine did not recover. She still remained in the infirmary.

The sisters had at first only received and nursed "that woman" with repugnance. Those who have seen the bas-reliefs of Rheims will recall the inflation of the lower lip of the wise virgins as they survey the foolish virgins. The ancient scorn of the vestals for the ambubajae is one of the most profound instincts of feminine dignity; the sisters felt it with the double force contributed by religion. But in a few days Fantine disarmed them. She said all kinds of humble and gentle things, and the mother in her provoked tenderness. One day the sisters heard her say amid her fever: "I have been a sinner; but when I have my child beside me, it will be a sign that God has pardoned me. While I was leading a bad life, I should not have liked to have my Cosette with me; I could not have borne her sad, astonished eyes. It was for her sake that I did evil, and that is why God pardons me. I shall feel the benediction of the good God when Cosette is here. I shall gaze at her; it will do me good to see that innocent creature. She knows nothing at all. She is an angel, you see, my sisters. At that age the wings have not fallen off."

M. Madeleine went to see her twice a day, and each time she asked him:—

"Shall I see my Cosette soon?"

He answered:—

"Tomorrow, perhaps. She may arrive at any moment. I am expecting her."

And the mother's pale face grew radiant.

"Oh!" she said, "how happy I am going to be!"

We have just said that she did not recover her health. On the contrary, her condition seemed to become more grave from week to week. That handful of snow applied to her bare skin between her shoulder-blades had brought about a sudden suppression of perspiration, as a consequence of which the malady which had been smouldering within her for many years was violently developed at last. At that time people were beginning to follow the fine Laennec's fine suggestions in the study and treatment of chest maladies. The doctor sounded Fantine's chest and shook his head.

M. Madeleine said to the doctor:—

"Well?"

"Has she not a child which she desires to see?" said the doctor.

"Yes."

"Well! Make haste and get it here!"

M. Madeleine shuddered.

Fantine inquired:—

"What did the doctor say?"

M. Madeleine forced himself to smile.

"He said that your child was to be brought speedily. That that would restore your health."

"Oh!" she rejoined, "he is right! But what do those Thenardiers mean by keeping my Cosette from me! Oh! she is coming. At last I behold happiness close beside me!"

In the meantime Thenardier did not "let go of the child," and gave a hundred insufficient reasons for it. Cosette was not quite well enough to take a journey in the winter. And then, there still remained some petty but pressing debts in the neighborhood, and they were collecting the bills for them, etc., etc.

"I shall send some one to fetch Cosette!" said Father Madeleine. "If necessary, I will go myself."

He wrote the following letter to Fantine's dictation, and made her sign it:—

292

"MONSIEUR THENARDIER:—

You will deliver Cosette to this person.
You will be paid for all the little things.
I have the honor to salute you with respect.

"FANTINE."

In the meantime a serious incident occurred. Carve as we will the mysterious block of which our life is made, the black vein of destiny constantly reappears in it.

CHAPTER II

HOW JEAN MAY BECOME CHAMP

One morning M. Madeleine was in his study, occupied in arranging in advance some pressing matters connected with the mayor's office, in case he should decide to take the trip to Montfermeil, when he was informed that Police Inspector Javert was desirous of speaking with him. Madeleine could not refrain from a disagreeable impression on hearing this name. Javert had avoided him more than ever since the affair of the police-station, and M. Madeleine had not seen him.

"Admit him," he said.

Javert entered.

M. Madeleine had retained his seat near the fire, pen in hand, his eyes fixed on the docket which he was turning over and annotating, and which contained the trials of the commission on highways for the infraction of police regulations. He did not disturb himself on Javert's account. He could not help thinking of poor Fantine, and it suited him to be glacial in his manner.

Javert bestowed a respectful salute on the mayor, whose back was turned to him. The mayor did not look at him, but went on annotating this docket.

Javert advanced two or three paces into the study, and halted, without breaking the silence.

If any physiognomist who had been familiar with Javert, and who had made a lengthy study of this savage in the service of civilization, this singular composite of the Roman, the Spartan, the monk, and the corporal, this spy who was incapable of a lie, this unspotted police agent—if any physiognomist had known his secret and long-cherished aversion for M. Madeleine, his conflict with the mayor on the subject of Fantine, and had examined Javert at that moment, he would have said to himself, "What has taken place?" It was evident to any one acquainted with that clear, upright, sincere, honest, austere, and ferocious conscience, that Javert had but just gone through some great interior struggle. Javert had nothing in his soul which he had not also in his countenance. Like violent people in general, he was subject to abrupt changes of opinion. His physiognomy had never been more peculiar and startling. On entering he bowed to M. Madeleine with a look in which there was neither rancor, anger, nor distrust; he halted a few paces in the rear of the mayor's arm-chair, and there he stood, perfectly erect, in an attitude almost of discipline, with the cold, ingenuous roughness of a man who has never been gentle and who has always been patient; he waited without uttering a word, without making a movement, in genuine humility and tranquil resignation, calm, serious, hat in hand, with eyes cast down, and an expression which was half-way between that of a soldier in the presence of his officer and a criminal in the presence of his judge, until it should please the mayor to turn round. All the sentiments as well as all the memories which one might have attributed to him had disappeared. That face, as impenetrable and simple as granite, no longer bore any trace of anything but a melancholy depression. His whole person breathed lowliness and firmness and an indescribable courageous despondency.

At last the mayor laid down his pen and turned half round.

"Well! What is it? What is the matter, Javert?"

Javert remained silent for an instant as though collecting his ideas, then raised his voice with a sort of sad solemnity, which did not, however, preclude simplicity.

"This is the matter, Mr. Mayor; a culpable act has been committed."

"What act?"

"An inferior agent of the authorities has failed in respect, and in the gravest manner, towards a magistrate. I have come to bring the fact to your knowledge, as it is my duty to do."

"Who is the agent?" asked M. Madeleine.

"I," said Javert.

"You?"

"I."

"And who is the magistrate who has reason to complain of the agent?"

"You, Mr. Mayor."

M. Madeleine sat erect in his arm-chair. Javert went on, with a severe air and his eyes still cast down.

"Mr. Mayor, I have come to request you to instigate the authorities to dismiss me."

M. Madeleine opened his mouth in amazement. Javert interrupted him:—

"You will say that I might have handed in my resignation, but that does not suffice. Handing in one's resignation is honorable. I have failed in my duty; I ought to be punished; I must be turned out."

And after a pause he added:—

"Mr. Mayor, you were severe with me the other day, and unjustly. Be so today, with justice."

"Come, now! Why?" exclaimed M. Madeleine. "What nonsense is this? What is the meaning of this? What culpable act have you been guilty of towards me? What have you done to me? What are your wrongs with regard to me? You accuse yourself; you wish to be superseded—"

"Turned out," said Javert.

"Turned out; so it be, then. That is well. I do not understand."

"You shall understand, Mr. Mayor."

Javert sighed from the very bottom of his chest, and resumed, still coldly and sadly:—

"Mr. Mayor, six weeks ago, in consequence of the scene over that woman, I was furious, and I informed against you."

"Informed against me!"

"At the Prefecture of Police in Paris."

M. Madeleine, who was not in the habit of laughing much oftener than Javert himself, burst out laughing now:—

"As a mayor who had encroached on the province of the police?"

"As an ex-convict."

The mayor turned livid.

Javert, who had not raised his eyes, went on:—

"I thought it was so. I had had an idea for a long time; a resemblance; inquiries which you had caused to be made at Faverolles; the strength of your loins; the adventure with old Fauchelevant; your skill in marksmanship; your leg, which you drag a little;—I hardly know what all,—absurdities! But, at all events, I took you for a certain Jean Valjean."

"A certain—What did you say the name was?"

"Jean Valjean. He was a convict whom I was in the habit of seeing twenty years ago, when I was adjutant-guard of convicts at Toulon. On leaving the galleys, this Jean Valjean, as it appears, robbed a bishop; then he committed another theft, accompanied with violence, on a public highway on the person of a little Savoyard. He disappeared eight years ago, no one knows how, and he has been sought, I fancied. In short, I did this thing! Wrath impelled me; I denounced you at the Prefecture!"

M. Madeleine, who had taken up the docket again several moments before this, resumed with an air of perfect indifference:—

"And what reply did you receive?"

"That I was mad."

"Well?"

"Well, they were right."

"It is lucky that you recognize the fact."

"I am forced to do so, since the real Jean Valjean has been found."

The sheet of paper which M. Madeleine was holding dropped from his hand; he raised his head, gazed fixedly at Javert, and said with his indescribable accent:—

"Ah!"

Javert continued:—

"This is the way it is, Mr. Mayor. It seems that there was in the neighborhood near Ailly-le-Haut-Clocher an old fellow who was called Father Champmathieu. He was a very wretched creature. No one paid any attention to him. No one knows what such people subsist on. Lately, last autumn, Father Champmathieu was arrested for the theft of some cider apples from—Well, no matter, a theft had been committed, a wall scaled, branches of trees broken. My Champmathieu was arrested. He still had the branch of apple-tree in his hand. The scamp is locked up. Up to this point it was merely an affair of a misdemeanor. But here is where Providence intervened.

"The jail being in a bad condition, the examining magistrate finds it convenient to transfer Champmathieu to Arras, where the departmental prison is situated. In this prison at Arras there is an ex-convict named Brevet, who is detained for I know not what, and who has been appointed turnkey of the house, because of good behavior. Mr. Mayor, no sooner had Champmathieu arrived than Brevet exclaims: 'Eh! Why, I know that man! He is a fagot![4] Take a good look at me, my good man! You are Jean Valjean!' 'Jean Valjean! who's Jean Valjean?' Champmathieu feigns astonishment. 'Don't play the innocent dodge,' says Brevet. 'You are Jean Valjean! You have been in the galleys of Toulon; it was twenty years ago; we were there together.' Champmathieu denies it. Parbleu! You understand. The case is investigated. The thing was well ventilated for me. This is what they discovered: This Champmathieu had been, thirty years ago, a pruner of trees in various localities, notably at Faverolles. There all trace of him was lost. A long time afterwards he was seen again in Auvergne; then in Paris, where he is said to have been a wheelwright, and to have had a daughter, who was a laundress; but that has not been proved. Now, before going to the galleys for theft, what was Jean Valjean? A pruner of trees. Where? At Faverolles. Another fact. This Valjean's Christian name was Jean, and his mother's surname was Mathieu. What more natural to suppose than that, on emerging from the galleys, he should have taken his mother's name for the purpose of concealing himself, and have called himself Jean Mathieu? He goes to Auvergne. The local pronunciation turns Jean into Chan—he is called Chan Mathieu. Our man offers no opposition, and behold him transformed into Champmathieu. You follow me, do you not? Inquiries were made at Faverolles. The family of Jean Valjean is no longer there. It is not known where they have gone. You know that among those classes a family often disappears. Search was made, and nothing was found. When such people are not mud, they are dust. And then, as the beginning of the story dates thirty years back, there is no longer any one at Faverolles who knew Jean Valjean. Inquiries were made at Toulon. Besides Brevet, there are only two convicts in existence who have seen Jean Valjean; they are Cochepaille and Chenildieu, and are sentenced for life. They are taken from the galleys and confronted with the pretended Champmathieu. They do not hesitate; he is Jean Valjean for them as well as for Brevet. The same age,—he is fifty-four,—the same height, the same air, the same man; in short, it is he. It was precisely at this moment that I forwarded my denunciation to the Prefecture in Paris. I was told that I had lost my reason, and that Jean Valjean is at Arras, in the power of the authorities. You can imagine whether this surprised me, when I thought that I had that same Jean Valjean here. I write to the examining judge; he sends for me; Champmathieu is conducted to me—"

4 An ex-convict.

"Well?" interposed M. Madeleine.
Javert replied, his face incorruptible, and as melancholy as ever:—

"Mr. Mayor, the truth is the truth. I am sorry; but that man is Jean Valjean. I recognized him also."

M. Madeleine resumed in, a very low voice:—

"You are sure?"

Javert began to laugh, with that mournful laugh which comes from profound conviction.

"O! Sure!"

He stood there thoughtfully for a moment, mechanically taking pinches of powdered wood for blotting ink from the wooden bowl which stood on the table, and he added:—

"And even now that I have seen the real Jean Valjean, I do not see how I could have thought otherwise. I beg your pardon, Mr. Mayor."

Javert, as he addressed these grave and supplicating words to the man, who six weeks before had humiliated him in the presence of the whole station-house, and bade him "leave the room,"—Javert, that haughty man, was unconsciously full of simplicity and dignity,—M. Madeleine made no other reply to his prayer than the abrupt question:—

"And what does this man say?"

"Ah! Indeed, Mr. Mayor, it's a bad business. If he is Jean Valjean, he has his previous conviction against him. To climb a wall, to break a branch, to purloin apples, is a mischievous trick in a child; for a man it is a misdemeanor; for a convict it is a crime. Robbing and housebreaking—it is all there. It is no longer a question of correctional police; it is a matter for the Court of Assizes. It is no longer a matter of a few days in prison; it is the galleys for life. And then, there is the affair with the little Savoyard, who will return, I hope. The deuce! there is plenty to dispute in the matter, is there not? Yes, for any one but Jean Valjean. But Jean Valjean is a sly dog. That is the way I recognized him. Any other man would have felt that things were getting hot for him; he would struggle, he would cry out—the kettle sings before the fire; he would not be Jean Valjean, et cetera. But he has not the appearance of understanding; he says, 'I am Champmathieu, and I won't depart from that!' He has an astonished air, he pretends to be stupid; it is far better. Oh! the rogue is clever! But it makes no difference. The proofs are there. He has been recognized by four persons; the old scamp will be condemned. The case has been taken to the Assizes at Arras. I shall go there to give my testimony. I have been summoned."

M. Madeleine had turned to his desk again, and taken up his docket, and was turning over the leaves tranquilly, reading and writing by turns, like a busy man. He turned to Javert:—

"That will do, Javert. In truth, all these details interest me but little. We are wasting our time, and we have pressing business on hand. Javert, you will betake yourself at once to the house of the woman Buseaupied, who sells herbs at the corner of the Rue Saint-Saulve. You will tell her that she must enter her complaint against carter Pierre Chesnelong. The man is a brute, who came near crushing this woman and her child. He must be punished. You will then go to M. Charcellay, Rue Montre-de-Champigny. He complained that there is a gutter on the adjoining house which discharges rain-water on his premises, and is undermining the foundations of his house. After that, you will verify the infractions of police regulations which have been reported to me in the Rue Guibourg, at Widow Doris's, and Rue du Garraud-Blanc, at Madame Renee le Bosse's, and you will prepare documents. But I am giving you a great deal of work. Are you not to be absent? Did you not tell me that you were going to Arras on that matter in a week or ten days?"

"Sooner than that, Mr. Mayor."

"On what day, then?"

"Why, I thought that I had said to Monsieur le Maire that the case was to be tried tomorrow, and that I am to set out by diligence tonight."

M. Madeleine made an imperceptible movement.

"And how long will the case last?"

"One day, at the most. The judgment will be pronounced tomorrow evening at latest. But I shall not wait for the sentence, which is certain; I shall return here as soon as my deposition has been taken."

"That is well," said M. Madeleine.

And he dismissed Javert with a wave of the hand.

Javert did not withdraw.

"Excuse me, Mr. Mayor," said he.

"What is it now?" demanded M. Madeleine.

"Mr. Mayor, there is still something of which I must remind you."

"What is it?"

"That I must be dismissed."

M. Madeleine rose.

"Javert, you are a man of honor, and I esteem you. You exaggerate your fault. Moreover, this is an offence which concerns me. Javert, you deserve promotion instead of degradation. I wish you to retain your post."

Javert gazed at M. Madeleine with his candid eyes, in whose depths his not very enlightened but pure and rigid conscience seemed visible, and said in a tranquil voice:—

"Mr. Mayor, I cannot grant you that."

"I repeat," replied M. Madeleine, "that the matter concerns me."

But Javert, heeding his own thought only, continued:—

"So far as exaggeration is concerned, I am not exaggerating. This is the way I reason: I have suspected you unjustly. That is nothing. It is our right to cherish suspicion, although suspicion directed above ourselves is an abuse. But without proofs, in a fit of rage, with the object of wreaking my vengeance, I have denounced you as a convict, you, a respectable man, a mayor, a magistrate! That is serious, very serious. I have insulted authority in your person, I, an agent of the authorities! If one of my subordinates had done what I have done, I should have declared him unworthy of the service, and have expelled him. Well? Stop, Mr. Mayor; one word more. I have often been severe in the course of my life towards others. That is just. I have done well. Now, if I were not severe towards myself, all the justice that I have done would become injustice. Ought I to spare myself more than others? No! What! I should be good for nothing but to chastise others, and not myself! Why, I should be a blackguard!

Those who say, 'That blackguard of a Javert!' would be in the right. Mr. Mayor, I do not desire that you should treat me kindly; your kindness roused sufficient bad blood in me when it was directed to others. I want none of it for myself. The kindness which consists in upholding a woman of the town against a citizen, the police agent against the mayor, the man who is down against the man who is up in the world, is what I call false kindness. That is the sort of kindness which disorganizes society. Good God! it is very easy to be kind; the difficulty lies in being just. Come! if you had been what I thought you, I should not have been kind to you, not I! You would have seen! Mr. Mayor, I must treat myself as I would treat any other man. When I have subdued malefactors, when I have proceeded with vigor against rascals, I have often said to myself, 'If you flinch, if I ever catch you in fault, you may rest at your ease!' I have flinched, I have caught myself in a fault. So much the worse! Come, discharged, cashiered, expelled! That is well. I have arms. I will till the soil; it makes no difference to me. Mr. Mayor, the good of the service demands an example. I simply require the discharge of Inspector Javert."

All this was uttered in a proud, humble, despairing, yet convinced tone, which lent indescribable grandeur to this singular, honest man.

"We shall see," said M. Madeleine.

And he offered him his hand.

Javert recoiled, and said in a wild voice:—

"Excuse me, Mr. Mayor, but this must not be. A mayor does not offer his hand to a police spy."

He added between his teeth:—

"A police spy, yes; from the moment when I have misused the police. I am no more than a police spy."

Then he bowed profoundly, and directed his steps towards the door.

There he wheeled round, and with eyes still downcast:—

"Mr. Mayor," he said, "I shall continue to serve until I am superseded."

He withdrew. M. Madeleine remained thoughtfully listening to the firm, sure step, which died away on the pavement of the corridor.

BOOK SEVENTH.

THE CHAMPMATHIEU AFFAIR

CHAPTER I

SISTER SIMPLICE

The incidents the reader is about to peruse were not all known at M. sur M. But the small portion of them which became known left such a memory in that town that a serious gap would exist in this book if we did not narrate them in their most minute details. Among these details the reader will encounter two or three improbable circumstances, which we preserve out of respect for the truth.

On the afternoon following the visit of Javert, M. Madeleine went to see Fantine according to his wont.

Before entering Fantine's room, he had Sister Simplice summoned.

The two nuns who performed the services of nurse in the infirmary, Lazariste ladies, like all sisters of charity, bore the names of Sister Perpetue and Sister Simplice.

Sister Perpetue was an ordinary villager, a sister of charity in a coarse style, who had entered the service of God as one enters any other service. She was a nun as other women are cooks. This type is not so very rare. The monastic orders gladly accept this heavy peasant earthenware, which is easily fashioned into a Capuchin or an Ursuline. These rustics are utilized for the rough work of devotion. The transition from a drover to a Carmelite is not in the least violent; the one turns into the other without much effort; the fund of ignorance common to the village and the cloister is a preparation ready at hand, and places the boor at once on the same footing as the monk: a little more amplitude in the smock, and it becomes a frock. Sister Perpetue was a robust nun from Marines near Pontoise, who chattered her patois, droned, grumbled, sugared the potion according to the bigotry or the hypocrisy of the invalid, treated her patients abruptly, roughly, was crabbed with the dying, almost flung God in their faces, stoned their death agony with prayers mumbled in a rage; was bold, honest, and ruddy.

Sister Simplice was white, with a waxen pallor. Beside Sister Perpetue, she was the taper beside the candle. Vincent de Paul has divinely traced the features of the Sister of Charity in these admirable words, in which he mingles as much freedom as servitude: "They shall have for their convent only the house of the sick; for cell only a hired room; for chapel only their parish church; for cloister only the streets of the town and the wards of the hospitals; for enclosure only obedience; for gratings only the fear of God; for veil only modesty." This ideal was realized in the living person of Sister Simplice: she had never been young, and it seemed as though she would never grow old. No one could have told Sister Simplice's age. She was a person—we dare not say a woman—who was gentle, austere, well-bred, cold, and who had never lied. She was so gentle that she appeared fragile; but she was more solid than granite. She touched the unhappy with fingers that were charmingly pure and fine. There was, so to speak, silence in her speech; she said just what was necessary, and she possessed a tone of voice which would have equally edified a confessional or enchanted a drawing-room. This delicacy accommodated itself to the serge gown, finding in this harsh contact a continual reminder of heaven and of God. Let us emphasize one detail. Never to have lied, never to have said, for any interest whatever, even in indifference, any single thing which was not the truth, the sacred truth, was Sister Simplice's distinctive trait; it was the accent of her virtue. She was almost renowned in the congregation for this imperturbable veracity. The Abbe Sicard speaks of Sister Simplice in a letter to the deaf-mute Massieu. However pure and sincere we may be, we all bear upon our candor the crack of the little, innocent lie. She did not. Little lie, innocent lie—does such a thing exist? To lie is the absolute form of evil. To lie a little is not possible: he who lies, lies the whole lie. To lie is the very face of the demon. Satan has two names; he is called Satan and Lying. That is what she thought; and as she thought, so she did. The result was the whiteness which we have mentioned—a whiteness which covered even her lips and her eyes with radiance. Her smile was white, her glance was white. There was not a single spider's web, not a grain of dust, on the glass window of that conscience. On entering the order of Saint Vincent de Paul, she had taken the name of Simplice by special choice. Simplice of Sicily, as we know, is the saint who preferred to allow both her breasts to be torn off rather than to say that she had been born at Segesta when she had been born at Syracuse—a lie which would have saved her. This patron saint suited this soul.

Sister Simplice, on her entrance into the order, had had two faults which she had gradually corrected: she had a taste for dainties, and she liked to receive letters. She never read anything but a book of prayers printed in Latin, in coarse type. She did not understand Latin, but she understood the book.

This pious woman had conceived an affection for Fantine, probably feeling a latent virtue there, and she had devoted herself almost exclusively to her care.

M. Madeleine took Sister Simplice apart and recommended Fantine to her in a singular tone, which the sister recalled later on.

On leaving the sister, he approached Fantine.

Fantine awaited M. Madeleine's appearance every day as one awaits a ray of warmth and joy. She said to the sisters, "I only live when Monsieur le Maire is here."

She had a great deal of fever that day. As soon as she saw M. Madeleine she asked him:—

"And Cosette?"

He replied with a smile:—

"Soon."

M. Madeleine was the same as usual with Fantine. Only he remained an hour instead of half an hour, to Fantine's great delight. He urged every one repeatedly not to allow the invalid to want for anything. It was noticed that there was a moment when his countenance became very sombre. But this was explained when it became known that the doctor had bent down to his ear and said to him, "She is losing ground fast."

Then he returned to the town-hall, and the clerk observed him attentively examining a road map of France which hung in his study. He wrote a few figures on a bit of paper with a pencil.

CHAPTER II

THE PERSPICACITY OF MASTER SCAUFFLAIRE

From the town-hall he betook himself to the extremity of the town, to a Fleming named Master Scaufflaer, French Scaufflaire, who let out "horses and cabriolets as desired."

In order to reach this Scaufflaire, the shortest way was to take the little-frequented street in which was situated the parsonage of the parish in which M. Madeleine resided. The cure was, it was said, a worthy, respectable, and sensible man. At the moment when M. Madeleine arrived in front of the parsonage there was but one passer-by in the street, and this person noticed this: After the mayor had passed the priest's house he halted, stood motionless, then turned about, and retraced his steps to the door of the parsonage, which had an iron knocker. He laid his hand quickly on the knocker and lifted it; then he paused again and stopped short, as though in thought, and after the lapse of a few seconds, instead of allowing the knocker to fall abruptly, he placed it gently, and resumed his way with a sort of haste which had not been apparent previously.

M. Madeleine found Master Scaufflaire at home, engaged in stitching a harness over.

"Master Scaufflaire," he inquired, "have you a good horse?"

"Mr. Mayor," said the Fleming, "all my horses are good. What do you mean by a good horse?"

"I mean a horse which can travel twenty leagues in a day."

"The deuce!" said the Fleming. "Twenty leagues!"

"Yes."

"Hitched to a cabriolet?"

"Yes."

"And how long can he rest at the end of his journey?"

"He must be able to set out again on the next day if necessary."

"To traverse the same road?"

"Yes."

"The deuce! the deuce! And it is twenty leagues?"

M. Madeleine drew from his pocket the paper on which he had pencilled some figures. He showed it to the Fleming. The figures were 5, 6, 8 1/2.

"You see," he said, "total, nineteen and a half; as well say twenty leagues."

"Mr. Mayor," returned the Fleming, "I have just what you want. My little white horse—you may have seen him pass occasionally; he is a small beast from Lower Boulonnais. He is full of fire. They wanted to make a saddle-horse of him at first. Bah! He reared, he kicked, he laid everybody flat on the ground. He was thought to be vicious, and no one knew what to do with him. I bought him. I harnessed him to a carriage. That is what he wanted, sir; he is as gentle as a girl; he goes like the wind. Ah! indeed he must not be mounted. It does not suit his ideas to be a saddle-horse. Every one has his ambition. 'Draw? Yes. Carry? No.' We must suppose that is what he said to himself."

"And he will accomplish the trip?"

"Your twenty leagues all at a full trot, and in less than eight hours. But here are the conditions."

"State them."

"In the first place, you will give him half an hour's breathing spell midway of the road; he will eat; and some one must be by while he is eating to prevent the stable boy of the inn from stealing his oats; for I have noticed that in inns the oats are more often drunk by the stable men than eaten by the horses."

312

"Some one will be by."

"In the second place—is the cabriolet for Monsieur le Maire?"

"Yes."

"Does Monsieur le Maire know how to drive?"

"Yes."

"Well, Monsieur le Maire will travel alone and without baggage, in order not to overload the horse?"

"Agreed."

"But as Monsieur le Maire will have no one with him, he will be obliged to take the trouble himself of seeing that the oats are not stolen."

"That is understood."

"I am to have thirty francs a day. The days of rest to be paid for also—not a farthing less; and the beast's food to be at Monsieur le Maire's expense."

M. Madeleine drew three napoleons from his purse and laid them on the table.

"Here is the pay for two days in advance."

"Fourthly, for such a journey a cabriolet would be too heavy, and would fatigue the horse. Monsieur le Maire must consent to travel in a little tilbury that I own."

"I consent to that."

"It is light, but it has no cover."

"That makes no difference to me."

"Has Monsieur le Maire reflected that we are in the middle of winter?"

M. Madeleine did not reply. The Fleming resumed:—

"That it is very cold?"

M. Madeleine preserved silence.

Master Scaufflaire continued:—

"That it may rain?"

M. Madeleine raised his head and said:—

"The tilbury and the horse will be in front of my door tomorrow morning at half-past four o'clock."

"Of course, Monsieur le Maire," replied Scaufflaire; then, scratching a speck in the wood of the table with his thumb-nail, he resumed with that careless air which the Flemings understand so well how to mingle with their shrewdness:—

"But this is what I am thinking of now: Monsieur le Maire has not told me where he is going. Where is Monsieur le Maire going?"

He had been thinking of nothing else since the beginning of the conversation, but he did not know why he had not dared to put the question.

"Are your horse's forelegs good?" said M. Madeleine.

"Yes, Monsieur le Maire. You must hold him in a little when going down hill. Are there many descends between here and the place whither you are going?"

"Do not forget to be at my door at precisely half-past four o'clock tomorrow morning," replied M. Madeleine; and he took his departure.

The Fleming remained "utterly stupid," as he himself said some time afterwards.

The mayor had been gone two or three minutes when the door opened again; it was the mayor once more.

He still wore the same impassive and preoccupied air.

"Monsieur Scaufflaire," said he, "at what sum do you estimate the value of the horse and tilbury which you are to let to me,—the one bearing the other?"

"The one dragging the other, Monsieur le Maire," said the Fleming, with a broad smile.

"So be it. Well?"

"Does Monsieur le Maire wish to purchase them or me?"

"No; but I wish to guarantee you in any case. You shall give me back the sum at my return. At what value do you estimate your horse and cabriolet?"

"Five hundred francs, Monsieur le Maire."

"Here it is."

M. Madeleine laid a bank-bill on the table, then left the room; and this time he did not return.

Master Scaufflaire experienced a frightful regret that he had not said a thousand francs. Besides the horse and tilbury together were worth but a hundred crowns.

The Fleming called his wife, and related the affair to her. "Where the devil could Monsieur le Maire be going?" They held counsel together. "He is going to Paris," said the wife. "I don't believe it," said the husband.

M. Madeleine had forgotten the paper with the figures on it, and it lay on the chimney-piece. The Fleming picked it up and studied it. "Five, six, eight and a half? That must designate the posting relays." He turned to his wife:—

"I have found out."

"What?"

"It is five leagues from here to Hesdin, six from Hesdin to Saint-Pol, eight and a half from Saint-Pol to Arras. He is going to Arras."

Meanwhile, M. Madeleine had returned home. He had taken the longest way to return from Master Scaufflaire's, as though the parsonage door had been a temptation for him, and he had wished to avoid it. He ascended to his room, and there he shut himself up, which was a very simple act, since he liked to go to bed early. Nevertheless, the portress of the factory, who was, at the same time, M. Madeleine's only servant, noticed that the latter's light was extinguished at half-past eight, and she mentioned it to the cashier when he came home, adding:—

"Is Monsieur le Maire ill? I thought he had a rather singular air."

This cashier occupied a room situated directly under M. Madeleine's chamber. He paid no heed to the portress's words, but went to bed and to sleep. Towards midnight he woke up with a start; in his sleep he had heard a noise above his head. He listened; it was a footstep pacing back and forth, as though some one were walking in the room above him. He listened more attentively, and recognized M. Madeleine's step. This struck him as strange; usually, there was no noise in M. Madeleine's chamber until he rose in the morning. A moment later the cashier heard a noise which resembled that of a cupboard being opened, and then shut again; then a piece of furniture was disarranged; then a pause ensued; then the step began again. The cashier sat up in bed, quite awake now, and staring; and through his window-panes he saw the reddish gleam of a lighted window reflected on the opposite wall; from the direction of the rays, it could only come from the window of M. Madeleine's chamber. The reflection wavered, as though it came rather from a fire which had been lighted than from a candle. The shadow of the window-frame was not shown, which indicated that the window was wide open. The fact that this window was open in such cold weather was surprising. The cashier fell asleep again. An hour or two later he waked again. The same step was still passing slowly and regularly back and forth overhead.

The reflection was still visible on the wall, but now it was pale and peaceful, like the reflection of a lamp or of a candle. The window was still open.

This is what had taken place in M. Madeleine's room.

CHAPTER III

A TEMPEST IN A SKULL

The reader has, no doubt, already divined that M. Madeleine is no other than Jean Valjean.

We have already gazed into the depths of this conscience; the moment has now come when we must take another look into it. We do so not without emotion and trepidation. There is nothing more terrible in existence than this sort of contemplation. The eye of the spirit can nowhere find more dazzling brilliance and more shadow than in man; it can fix itself on no other thing which is more formidable, more complicated, more mysterious, and more infinite. There is a spectacle more grand than the sea; it is heaven: there is a spectacle more grand than heaven; it is the inmost recesses of the soul.

To make the poem of the human conscience, were it only with reference to a single man, were it only in connection with the basest of men, would be to blend all epics into one superior and definitive epic. Conscience is the chaos of chimeras, of lusts, and of temptations; the furnace of dreams; the lair of ideas of which we are ashamed; it is the pandemonium of sophisms; it is the battlefield of the passions. Penetrate, at certain hours, past the livid face of a human being who is engaged in reflection, and look behind, gaze into that soul, gaze into that obscurity. There, beneath that external silence, battles of giants, like those recorded in Homer, are in progress; skirmishes of dragons and hydras and swarms of phantoms, as in Milton; visionary circles, as in Dante. What a solemn thing is this infinity which every man bears within him, and which he measures with despair against the caprices of his brain and the actions of his life!

Alighieri one day met with a sinister-looking door, before which he hesitated. Here is one before us, upon whose threshold we hesitate. Let us enter, nevertheless.

We have but little to add to what the reader already knows of what had happened to Jean Valjean after the adventure with Little Gervais. From that moment forth he was, as we have seen, a totally different man. What the Bishop had wished to make of him, that he carried out. It was more than a transformation; it was a transfiguration.

He succeeded in disappearing, sold the Bishop's silver, reserving only the candlesticks as a souvenir, crept from town to town, traversed France, came to M. sur M., conceived the idea which we have mentioned, accomplished what we have related, succeeded in rendering himself safe from seizure and inaccessible, and, thenceforth, established at M. sur M., happy in feeling his conscience saddened by the past and the first half of his existence belied by the last, he lived in peace, reassured and hopeful, having henceforth only two thoughts,—to conceal his name and to sanctify his life; to escape men and to return to God.

These two thoughts were so closely intertwined in his mind that they formed but a single one there; both were equally absorbing and imperative and ruled his slightest actions. In general, they conspired to regulate the conduct of his life; they turned him towards the gloom; they rendered him kindly and simple; they counselled him to the same things. Sometimes, however, they conflicted. In that case, as the reader will remember, the man whom all the country of M. sur M. called M. Madeleine did not hesitate to sacrifice the first to the second—his security to his virtue. Thus, in spite of all his reserve and all his prudence, he had preserved the Bishop's candlesticks, worn mourning for him, summoned and interrogated all the little Savoyards who passed that way, collected information regarding the families at Faverolles, and saved old Fauchelevent's life, despite the disquieting insinuations of Javert. It seemed, as we have already remarked, as though he thought, following the example of all those who have been wise, holy, and just, that his first duty was not towards himself.

At the same time, it must be confessed, nothing just like this had yet presented itself.

Never had the two ideas which governed the unhappy man whose sufferings we are narrating, engaged in so serious a struggle. He understood this confusedly but profoundly at the very first words pronounced by Javert, when the latter entered his study. At the moment when that name, which he had buried beneath so many layers, was so strangely articulated, he was struck with stupor, and as though intoxicated with the sinister eccentricity of his destiny; and through this stupor he felt that shudder which precedes great shocks. He bent like an oak at the approach of a storm, like a soldier at the approach of an assault. He felt shadows filled with thunders and lightnings descending upon his head. As he listened to Javert, the first thought which occurred to him was to go, to run and denounce himself, to take that Champmathieu out of prison and place himself there; this was as painful and as poignant as an incision in the living flesh. Then it passed away, and he said to himself, "We will see! We will see!" He repressed this first, generous instinct, and recoiled before heroism.

It would be beautiful, no doubt, after the Bishop's holy words, after so many years of repentance and abnegation, in the midst of a penitence admirably begun, if this man had not flinched for an instant, even in the presence of so terrible a conjecture, but had continued to walk with the same step towards this yawning precipice, at the bottom of which lay heaven; that would have been beautiful; but it was not thus. We must render an account of the things which went on in this soul, and we can only tell what there was there. He was carried away, at first, by the instinct of self-preservation; he rallied all his ideas in haste, stifled his emotions, took into consideration Javert's presence, that great danger, postponed all decision with the firmness of terror, shook off thought as to what he had to do, and resumed his calmness as a warrior picks up his buckler.

He remained in this state during the rest of the day, a whirlwind within, a profound tranquillity without. He took no "preservative measures," as they may be called. Everything was still confused, and jostling together in his brain. His trouble was so great that he could not perceive the form of a single idea distinctly, and he could have told nothing about himself, except that he had received a great blow.

He repaired to Fantine's bed of suffering, as usual, and prolonged his visit, through a kindly instinct, telling himself that he must behave thus, and recommend her well to the sisters, in case he should be obliged to be absent himself. He had a vague feeling that he might be obliged to go to Arras; and without having the least in the world made up his mind to this trip, he said to himself that being, as he was, beyond the shadow of any suspicion, there could be nothing out of the way in being a witness to what was to take place, and he engaged the tilbury from Scaufflaire in order to be prepared in any event.

He dined with a good deal of appetite.

On returning to his room, he communed with himself.

He examined the situation, and found it unprecedented; so unprecedented that in the midst of his revery he rose from his chair, moved by some inexplicable impulse of anxiety, and bolted his door. He feared lest something more should enter. He was barricading himself against possibilities.

A moment later he extinguished his light; it embarrassed him.

It seemed to him as though he might be seen.

By whom?

Alas! That on which he desired to close the door had already entered; that which he desired to blind was staring him in the face,—his conscience.

His conscience; that is to say, God.

Nevertheless, he deluded himself at first; he had a feeling of security and of solitude; the bolt once drawn, he thought himself impregnable; the candle extinguished, he felt himself invisible. Then he took possession of himself: he set his elbows on the table, leaned his head on his hand, and began to meditate in the dark.

"Where do I stand? Am not I dreaming? What have I heard? Is it really true that I have seen that Javert, and that he spoke to me in that manner? Who can that Champmathieu be? So he resembles me! Is it possible? When I reflect that yesterday I was so tranquil, and so far from suspecting anything! What was I doing yesterday at this hour? What is there in this incident? What will the end be? What is to be done?"

This was the torment in which he found himself. His brain had lost its power of retaining ideas; they passed like waves, and he clutched his brow in both hands to arrest them.

Nothing but anguish extricated itself from this tumult which overwhelmed his will and his reason, and from which he sought to draw proof and resolution.

His head was burning. He went to the window and threw it wide open. There were no stars in the sky. He returned and seated himself at the table.

The first hour passed in this manner.

Gradually, however, vague outlines began to take form and to fix themselves in his meditation, and he was able to catch a glimpse with precision of the reality,—not the whole situation, but some of the details. He began by recognizing the fact that, critical and extraordinary as was this situation, he was completely master of it.

This only caused an increase of his stupor.

Independently of the severe and religious aim which he had assigned to his actions, all that he had made up to that day had been nothing but a hole in which to bury his name. That which he had always feared most of all in his hours of self-communion, during his sleepless nights, was to ever hear that name pronounced; he had said to himself, that that would be the end of all things for him; that on the day when that name made its reappearance it would cause his new life to vanish from about him, and—who knows?—perhaps even his new soul within him, also. He shuddered at the very thought that this was possible. Assuredly, if any one had said to him at such moments that the hour would come when that name would ring in his ears, when the hideous words, Jean Valjean, would suddenly emerge from the darkness and rise in front of him, when that formidable light, capable of dissipating the mystery in which he had enveloped himself, would suddenly blaze forth above his head, and that that name would not menace him, that that light would but produce an obscurity more dense, that this rent veil would but increase the mystery, that this earthquake would solidify his edifice, that this prodigious incident would have no other result, so far as he was concerned, if so it seemed good to him, than that of rendering his existence at once clearer and more impenetrable, and that, out of his confrontation with the phantom of Jean Valjean, the good and worthy citizen Monsieur Madeleine would emerge more honored, more peaceful, and more respected than ever—if any one had told him that, he would have tossed his head and regarded the words as those of a madman. Well, all this was precisely what had just come to pass; all that accumulation of impossibilities was a fact, and God had permitted these wild fancies to become real things!

His revery continued to grow clearer. He came more and more to an understanding of his position.

It seemed to him that he had but just waked up from some inexplicable dream, and that he found himself slipping down a declivity in the middle of the night, erect, shivering, holding back all in vain, on the very brink of the abyss. He distinctly perceived in the darkness a stranger, a man unknown to him, whom destiny had mistaken for him, and whom she was thrusting into the gulf in his stead; in order that the gulf might close once more, it was necessary that some one, himself or that other man, should fall into it: he had only let things take their course.

The light became complete, and he acknowledged this to himself: That his place was empty in the galleys; that do what he would, it was still awaiting him; that the theft from little Gervais had led him back to it; that this vacant place would await him, and draw him on until he filled it; that this was inevitable and fatal; and then he said to himself, "that, at this moment, he had a substitute; that it appeared that a certain Champmathieu had that ill luck, and that, as regards himself, being present in the galleys in the person of that Champmathieu, present in society under the name of M. Madeleine, he had nothing more to fear, provided that he did not prevent men from sealing over the head of that Champmathieu this stone of infamy which, like the stone of the sepulchre, falls once, never to rise again."

All this was so strange and so violent, that there suddenly took place in him that indescribable movement, which no man feels more than two or three times in the course of his life, a sort of convulsion of the conscience which stirs up all that there is doubtful in the heart, which is composed of irony, of joy, and of despair, and which may be called an outburst of inward laughter.

He hastily relighted his candle.

"Well, what then?" he said to himself; "what am I afraid of? What is there in all that for me to think about? I am safe; all is over. I had but one partly open door through which my past might invade my life, and behold that door is walled up forever! That Javert, who has been annoying me so long; that terrible instinct which seemed to have divined me, which had divined me—good God! and which followed me everywhere; that frightful hunting-dog, always making a point at me, is thrown off the scent, engaged elsewhere, absolutely turned from the trail: henceforth he is satisfied; he will leave me in peace; he has his Jean Valjean. Who knows? it is even probable that he will wish to leave town! And all this has been brought about without any aid from me, and I count for nothing in it! Ah! but where is the misfortune in this? Upon my honor, people would think, to see me, that some catastrophe had happened to me! After all, if it does bring harm to some one, that is not my fault in the least: it is Providence which has done it all; it is because it wishes it so to be, evidently. Have I the right to disarrange what it has arranged? What do I ask now? Why should I meddle? It does not concern me; what! I am not satisfied: but what more do I want? The goal to which I have aspired for so many years, the dream of my nights, the object of my prayers to Heaven,—security,—I have now attained; it is God who wills it; I can do nothing against the will of God, and why does God will it? In order that I may continue what I have begun, that I may do good, that I may one day be a grand and encouraging example, that it may be said at last, that a little happiness has been attached to the penance which I have undergone, and to that virtue to which I have returned. Really, I do not understand why I was afraid, a little while ago, to enter the house of that good cure, and to ask his advice; this is evidently what he would have said to me: It is settled; let things take their course; let the good God do as he likes!"

Thus did he address himself in the depths of his own conscience, bending over what may be called his own abyss; he rose from his chair, and began to pace the room: "Come," said he, "let us think no more about it; my resolve is taken!" but he felt no joy.

Quite the reverse.

One can no more prevent thought from recurring to an idea than one can the sea from returning to the shore: the sailor calls it the tide; the guilty man calls it remorse; God upheaves the soul as he does the ocean.

After the expiration of a few moments, do what he would, he resumed the gloomy dialogue in which it was he who spoke and he who listened, saying that which he would have preferred to ignore, and listened to that which he would have preferred not to hear, yielding to that mysterious power which said to him: "Think!" as it said to another condemned man, two thousand years ago, "March on!"

Before proceeding further, and in order to make ourselves fully understood, let us insist upon one necessary observation.

It is certain that people do talk to themselves; there is no living being who has not done it. It may even be said that the word is never a more magnificent mystery than when it goes from thought to conscience within a man, and when it returns from conscience to thought; it is in this sense only that the words so often employed in this chapter, he said, he exclaimed, must be understood; one speaks to one's self, talks to one's self, exclaims to one's self without breaking the external silence; there is a great tumult; everything about us talks except the mouth. The realities of the soul are none the less realities because they are not visible and palpable.

So he asked himself where he stood. He interrogated himself upon that "settled resolve." He confessed to himself that all that he had just arranged in his mind was monstrous, that "to let things take their course, to let the good God do as he liked," was simply horrible; to allow this error of fate and of men to be carried out, not to hinder it, to lend himself to it through his silence, to do nothing, in short, was to do everything! that this was hypocritical baseness in the last degree! that it was a base, cowardly, sneaking, abject, hideous crime!

For the first time in eight years, the wretched man had just tasted the bitter savor of an evil thought and of an evil action.

He spit it out with disgust.

He continued to question himself. He asked himself severely what he had meant by this, "My object is attained!" He declared to himself that his life really had an object; but what object? To conceal his name? To deceive the police? Was it for so petty a thing that he had done all that he had done? Had he not another and a grand object, which was the true one—to save, not his person, but his soul; to become honest and good once more; to be a just man? Was it not that above all, that alone, which he had always desired, which the Bishop had enjoined upon him—to shut the door on his past? But he was not shutting it! great God! he was re-opening it by committing an infamous action! He was becoming a thief once more, and the most odious of thieves! He was robbing

325

another of his existence, his life, his peace, his place in the sunshine. He was becoming an assassin. He was murdering, morally murdering, a wretched man. He was inflicting on him that frightful living death, that death beneath the open sky, which is called the galleys. On the other hand, to surrender himself to save that man, struck down with so melancholy an error, to resume his own name, to become once more, out of duty, the convict Jean Valjean, that was, in truth, to achieve his resurrection, and to close forever that hell whence he had just emerged; to fall back there in appearance was to escape from it in reality. This must be done! He had done nothing if he did not do all this; his whole life was useless; all his penitence was wasted. There was no longer any need of saying, "What is the use?" He felt that the Bishop was there, that the Bishop was present all the more because he was dead, that the Bishop was gazing fixedly at him, that henceforth Mayor Madeleine, with all his virtues, would be abominable to him, and that the convict Jean Valjean would be pure and admirable in his sight; that men beheld his mask, but that the Bishop saw his face; that men saw his life, but that the Bishop beheld his conscience. So he must go to Arras, deliver the false Jean Valjean, and denounce the real one. Alas! that was the greatest of sacrifices, the most poignant of victories, the last step to take; but it must be done. Sad fate! he would enter into sanctity only in the eyes of God when he returned to infamy in the eyes of men.

"Well," said he, "let us decide upon this; let us do our duty; let us save this man." He uttered these words aloud, without perceiving that he was speaking aloud.

He took his books, verified them, and put them in order. He flung in the fire a bundle of bills which he had against petty and embarrassed tradesmen. He wrote and sealed a letter, and on the envelope it might have been read, had there been any one in his chamber at the moment, To Monsieur Laffitte, Banker, Rue d'Artois, Paris. He drew from his secretary a pocket-book which contained several bank-notes and the passport of which he had made use that same year when he went to the elections.

Any one who had seen him during the execution of these various acts, into which there entered such grave thought, would have had no suspicion of what was going on within him. Only occasionally did his lips move; at other times he raised his head and fixed his gaze upon some point of the wall, as though there existed at that point something which he wished to elucidate or interrogate.

When he had finished the letter to M. Laffitte, he put it into his pocket, together with the pocket-book, and began his walk once more.

His revery had not swerved from its course. He continued to see his duty clearly, written in luminous letters, which flamed before his eyes and changed its place as he altered the direction of his glance:—

"Go! Tell your name! Denounce yourself!"

In the same way he beheld, as though they had passed before him in visible forms, the two ideas which had, up to that time, formed the double rule of his soul,—the concealment of his name, the sanctification of his life. For the first time they appeared to him as absolutely distinct, and he perceived the distance which separated them. He recognized the fact that one of these ideas was, necessarily, good, while the other might become bad; that the first was self-devotion, and that the other was personality; that the one said, my neighbor, and that the other said, myself; that one emanated from the light, and the other from darkness.

They were antagonistic. He saw them in conflict. In proportion as he meditated, they grew before the eyes of his spirit. They had now attained colossal statures, and it seemed to him that he beheld within himself, in that infinity of which we were recently speaking, in the midst of the darkness and the lights, a goddess and a giant contending.

He was filled with terror; but it seemed to him that the good thought was getting the upper hand.

He felt that he was on the brink of the second decisive crisis of his conscience and of his destiny; that the Bishop had marked the first phase of his new life, and that Champmathieu marked the second. After the grand crisis, the grand test.

But the fever, allayed for an instant, gradually resumed possession of him. A thousand thoughts traversed his mind, but they continued to fortify him in his resolution.

One moment he said to himself that he was, perhaps, taking the matter too keenly; that, after all, this Champmathieu was not interesting, and that he had actually been guilty of theft.

He answered himself: "If this man has, indeed, stolen a few apples, that means a month in prison. It is a long way from that to the galleys. And who knows? Did he steal? Has it been proved? The name of Jean Valjean overwhelms him, and seems to dispense with proofs. Do not the attorneys for the Crown always proceed in this manner? He is supposed to be a thief because he is known to be a convict."

In another instant the thought had occurred to him that, when he denounced himself, the heroism of his deed might, perhaps, be taken into consideration, and his honest life for the last seven years, and what he had done for the district, and that they would have mercy on him.

But this supposition vanished very quickly, and he smiled bitterly as he remembered that the theft of the forty sous from little Gervais put him in the position of a man guilty of a second offence after conviction, that this affair would certainly come up, and, according to the precise terms of the law, would render him liable to penal servitude for life.

He turned aside from all illusions, detached himself more and more from earth, and sought strength and consolation elsewhere. He told himself that he must do his duty; that perhaps he should not be more unhappy after doing his duty than after having avoided it; that if he allowed things to take their own course, if he remained at M. sur M., his consideration, his good name, his good works, the deference and veneration paid to him, his charity, his wealth, his popularity, his virtue, would be seasoned with a crime. And what would be the taste of all these holy things when bound up with this hideous thing? while, if he accomplished his sacrifice, a celestial idea would be mingled with the galleys, the post, the iron necklet, the green cap, unceasing toil, and pitiless shame.

At length he told himself that it must be so, that his destiny was thus allotted, that he had not authority to alter the arrangements made on high, that, in any case, he must make his choice: virtue without and abomination within, or holiness within and infamy without.

The stirring up of these lugubrious ideas did not cause his courage to fail, but his brain grow weary. He began to think of other things, of indifferent matters, in spite of himself.

The veins in his temples throbbed violently; he still paced to and fro; midnight sounded first from the parish church, then from the town-hall; he counted the twelve strokes of the two clocks, and compared the sounds of the two bells; he recalled in this connection the fact that, a few days previously, he had seen in an ironmonger's shop an ancient clock for sale, upon which was written the name, Antoine-Albin de Romainville.

He was cold; he lighted a small fire; it did not occur to him to close the window.

In the meantime he had relapsed into his stupor; he was obliged to make a tolerably vigorous effort to recall what had been the subject of his thoughts before midnight had struck; he finally succeeded in doing this.

"Ah! yes," he said to himself, "I had resolved to inform against myself."

And then, all of a sudden, he thought of Fantine.

"Hold!" said he, "and what about that poor woman?"

Here a fresh crisis declared itself.

Fantine, by appearing thus abruptly in his revery, produced the effect of an unexpected ray of light; it seemed to him as though everything about him were undergoing a change of aspect: he exclaimed:—

"Ah! but I have hitherto considered no one but myself; it is proper for me to hold my tongue or to denounce myself, to conceal my person or to save my soul, to be a despicable and respected magistrate, or an infamous and venerable convict; it is I, it is always I and nothing but I: but, good God! all this is egotism; these are diverse forms of egotism, but it is egotism all the same. What if I were to think a little about others? The highest holiness is to think of others; come, let us examine the matter. The *I* excepted, the *I* effaced, the *I* forgotten, what would be the result of all this? What if I denounce myself? I am arrested; this Champmathieu is released; I am put back in the galleys; that is well—and what then? What is going on here? Ah! here is a country, a town, here are factories, an industry, workers, both men and women, aged grandsires, children, poor people! All this I have created; all these I provide with their living; everywhere where there is a smoking chimney, it is I who have placed the brand on the hearth and meat in the pot; I have created ease, circulation, credit; before me there was nothing; I have elevated, vivified, informed with life, fecundated, stimulated, enriched the whole country-side; lacking me, the soul is lacking; I take myself off, everything dies: and this woman, who has suffered so much, who possesses so many merits in spite of her fall; the cause of all whose misery I have unwittingly been! And that child whom I meant to go in search of, whom I have promised to her mother; do I not also owe something to this woman, in reparation for the evil which I have done her? If I disappear, what happens? The mother dies; the child becomes what it can; that is what will take place, if I denounce myself. If I do not denounce myself? come, let us see how it will be if I do not denounce myself."

After putting this question to himself, he paused; he seemed to undergo a momentary hesitation and trepidation; but it did not last long, and he answered himself calmly:—

"Well, this man is going to the galleys; it is true, but what the deuce! he has stolen! There is no use in my saying that he has not been guilty of theft, for he has! I remain here; I go on: in ten years I shall have made ten millions; I scatter them over the country; I have nothing of my own; what is that to me? It is not for myself that I am doing it; the prosperity of all goes on augmenting; industries are aroused and animated; factories and shops are multiplied; families, a hundred families, a thousand families, are happy; the district becomes populated; villages spring up where there were only farms before; farms rise where there was nothing; wretchedness disappears, and with wretchedness debauchery, prostitution, theft, murder; all vices disappear, all crimes: and this poor mother rears her child; and behold a whole country rich and honest! Ah! I was a fool! I was absurd! what was that I was saying about denouncing myself? I really must pay attention and not be precipitate about anything. What! because it would have pleased me to play the grand and generous; this is melodrama, after all; because I should have thought of no one but myself, the idea! for the sake of saving from a punishment, a trifle exaggerated, perhaps, but just at bottom, no one knows whom, a thief, a good-for-nothing, evidently, a whole country-side must perish! a poor woman must die in the hospital! a poor little girl must die in the street! like dogs; ah, this is abominable! And without the mother even having seen her child once more, almost without the child's having known her mother; and all that for the sake of an old wretch of an apple-thief who, most assuredly, has deserved the galleys for something else, if not for that; fine scruples, indeed, which save a guilty man and sacrifice the innocent, which save an old vagabond who has only a few years to live at most, and who will not be more unhappy in the galleys than in his hovel, and which sacrifice a whole population, mothers, wives, children. This poor little Cosette who has no one in the world but me, and who is, no doubt, blue with cold at this moment in the den of those Thenardiers; those peoples are rascals; and I was going to neglect my duty towards all these poor creatures; and I was going off to denounce myself; and I was about to commit that unspeakable folly! Let us put it at the worst: suppose that there is a wrong action on my part in this, and that my conscience will reproach me for it some day, to accept, for the good of others, these reproaches which weigh only on myself; this evil action which compromises my soul alone; in that lies self-sacrifice; in that alone there is virtue."

He rose and resumed his march; this time, he seemed to be content.

Diamonds are found only in the dark places of the earth; truths are found only in the depths of thought. It seemed to him, that, after having descended into these depths, after having long groped among the darkest of these shadows, he had at last found one of these diamonds, one of these truths, and that he now held it in his hand, and he was dazzled as he gazed upon it.

"Yes," he thought, "this is right; I am on the right road; I have the solution; I must end by holding fast to something; my resolve is taken; let things take their course; let us no longer vacillate; let us no longer hang back; this is for the interest of all, not for my own; I am Madeleine, and Madeleine I remain. Woe to the man who is Jean Valjean! I am no longer he; I do not know that man; I no longer know anything; it turns out that some one is Jean Valjean at the present moment; let him look out for himself; that does not concern me; it is a fatal name which was floating abroad in the night; if it halts and descends on a head, so much the worse for that head."

He looked into the little mirror which hung above his chimney-piece, and said:—

"Hold! it has relieved me to come to a decision; I am quite another man now."

He proceeded a few paces further, then he stopped short.

"Come!" he said, "I must not flinch before any of the consequences of the resolution which I have once adopted; there are still threads which attach me to that Jean Valjean; they must be broken; in this very room there are objects which would betray me, dumb things which would bear witness against me; it is settled; all these things must disappear."

He fumbled in his pocket, drew out his purse, opened it, and took out a small key; he inserted the key in a lock whose aperture could hardly be seen, so hidden was it in the most sombre tones of the design which covered the wall-paper; a secret receptacle opened, a sort of false cupboard constructed in the angle between the wall and the chimney-piece; in this hiding-place there were some rags—a blue linen blouse, an old pair of trousers, an old knapsack, and a huge thorn cudgel shod with iron at both ends. Those who had seen Jean Valjean at the epoch when he passed through D—in October, 1815, could easily have recognized all the pieces of this miserable outfit.

He had preserved them as he had preserved the silver candlesticks, in order to remind himself continually of his starting-point, but he had concealed all that came from the galleys, and he had allowed the candlesticks which came from the Bishop to be seen.

He cast a furtive glance towards the door, as though he feared that it would open in spite of the bolt which fastened it; then, with a quick and abrupt movement, he took the whole in his arms at once, without bestowing so much as a glance on the things which he had so religiously and so perilously preserved for so many years, and flung them all, rags, cudgel, knapsack, into the fire.

He closed the false cupboard again, and with redoubled precautions, henceforth unnecessary, since it was now empty, he concealed the door behind a heavy piece of furniture, which he pushed in front of it.

After the lapse of a few seconds, the room and the opposite wall were lighted up with a fierce, red, tremulous glow. Everything was on fire; the thorn cudgel snapped and threw out sparks to the middle of the chamber.

As the knapsack was consumed, together with the hideous rags which it contained, it revealed something which sparkled in the ashes. By bending over, one could have readily recognized a coin,—no doubt the forty-sou piece stolen from the little Savoyard.

He did not look at the fire, but paced back and forth with the same step.

All at once his eye fell on the two silver candlesticks, which shone vaguely on the chimney-piece, through the glow.

"Hold!" he thought; "the whole of Jean Valjean is still in them. They must be destroyed also."

He seized the two candlesticks.

There was still fire enough to allow of their being put out of shape, and converted into a sort of unrecognizable bar of metal.

He bent over the hearth and warmed himself for a moment. He felt a sense of real comfort. "How good warmth is!" said he.

He stirred the live coals with one of the candlesticks.

A minute more, and they were both in the fire.

At that moment it seemed to him that he heard a voice within him shouting: "Jean Valjean! Jean Valjean!"

His hair rose upright: he became like a man who is listening to some terrible thing.

"Yes, that's it! finish!" said the voice. "Complete what you are about! Destroy these candlesticks! Annihilate this souvenir! Forget the Bishop! Forget everything! Destroy this Champmathieu, do! That is right! Applaud yourself! So it is settled, resolved, fixed, agreed: here is an old man who does not know what is wanted of him, who has, perhaps, done nothing, an innocent man, whose whole misfortune lies in your name, upon whom your name weighs like a crime, who is about to be taken for you, who will be condemned, who will finish his days in abjectness and horror. That is good! Be an honest man yourself; remain Monsieur le Maire; remain honorable and honored; enrich the town; nourish the indigent; rear the orphan; live happy, virtuous, and admired; and, during this time, while you are here in the midst of joy and light, there will be a man who will wear your red blouse, who will bear your name in ignominy, and who will drag your chain in the galleys. Yes, it is well arranged thus. Ah, wretch!"

The perspiration streamed from his brow. He fixed a haggard eye on the candlesticks. But that within him which had spoken had not finished. The voice continued:—

"Jean Valjean, there will be around you many voices, which will make a great noise, which will talk very loud, and which will bless you, and only one which no one will hear, and which will curse you in the dark. Well! listen, infamous man! All those benedictions will fall back before they reach heaven, and only the malediction will ascend to God."

This voice, feeble at first, and which had proceeded from the most obscure depths of his conscience, had gradually become startling and formidable, and he now heard it in his very ear. It seemed to him that it had detached itself from him, and that it was now speaking outside of him. He thought that he heard the last words so distinctly, that he glanced around the room in a sort of terror.

"Is there any one here?" he demanded aloud, in utter bewilderment.

Then he resumed, with a laugh which resembled that of an idiot:—

"How stupid I am! There can be no one!"

There was some one; but the person who was there was of those whom the human eye cannot see.

He placed the candlesticks on the chimney-piece.

Then he resumed his monotonous and lugubrious tramp, which troubled the dreams of the sleeping man beneath him, and awoke him with a start.

This tramping to and fro soothed and at the same time intoxicated him. It sometimes seems, on supreme occasions, as though people moved about for the purpose of asking advice of everything that they may encounter by change of place. After the lapse of a few minutes he no longer knew his position.

He now recoiled in equal terror before both the resolutions at which he had arrived in turn. The two ideas which counselled him appeared to him equally fatal. What a fatality! What conjunction that that Champmathieu should have been taken for him; to be overwhelmed by precisely the means which Providence seemed to have employed, at first, to strengthen his position!

There was a moment when he reflected on the future. Denounce himself, great God! Deliver himself up! With immense despair he faced all that he should be obliged to leave, all that he should be obliged to take up once more. He should have to bid farewell to that existence which was so good, so pure, so radiant, to the respect of all, to honor, to liberty. He should never more stroll in the fields; he should never more hear the birds sing in the month of May; he should never more bestow alms on the little children; he should never more experience the sweetness of having glances of gratitude and love fixed upon him; he should quit that house which he had built, that little chamber! Everything seemed charming to him at that moment. Never again should he read those books; never more should he write on that little table of white wood; his old portress, the only servant whom he kept, would never more bring him his coffee in the morning. Great God! instead of that, the convict gang, the iron necklet, the red waistcoat, the chain on his ankle, fatigue, the cell, the camp bed all those horrors which he knew so well! At his age, after having been what he was! If he were only young again! but to be addressed in his old age as "thou" by any one who pleased; to be searched by the convict-guard; to receive the galley-sergeant's cudgellings; to wear iron-bound shoes on his bare feet; to have to stretch out his leg night and morning to the hammer of the roundsman who visits the gang; to submit to the curiosity of strangers, who would be told: "That man yonder is the famous Jean Valjean, who was mayor of M. sur M."; and at night, dripping with perspiration, overwhelmed with lassitude, their green caps drawn over their eyes, to remount, two by two, the ladder staircase of the galleys beneath the sergeant's whip. Oh, what misery! Can destiny, then, be as malicious as an intelligent being, and become as monstrous as the human heart?

And do what he would, he always fell back upon the heartrending dilemma which lay at the foundation of his revery: "Should he remain in paradise and become a demon? Should he return to hell and become an angel?"

What was to be done? Great God! what was to be done?

The torment from which he had escaped with so much difficulty was unchained afresh within him. His ideas began to grow confused once more; they assumed a kind of stupefied and mechanical quality which is peculiar to despair. The name of Romainville recurred incessantly to his mind, with the two verses of a song which he had heard in the past. He thought that Romainville was a little grove near Paris, where young lovers go to pluck lilacs in the month of April.

He wavered outwardly as well as inwardly. He walked like a little child who is permitted to toddle alone.

At intervals, as he combated his lassitude, he made an effort to recover the mastery of his mind. He tried to put to himself, for the last time, and definitely, the problem over which he had, in a manner, fallen prostrate with fatigue: Ought he to denounce himself? Ought he to hold his peace? He could not manage to see anything distinctly. The vague aspects of all the courses of reasoning which had been sketched out by his meditations quivered and vanished, one after the other, into smoke. He only felt that, to whatever course of action he made up his mind, something in him must die, and that of necessity, and without his being able to escape the fact; that he was entering a sepulchre on the right hand as much as on the left; that he was passing through a death agony,—the agony of his happiness, or the agony of his virtue.

Alas! all his resolution had again taken possession of him. He was no further advanced than at the beginning.

Thus did this unhappy soul struggle in its anguish. Eighteen hundred years before this unfortunate man, the mysterious Being in whom are summed up all the sanctities and all the sufferings of humanity had also long thrust aside with his hand, while the olive-trees quivered in the wild wind of the infinite, the terrible cup which appeared to Him dripping with darkness and overflowing with shadows in the depths all studded with stars.

CHAPTER IV

FORMS ASSUMED BY SUFFERING DURING SLEEP

Three o'clock in the morning had just struck, and he had been walking thus for five hours, almost uninterruptedly, when he at length allowed himself to drop into his chair.

There he fell asleep and had a dream.

This dream, like the majority of dreams, bore no relation to the situation, except by its painful and heart-rending character, but it made an impression on him. This nightmare struck him so forcibly that he wrote it down later on. It is one of the papers in his own handwriting which he has bequeathed to us. We think that we have here reproduced the thing in strict accordance with the text.

Of whatever nature this dream may be, the history of this night would be incomplete if we were to omit it: it is the gloomy adventure of an ailing soul.

Here it is. On the envelope we find this line inscribed, "The Dream I had that Night."

"I was in a plain; a vast, gloomy plain, where there was no grass. It did not seem to me to be daylight nor yet night.

"I was walking with my brother, the brother of my childish years, the brother of whom, I must say, I never think, and whom I now hardly remember.

"We were conversing and we met some passers-by. We were talking of a neighbor of ours in former days, who had always worked with her window open from the time when she came to live on the street. As we talked we felt cold because of that open window.

"There were no trees in the plain. We saw a man passing close to us. He was entirely nude, of the hue of ashes, and mounted on a horse which was earth color. The man had no hair; we could see his skull and the veins on it. In his hand he held a switch which was as supple as a vine-shoot and as heavy as iron. This horseman passed and said nothing to us.

"My brother said to me, 'Let us take to the hollow road.'

"There existed a hollow way wherein one saw neither a single shrub nor a spear of moss. Everything was dirt-colored, even the sky. After proceeding a few paces, I received no reply when I spoke: I perceived that my brother was no longer with me.

"I entered a village which I espied. I reflected that it must be Romainville. (Why Romainville?)[5]

5 This parenthesis is due to Jean Valjean.

"The first street that I entered was deserted. I entered a second street. Behind the angle formed by the two streets, a man was standing erect against the wall. I said to this Man:—

"'What country is this? Where am I?' The man made no reply. I saw the door of a house open, and I entered.

"The first chamber was deserted. I entered the second. Behind the door of this chamber a man was standing erect against the wall. I inquired of this man, 'Whose house is this? Where am I?' The man replied not.

"The house had a garden. I quitted the house and entered the garden. The garden was deserted. Behind the first tree I found a man standing upright. I said to this man, 'What garden is this? Where am I?' The man did not answer.

"I strolled into the village, and perceived that it was a town. All the streets were deserted, all the doors were open. Not a single living being was passing in the streets, walking through the chambers or strolling in the gardens. But behind each angle of the walls, behind each door, behind each tree, stood a silent man. Only one was to be seen at a time. These men watched me pass.

"I left the town and began to ramble about the fields.

"After the lapse of some time I turned back and saw a great crowd coming up behind me. I recognized all the men whom I had seen in that town. They had strange heads. They did not seem to be in a hurry, yet they walked faster than I did. They made no noise as they walked. In an instant this crowd had overtaken and surrounded me. The faces of these men were earthen in hue.

"Then the first one whom I had seen and questioned on entering the town said to me:—

"'Whither are you going! Do you not know that you have been dead this long time?'

"I opened my mouth to reply, and I perceived that there was no one near me."

He woke. He was icy cold. A wind which was chill like the breeze of dawn was rattling the leaves of the window, which had been left open on their hinges. The fire was out. The candle was nearing its end. It was still black night.

He rose, he went to the window. There were no stars in the sky even yet.

From his window the yard of the house and the street were visible. A sharp, harsh noise, which made him drop his eyes, resounded from the earth.

Below him he perceived two red stars, whose rays lengthened and shortened in a singular manner through the darkness.

As his thoughts were still half immersed in the mists of sleep, "Hold!" said he, "there are no stars in the sky. They are on earth now."

But this confusion vanished; a second sound similar to the first roused him thoroughly; he looked and recognized the fact that these two stars were the lanterns of a carriage. By the light which they cast he was able to distinguish the form of this vehicle. It was a tilbury harnessed to a small white horse. The noise which he had heard was the trampling of the horse's hoofs on the pavement.

"What vehicle is this?" he said to himself. "Who is coming here so early in the morning?"

At that moment there came a light tap on the door of his chamber.

He shuddered from head to foot, and cried in a terrible voice:—

"Who is there?"

Some one said:—

"I, Monsieur le Maire."

He recognized the voice of the old woman who was his portress.

"Well!" he replied, "what is it?"

"Monsieur le Maire, it is just five o'clock in the morning."

"What is that to me?"

"The cabriolet is here, Monsieur le Maire."

"What cabriolet?"

"The tilbury."

"What tilbury?"

"Did not Monsieur le Maire order a tilbury?"

"No," said he.

"The coachman says that he has come for Monsieur le Maire."

"What coachman?"

"M. Scaufflaire's coachman."

"M. Scaufflaire?"

That name sent a shudder over him, as though a flash of lightning had passed in front of his face.

"Ah! yes," he resumed; "M. Scaufflaire!"

If the old woman could have seen him at that moment, she would have been frightened.

A tolerably long silence ensued. He examined the flame of the candle with a stupid air, and from around the wick he took some of the burning wax, which he rolled between his fingers. The old woman waited for him. She even ventured to uplift her voice once more:—

"What am I to say, Monsieur le Maire?"

"Say that it is well, and that I am coming down."

CHAPTER V

HINDRANCES

The posting service from Arras to M. sur M. was still operated at this period by small mail-wagons of the time of the Empire. These mail-wagons were two-wheeled cabriolets, upholstered inside with fawn-colored leather, hung on springs, and having but two seats, one for the postboy, the other for the traveller. The wheels were armed with those long, offensive axles which keep other vehicles at a distance, and which may still be seen on the road in Germany. The despatch box, an immense oblong coffer, was placed behind the vehicle and formed a part of it. This coffer was painted black, and the cabriolet yellow.

These vehicles, which have no counterparts nowadays, had something distorted and hunchbacked about them; and when one saw them passing in the distance, and climbing up some road to the horizon, they resembled the insects which are called, I think, termites, and which, though with but little corselet, drag a great train behind them. But they travelled at a very rapid rate. The post-wagon which set out from Arras at one o'clock every night, after the mail from Paris had passed, arrived at M. sur M. a little before five o'clock in the morning.

That night the wagon which was descending to M. sur M. by the Hesdin road, collided at the corner of a street, just as it was entering the town, with a little tilbury harnessed to a white horse, which was going in the opposite direction, and in which there was but one person, a man enveloped in a mantle. The wheel of the tilbury received quite a violent shock. The postman shouted to the man to stop, but the traveller paid no heed and pursued his road at full gallop.

"That man is in a devilish hurry!" said the postman.

The man thus hastening on was the one whom we have just seen struggling in convulsions which are certainly deserving of pity.

Whither was he going? He could not have told. Why was he hastening? He did not know. He was driving at random, straight ahead. Whither? To Arras, no doubt; but he might have been going elsewhere as well. At times he was conscious of it, and he shuddered. He plunged into the night as into a gulf. Something urged him forward; something drew him on. No one could have told what was taking place within him; every one will understand it. What man is there who has not entered, at least once in his life, into that obscure cavern of the unknown?

However, he had resolved on nothing, decided nothing, formed no plan, done nothing. None of the actions of his conscience had been decisive. He was, more than ever, as he had been at the first moment.

Why was he going to Arras?

He repeated what he had already said to himself when he had hired Scaufflaire's cabriolet: that, whatever the result was to be, there was no reason why he should not see with his own eyes, and judge of matters for himself; that this was even prudent; that he must know what took place; that no decision could be arrived at without having observed and scrutinized; that one made mountains out of everything from a distance; that, at any rate, when he should have seen that Champmathieu, some wretch, his conscience would probably be greatly relieved to allow him to go to the galleys in his stead; that Javert would indeed be there; and that Brevet, that Chenildieu, that Cochepaille, old convicts who had known him; but they certainly would not recognize him;—bah! what an idea! that Javert was a hundred leagues from suspecting the truth; that all conjectures and all suppositions were fixed on Champmathieu, and that there is nothing so headstrong as suppositions and conjectures; that accordingly there was no danger.

That it was, no doubt, a dark moment, but that he should emerge from it; that, after all, he held his destiny, however bad it might be, in his own hand; that he was master of it. He clung to this thought.

At bottom, to tell the whole truth, he would have preferred not to go to Arras.

Nevertheless, he was going thither.

As he meditated, he whipped up his horse, which was proceeding at that fine, regular, and even trot which accomplishes two leagues and a half an hour.

In proportion as the cabriolet advanced, he felt something within him draw back.

At daybreak he was in the open country; the town of M. sur M. lay far behind him. He watched the horizon grow white; he stared at all the chilly figures of a winter's dawn as they passed before his eyes, but without seeing them. The morning has its spectres as well as the evening. He did not see them; but without his being aware of it, and by means of a sort of penetration which was almost physical, these black silhouettes of trees and of hills added some gloomy and sinister quality to the violent state of his soul.

Each time that he passed one of those isolated dwellings which sometimes border on the highway, he said to himself, "And yet there are people there within who are sleeping!"

The trot of the horse, the bells on the harness, the wheels on the road, produced a gentle, monotonous noise. These things are charming when one is joyous, and lugubrious when one is sad.

It was broad daylight when he arrived at Hesdin. He halted in front of the inn, to allow the horse a breathing spell, and to have him given some oats.

The horse belonged, as Scaufflaire had said, to that small race of the Boulonnais, which has too much head, too much belly, and not enough neck and shoulders, but which has a broad chest, a large crupper, thin, fine legs, and solid hoofs—a homely, but a robust and healthy race. The excellent beast had travelled five leagues in two hours, and had not a drop of sweat on his loins.

He did not get out of the tilbury. The stableman who brought the oats suddenly bent down and examined the left wheel.

"Are you going far in this condition?" said the man.

He replied, with an air of not having roused himself from his revery:—

"Why?"

"Have you come from a great distance?" went on the man.

"Five leagues."

"Ah!"

"Why do you say, 'Ah?'"

The man bent down once more, was silent for a moment, with his eyes fixed on the wheel; then he rose erect and said:—

"Because, though this wheel has travelled five leagues, it certainly will not travel another quarter of a league."

He sprang out of the tilbury.

"What is that you say, my friend?"

"I say that it is a miracle that you should have travelled five leagues without you and your horse rolling into some ditch on the highway. Just see here!"

The wheel really had suffered serious damage. The shock administered by the mail-wagon had split two spokes and strained the hub, so that the nut no longer held firm.

"My friend," he said to the stableman, "is there a wheelwright here?"

"Certainly, sir."

"Do me the service to go and fetch him."

"He is only a step from here. Hey! Master Bourgaillard!"

Master Bourgaillard, the wheelwright, was standing on his own threshold. He came, examined the wheel and made a grimace like a surgeon when the latter thinks a limb is broken.

"Can you repair this wheel immediately?"

"Yes, sir."

"When can I set out again?"

"Tomorrow."

"Tomorrow!"

"There is a long day's work on it. Are you in a hurry, sir?"

"In a very great hurry. I must set out again in an hour at the latest."

"Impossible, sir."

"I will pay whatever you ask."

"Impossible."

"Well, in two hours, then."

"Impossible today. Two new spokes and a hub must be made. Monsieur will not be able to start before tomorrow morning."

"The matter cannot wait until tomorrow. What if you were to replace this wheel instead of repairing it?"

"How so?"

"You are a wheelwright?"

"Certainly, sir."

"Have you not a wheel that you can sell me? Then I could start again at once."

"A spare wheel?"

"Yes."

"I have no wheel on hand that would fit your cabriolet. Two wheels make a pair. Two wheels cannot be put together hap-hazard."

"In that case, sell me a pair of wheels."

"Not all wheels fit all axles, sir."

"Try, nevertheless."

"It is useless, sir. I have nothing to sell but cart-wheels. We are but a poor country here."

"Have you a cabriolet that you can let me have?"

The wheelwright had seen at the first glance that the tilbury was a hired vehicle. He shrugged his shoulders.

"You treat the cabriolets that people let you so well! If I had one, I would not let it to you!"

"Well, sell it to me, then."

"I have none."

"What! not even a spring-cart? I am not hard to please, as you see."

"We live in a poor country. There is, in truth," added the wheelwright, "an old calash under the shed yonder, which belongs to a bourgeois of the town, who gave it to me to take care of, and who only uses it on the thirty-sixth of the month—never, that is to say. I might let that to you, for what matters it to me? But the bourgeois must not see it pass—and then, it is a calash; it would require two horses."

"I will take two post-horses."

"Where is Monsieur going?"

"To Arras."

"And Monsieur wishes to reach there today?"

"Yes, of course."

"By taking two post-horses?"

"Why not?"

"Does it make any difference whether Monsieur arrives at four o'clock tomorrow morning?"

"Certainly not."

"There is one thing to be said about that, you see, by taking post-horses—Monsieur has his passport?"

"Yes."

"Well, by taking post-horses, Monsieur cannot reach Arras before tomorrow. We are on a cross-road. The relays are badly served, the horses are in the fields. The season for ploughing is just beginning; heavy teams are required, and horses are seized upon everywhere, from the post as well as elsewhere. Monsieur will have to wait three or four hours at the least at every relay. And, then, they drive at a walk. There are many hills to ascend."

"Come then, I will go on horseback. Unharness the cabriolet. Some one can surely sell me a saddle in the neighborhood."

"Without doubt. But will this horse bear the saddle?"

"That is true; you remind me of that; he will not bear it."

"Then—"

"But I can surely hire a horse in the village?"

"A horse to travel to Arras at one stretch?"

"Yes."

"That would require such a horse as does not exist in these parts. You would have to buy it to begin with, because no one knows you. But you will not find one for sale nor to let, for five hundred francs, or for a thousand."

"What am I to do?"

"The best thing is to let me repair the wheel like an honest man, and set out on your journey tomorrow."

"Tomorrow will be too late."

"The deuce!"

"Is there not a mail-wagon which runs to Arras? When will it pass?"

"Tonight. Both the posts pass at night; the one going as well as the one coming."

"What! It will take you a day to mend this wheel?"

"A day, and a good long one."

"If you set two men to work?"

"If I set ten men to work."

"What if the spokes were to be tied together with ropes?"

"That could be done with the spokes, not with the hub; and the felly is in a bad state, too."

"Is there any one in this village who lets out teams?"

"No."

"Is there another wheelwright?"

The stableman and the wheelwright replied in concert, with a toss of the head

"No."

He felt an immense joy.

It was evident that Providence was intervening. That it was it who had broken the wheel of the tilbury and who was stopping him on the road. He had not yielded to this sort of first summons; he had just made every possible effort to continue the journey; he had loyally and scrupulously exhausted all means; he had been deterred neither by the season, nor fatigue, nor by the expense; he had nothing with which to reproach himself. If he went no further, that was no fault of his. It did not concern him further. It was no longer his fault. It was not the act of his own conscience, but the act of Providence.

He breathed again. He breathed freely and to the full extent of his lungs for the first time since Javert's visit. It seemed to him that the hand of iron which had held his heart in its grasp for the last twenty hours had just released him.

It seemed to him that God was for him now, and was manifesting Himself.

He said himself that he had done all he could, and that now he had nothing to do but retrace his steps quietly.

If his conversation with the wheelwright had taken place in a chamber of the inn, it would have had no witnesses, no one would have heard him, things would have rested there, and it is probable that we should not have had to relate any of the occurrences which the reader is about to peruse; but this conversation had taken place in the street. Any colloquy in the street inevitably attracts a crowd. There are always people who ask nothing better than to become spectators. While he was questioning the wheelwright, some people who were passing back and forth halted around them. After listening for a few minutes, a young lad, to whom no one had paid any heed, detached himself from the group and ran off.

At the moment when the traveller, after the inward deliberation which we have just described, resolved to retrace his steps, this child returned. He was accompanied by an old woman.

350

"Monsieur," said the woman, "my boy tells me that you wish to hire a cabriolet."

These simple words uttered by an old woman led by a child made the perspiration trickle down his limbs. He thought that he beheld the hand which had relaxed its grasp reappear in the darkness behind him, ready to seize him once more.

He answered:—

"Yes, my good woman; I am in search of a cabriolet which I can hire."

And he hastened to add:—

"But there is none in the place."

"Certainly there is," said the old woman.

"Where?" interpolated the wheelwright.

"At my house," replied the old woman.

He shuddered. The fatal hand had grasped him again.

The old woman really had in her shed a sort of basket spring-cart. The wheelwright and the stable-man, in despair at the prospect of the traveller escaping their clutches, interfered.

"It was a frightful old trap; it rests flat on the axle; it is an actual fact that the seats were suspended inside it by leather thongs; the rain came into it; the wheels were rusted and eaten with moisture; it would not go much further than the tilbury; a regular ramshackle old stage-wagon; the gentleman would make a great mistake if he trusted himself to it," etc., etc.

All this was true; but this trap, this ramshackle old vehicle, this thing, whatever it was, ran on its two wheels and could go to Arras.

He paid what was asked, left the tilbury with the wheelwright to be repaired, intending to reclaim it on his return, had the white horse put to the cart, climbed into it, and resumed the road which he had been travelling since morning.

At the moment when the cart moved off, he admitted that he had felt, a moment previously, a certain joy in the thought that he should not go whither he was now proceeding. He examined this joy with a sort of wrath, and found it absurd. Why should he feel joy at turning back? After all, he was taking this trip of his own free will. No one was forcing him to it.

And assuredly nothing would happen except what he should choose.

As he left Hesdin, he heard a voice shouting to him: "Stop! Stop!" He halted the cart with a vigorous movement which contained a feverish and convulsive element resembling hope.

It was the old woman's little boy.

"Monsieur," said the latter, "it was I who got the cart for you."

"Well?"

"You have not given me anything."

He who gave to all so readily thought this demand exorbitant and almost odious.

"Ah! it's you, you scamp?" said he; "you shall have nothing."

He whipped up his horse and set off at full speed.

He had lost a great deal of time at Hesdin. He wanted to make it good. The little horse was courageous, and pulled for two; but it was the month of February, there had been rain; the roads were bad. And then, it was no longer the tilbury. The cart was very heavy, and in addition, there were many ascents.

He took nearly four hours to go from Hesdin to Saint-Pol; four hours for five leagues.

At Saint-Pol he had the horse unharnessed at the first inn he came to and led to the stable; as he had promised Scaufflaire, he stood beside the manger while the horse was eating; he thought of sad and confusing things.

The inn-keeper's wife came to the stable.

"Does not Monsieur wish to breakfast?"

"Come, that is true; I even have a good appetite."

He followed the woman, who had a rosy, cheerful face; she led him to the public room where there were tables covered with waxed cloth.

352

"Make haste!" said he; "I must start again; I am in a hurry."

A big Flemish servant-maid placed his knife and fork in all haste; he looked at the girl with a sensation of comfort.

"That is what ailed me," he thought; "I had not breakfasted."

His breakfast was served; he seized the bread, took a mouthful, and then slowly replaced it on the table, and did not touch it again.

A carter was eating at another table; he said to this man:—

"Why is their bread so bitter here?"

The carter was a German and did not understand him.

He returned to the stable and remained near the horse.

An hour later he had quitted Saint-Pol and was directing his course towards Tinques, which is only five leagues from Arras.

What did he do during this journey? Of what was he thinking? As in the morning, he watched the trees, the thatched roofs, the tilled fields pass by, and the way in which the landscape, broken at every turn of the road, vanished; this is a sort of contemplation which sometimes suffices to the soul, and almost relieves it from thought. What is more melancholy and more profound than to see a thousand objects for the first and the last time? To travel is to be born and to die at every instant; perhaps, in the vaguest region of his mind, he did make comparisons between the shifting horizon and our human existence: all the things of life are perpetually fleeing before us; the dark and bright intervals are intermingled; after a dazzling moment, an eclipse; we look, we hasten, we stretch out our hands to grasp what is passing; each event is a turn in the road, and, all at once, we are old; we feel a shock; all is black; we distinguish an obscure door; the gloomy horse of life, which has been drawing us halts, and we see a veiled and unknown person unharnessing amid the shadows.

Twilight was falling when the children who were coming out of school beheld this traveller enter Tinques; it is true that the days were still short; he did not halt at Tinques; as he emerged from the village, a laborer, who was mending the road with stones, raised his head and said to him:—

"That horse is very much fatigued."

The poor beast was, in fact, going at a walk.

"Are you going to Arras?" added the road-mender.

"Yes."

"If you go on at that rate you will not arrive very early."

He stopped his horse, and asked the laborer:—

"How far is it from here to Arras?"

"Nearly seven good leagues."

"How is that? the posting guide only says five leagues and a quarter."

"Ah!" returned the road-mender, "so you don't know that the road is under repair? You will find it barred a quarter of an hour further on; there is no way to proceed further."

"Really?"

"You will take the road on the left, leading to Carency; you will cross the river; when you reach Camblin, you will turn to the right; that is the road to Mont-Saint-Eloy which leads to Arras."

"But it is night, and I shall lose my way."

"You do not belong in these parts?"

"No."

"And, besides, it is all cross-roads; stop! sir," resumed the road-mender; "shall I give you a piece of advice? your horse is tired; return to Tinques; there is a good inn there; sleep there; you can reach Arras tomorrow."

"I must be there this evening."

"That is different; but go to the inn all the same, and get an extra horse; the stable-boy will guide you through the cross-roads."

He followed the road-mender's advice, retraced his steps, and, half an hour later, he passed the same spot again, but this time at full speed, with a good horse to aid; a stable-boy, who called himself a postilion, was seated on the shaft of the cariole.

Still, he felt that he had lost time.

Night had fully come.

They turned into the cross-road; the way became frightfully bad; the cart lurched from one rut to the other; he said to the postilion:—

"Keep at a trot, and you shall have a double fee."

In one of the jolts, the whiffle-tree broke.

"There's the whiffle-tree broken, sir," said the postilion; "I don't know how to harness my horse now; this road is very bad at night; if you wish to return and sleep at Tinques, we could be in Arras early tomorrow morning."

He replied, "Have you a bit of rope and a knife?"

"Yes, sir."

He cut a branch from a tree and made a whiffle-tree of it.

This caused another loss of twenty minutes; but they set out again at a gallop.

The plain was gloomy; low-hanging, black, crisp fogs crept over the hills and wrenched themselves away like smoke: there were whitish gleams in the clouds; a strong breeze which blew in from the sea produced a sound in all quarters of the horizon, as of some one moving furniture; everything that could be seen assumed attitudes of terror. How many things shiver beneath these vast breaths of the night!

He was stiff with cold; he had eaten nothing since the night before; he vaguely recalled his other nocturnal trip in the vast plain in the neighborhood of D—, eight years previously, and it seemed but yesterday.

The hour struck from a distant tower; he asked the boy:—

"What time is it?"

"Seven o'clock, sir; we shall reach Arras at eight; we have but three leagues still to go."

At that moment, he for the first time indulged in this reflection, thinking it odd the while that it had not occurred to him sooner: that all this trouble which he was taking was, perhaps, useless; that he did not know so much as the hour of the trial; that he should, at least, have informed himself of that; that he was foolish to go thus straight ahead without knowing whether he would be of any service or not; then he sketched out some calculations in his mind: that, ordinarily, the sittings of the Court of Assizes began at nine o'clock in the morning; that it could not be a long affair; that the theft of the apples would be very brief; that there would then remain only a question of identity, four or five depositions, and very little for the lawyers to say; that he should arrive after all was over.

The postilion whipped up the horses; they had crossed the river and left Mont-Saint-Eloy behind them.

The night grew more profound.

CHAPTER VI

SISTER SIMPLICE PUT TO THE PROOF

But at that moment Fantine was joyous.

She had passed a very bad night; her cough was frightful; her fever had doubled in intensity; she had had dreams: in the morning, when the doctor paid his visit, she was delirious; he assumed an alarmed look, and ordered that he should be informed as soon as M. Madeleine arrived.

All the morning she was melancholy, said but little, and laid plaits in her sheets, murmuring the while, in a low voice, calculations which seemed to be calculations of distances. Her eyes were hollow and staring. They seemed almost extinguished at intervals, then lighted up again and shone like stars. It seems as though, at the approach of a certain dark hour, the light of heaven fills those who are quitting the light of earth.

Each time that Sister Simplice asked her how she felt, she replied invariably, "Well. I should like to see M. Madeleine."

Some months before this, at the moment when Fantine had just lost her last modesty, her last shame, and her last joy, she was the shadow of herself; now she was the spectre of herself. Physical suffering had completed the work of moral suffering. This creature of five and twenty had a wrinkled brow, flabby cheeks, pinched nostrils, teeth from which the gums had receded, a leaden complexion, a bony neck, prominent shoulder-blades, frail limbs, a clayey skin, and her golden hair was growing out sprinkled with gray. Alas! how illness improvises old-age!

At mid-day the physician returned, gave some directions, inquired whether the mayor had made his appearance at the infirmary, and shook his head.

M. Madeleine usually came to see the invalid at three o'clock. As exactness is kindness, he was exact.

About half-past two, Fantine began to be restless. In the course of twenty minutes, she asked the nun more than ten times, "What time is it, sister?"

Three o'clock struck. At the third stroke, Fantine sat up in bed; she who could, in general, hardly turn over, joined her yellow, fleshless hands in a sort of convulsive clasp, and the nun heard her utter one of those profound sighs which seem to throw off dejection. Then Fantine turned and looked at the door.

No one entered; the door did not open.

She remained thus for a quarter of an hour, her eyes riveted on the door, motionless and apparently holding her breath. The sister dared not speak to her. The clock struck a quarter past three. Fantine fell back on her pillow.

She said nothing, but began to plait the sheets once more.

Half an hour passed, then an hour, no one came; every time the clock struck, Fantine started up and looked towards the door, then fell back again.

Her thought was clearly perceptible, but she uttered no name, she made no complaint, she blamed no one. But she coughed in a melancholy way. One would have said that something dark was descending upon her. She was livid and her lips were blue. She smiled now and then.

Five o'clock struck. Then the sister heard her say, very low and gently, "He is wrong not to come today, since I am going away tomorrow."

Sister Simplice herself was surprised at M. Madeleine's delay.

In the meantime, Fantine was staring at the tester of her bed. She seemed to be endeavoring to recall something. All at once she began to sing in a voice as feeble as a breath. The nun listened. This is what Fantine was singing:—

"Lovely things we will buy
As we stroll the faubourgs through.
Roses are pink, corn-flowers are blue,
I love my love, corn-flowers are blue.

"Yestere'en the Virgin Mary came near my stove, in a broidered mantle clad, and said to me, 'Here, hide 'neath my veil the child whom you one day begged from me. Haste to the city, buy linen, buy a needle, buy thread.'

"Lovely things we will buy
As we stroll the faubourgs through.

"Dear Holy Virgin, beside my stove I have set a cradle with ribbons decked. God may give me his loveliest star; I prefer the child thou hast granted me. 'Madame, what shall I do with this linen fine?'—'Make of it clothes for thy new-born babe.'

"Roses are pink and corn-flowers are blue,
I love my love, and corn-flowers are blue.

"'Wash this linen.'—'Where?'—'In the stream. Make of it, soiling not, spoiling not, a petticoat fair with its bodice fine, which I will embroider and fill with flowers.'—'Madame, the child is no longer here; what is to be done?'—'Then make of it a winding-sheet in which to bury me.'

"Lovely things we will buy
As we stroll the faubourgs through,
Roses are pink, corn-flowers are blue,
I love my love, corn-flowers are blue."

This song was an old cradle romance with which she had, in former days, lulled her little Cosette to sleep, and which had never recurred to her mind in all the five years during which she had been parted from her child. She sang it in so sad a voice, and to so sweet an air, that it was enough to make any one, even a nun, weep. The sister, accustomed as she was to austerities, felt a tear spring to her eyes.

The clock struck six. Fantine did not seem to hear it. She no longer seemed to pay attention to anything about her.

Sister Simplice sent a serving-maid to inquire of the portress of the factory, whether the mayor had returned, and if he would not come to the infirmary soon. The girl returned in a few minutes.

Fantine was still motionless and seemed absorbed in her own thoughts.

The servant informed Sister Simplice in a very low tone, that the mayor had set out that morning before six o'clock, in a little tilbury harnessed to a white horse, cold as the weather was; that he had gone alone, without even a driver; that no one knew what road he had taken; that people said he had been seen to turn into the road to Arras; that others asserted that they had met him on the road to Paris. That when he went away he had been very gentle, as usual, and that he had merely told the portress not to expect him that night.

While the two women were whispering together, with their backs turned to Fantine's bed, the sister interrogating, the servant conjecturing, Fantine, with the feverish vivacity of certain organic maladies, which unite the free movements of health with the frightful emaciation of death, had raised herself to her knees in bed, with her shrivelled hands resting on the bolster, and her head thrust through the opening of the curtains, and was listening. All at once she cried:—

"You are speaking of M. Madeleine! Why are you talking so low? What is he doing? Why does he not come?"

Her voice was so abrupt and hoarse that the two women thought they heard the voice of a man; they wheeled round in affright.

"Answer me!" cried Fantine.

The servant stammered:—

"The portress told me that he could not come today."

"Be calm, my child," said the sister; "lie down again."

Fantine, without changing her attitude, continued in a loud voice, and with an accent that was both imperious and heart-rending:—

"He cannot come? Why not? You know the reason. You are whispering it to each other there. I want to know it."

The servant-maid hastened to say in the nun's ear, "Say that he is busy with the city council."

Sister Simplice blushed faintly, for it was a lie that the maid had proposed to her.

On the other hand, it seemed to her that the mere communication of the truth to the invalid would, without doubt, deal her a terrible blow, and that this was a serious matter in Fantine's present state. Her flush did not last long; the sister raised her calm, sad eyes to Fantine, and said, "Monsieur le Maire has gone away."

Fantine raised herself and crouched on her heels in the bed: her eyes sparkled; indescribable joy beamed from that melancholy face.

"Gone!" she cried; "he has gone to get Cosette."

Then she raised her arms to heaven, and her white face became ineffable; her lips moved; she was praying in a low voice.

When her prayer was finished, "Sister," she said, "I am willing to lie down again; I will do anything you wish; I was naughty just now; I beg your pardon for having spoken so loud; it is very wrong to talk loudly; I know that well, my good sister, but, you see, I am very happy: the good God is good; M. Madeleine is good; just think! he has gone to Montfermeil to get my little Cosette."

She lay down again, with the nun's assistance, helped the nun to arrange her pillow, and kissed the little silver cross which she wore on her neck, and which Sister Simplice had given her.

"My child," said the sister, "try to rest now, and do not talk any more."

Fantine took the sister's hand in her moist hands, and the latter was pained to feel that perspiration.

"He set out this morning for Paris; in fact, he need not even go through Paris; Montfermeil is a little to the left as you come thence. Do you remember how he said to me yesterday, when I spoke to him of Cosette, Soon, soon? He wants to give me a surprise, you know! he made me sign a letter so that she could be taken from the Thenardiers; they cannot say anything, can they? they will give back Cosette, for they have been paid; the authorities will not allow them to keep the child since they have received their pay. Do not make signs to me that I must not talk, sister! I am extremely happy; I am doing well; I am not ill at all any more; I am going to see Cosette again; I am even quite hungry; it is nearly five years since I saw her last; you cannot imagine how much attached one gets to children, and then, she will be so pretty; you will see! If you only knew what pretty little rosy fingers she had! In the first place, she will have very beautiful hands; she had ridiculous hands when she was only a year old; like this! she must be a big girl now; she is seven years old; she is quite a young lady; I call her Cosette, but her name is really Euphrasie. Stop! this morning I was looking at the dust on the chimney-piece, and I had a sort of idea come across me, like that, that I should see Cosette again soon. Mon Dieu! how wrong it is not to see one's children for years! One ought to reflect that life is not eternal. Oh, how good M. le Maire is to go! it is very cold! it is true; he had on his cloak, at least? he will be here tomorrow, will he not? tomorrow will be a festival day; tomorrow morning, sister, you must remind me to put on my little cap that has lace on it. What a place that Montfermeil is! I took that journey on foot once; it was very long for me, but the diligences go very quickly! he will be here tomorrow with Cosette: how far is it from here to Montfermeil?"

The sister, who had no idea of distances, replied, "Oh, I think that he will be here tomorrow."

"Tomorrow! tomorrow!" said Fantine, "I shall see Cosette tomorrow! you see, good sister of the good God, that I am no longer ill; I am mad; I could dance if any one wished it."

A person who had seen her a quarter of an hour previously would not have understood the change; she was all rosy now; she spoke in a lively and natural voice; her whole face was one smile; now and then she talked, she laughed softly; the joy of a mother is almost infantile.

"Well," resumed the nun, "now that you are happy, mind me, and do not talk any more."

Fantine laid her head on her pillow and said in a low voice: "Yes, lie down again; be good, for you are going to have your child; Sister Simplice is right; every one here is right."

And then, without stirring, without even moving her head, she began to stare all about her with wide-open eyes and a joyous air, and she said nothing more.

The sister drew the curtains together again, hoping that she would fall into a doze. Between seven and eight o'clock the doctor came; not hearing any sound, he thought Fantine was asleep, entered softly, and approached the bed on tiptoe; he opened the curtains a little, and, by the light of the taper, he saw Fantine's big eyes gazing at him.

She said to him, "She will be allowed to sleep beside me in a little bed, will she not, sir?"

The doctor thought that she was delirious. She added:—

"See! there is just room."

The doctor took Sister Simplice aside, and she explained matters to him; that M. Madeleine was absent for a day or two, and that in their doubt they had not thought it well to undeceive the invalid, who believed that the mayor had gone to Montfermeil; that it was possible, after all, that her guess was correct: the doctor approved.

He returned to Fantine's bed, and she went on:—

"You see, when she wakes up in the morning, I shall be able to say good morning to her, poor kitten, and when I cannot sleep at night, I can hear her asleep; her little gentle breathing will do me good."

"Give me your hand," said the doctor.

She stretched out her arm, and exclaimed with a laugh:—

"Ah, hold! in truth, you did not know it; I am cured; Cosette will arrive tomorrow."

The doctor was surprised; she was better; the pressure on her chest had decreased; her pulse had regained its strength; a sort of life had suddenly supervened and reanimated this poor, worn-out creature.

"Doctor," she went on, "did the sister tell you that M. le Maire has gone to get that mite of a child?"

The doctor recommended silence, and that all painful emotions should be avoided; he prescribed an infusion of pure chinchona, and, in case the fever should increase again during the night, a calming potion. As he took his departure, he said to the sister:—

"She is doing better; if good luck willed that the mayor should actually arrive tomorrow with the child, who knows? there are crises so astounding; great joy has been known to arrest maladies; I know well that this is an organic disease, and in an advanced state, but all those things are such mysteries: we may be able to save her."

CHAPTER VII

THE TRAVELLER ON HIS ARRIVAL TAKES PRECAUTIONS FOR DEPARTURE

It was nearly eight o'clock in the evening when the cart, which we left on the road, entered the porte-cochere of the Hotel de la Poste in Arras; the man whom we have been following up to this moment alighted from it, responded with an abstracted air to the attentions of the people of the inn, sent back the extra horse, and with his own hands led the little white horse to the stable; then he opened the door of a billiard-room which was situated on the ground floor, sat down there, and leaned his elbows on a table; he had taken fourteen hours for the journey which he had counted on making in six; he did himself the justice to acknowledge that it was not his fault, but at bottom, he was not sorry.

The landlady of the hotel entered.

"Does Monsieur wish a bed? Does Monsieur require supper?"

He made a sign of the head in the negative.

"The stableman says that Monsieur's horse is extremely fatigued."

Here he broke his silence.

"Will not the horse be in a condition to set out again tomorrow morning?"

"Oh, Monsieur! he must rest for two days at least."

He inquired:—

"Is not the posting-station located here?"

"Yes, sir."

The hostess conducted him to the office; he showed his passport, and inquired whether there was any way of returning that same night to M. sur M. by the mail-wagon; the seat beside the post-boy chanced to be vacant; he engaged it and paid for it. "Monsieur," said the clerk, "do not fail to be here ready to start at precisely one o'clock in the morning."

This done, he left the hotel and began to wander about the town.

He was not acquainted with Arras; the streets were dark, and he walked on at random; but he seemed bent upon not asking the way of the passers-by. He crossed the little river Crinchon, and found himself in a labyrinth of narrow alleys where he lost his way. A citizen was passing along with a lantern. After some hesitation, he decided to apply to this man, not without having first glanced behind and in front of him, as though he feared lest some one should hear the question which he was about to put.

"Monsieur," said he, "where is the court-house, if you please."

"You do not belong in town, sir?" replied the bourgeois, who was an oldish man; "well, follow me. I happen to be going in the direction of the court-house, that is to say, in the direction of the hotel of the prefecture; for the court-house is undergoing repairs just at this moment, and the courts are holding their sittings provisionally in the prefecture."

"Is it there that the Assizes are held?" he asked.

"Certainly, sir; you see, the prefecture of today was the bishop's palace before the Revolution. M. de Conzie, who was bishop in '82, built a grand hall there. It is in this grand hall that the court is held."

On the way, the bourgeois said to him:—

"If Monsieur desires to witness a case, it is rather late. The sittings generally close at six o'clock."

When they arrived on the grand square, however, the man pointed out to him four long windows all lighted up, in the front of a vast and gloomy building.

"Upon my word, sir, you are in luck; you have arrived in season. Do you see those four windows? That is the Court of Assizes. There is

366

light there, so they are not through. The matter must have been greatly protracted, and they are holding an evening session. Do you take an interest in this affair? Is it a criminal case? Are you a witness?"

He replied:—

"I have not come on any business; I only wish to speak to one of the lawyers."

"That is different," said the bourgeois. "Stop, sir; here is the door where the sentry stands. You have only to ascend the grand staircase."

He conformed to the bourgeois's directions, and a few minutes later he was in a hall containing many people, and where groups, intermingled with lawyers in their gowns, were whispering together here and there.

It is always a heart-breaking thing to see these congregations of men robed in black, murmuring together in low voices, on the threshold of the halls of justice. It is rare that charity and pity are the outcome of these words. Condemnations pronounced in advance are more likely to be the result. All these groups seem to the passing and thoughtful observer so many sombre hives where buzzing spirits construct in concert all sorts of dark edifices.

This spacious hall, illuminated by a single lamp, was the old hall of the episcopal palace, and served as the large hall of the palace of justice. A double-leaved door, which was closed at that moment, separated it from the large apartment where the court was sitting.

The obscurity was such that he did not fear to accost the first lawyer whom he met.

"What stage have they reached, sir?" he asked.

"It is finished," said the lawyer.

"Finished!"

This word was repeated in such accents that the lawyer turned round.

"Excuse me sir; perhaps you are a relative?"

"No; I know no one here. Has judgment been pronounced?"

"Of course. Nothing else was possible."

"To penal servitude?"

"For life."

He continued, in a voice so weak that it was barely audible:—

"Then his identity was established?"

"What identity?" replied the lawyer. "There was no identity to be established. The matter was very simple. The woman had murdered her child; the infanticide was proved; the jury threw out the question of premeditation, and she was condemned for life."

"So it was a woman?" said he.

"Why, certainly. The Limosin woman. Of what are you speaking?"

"Nothing. But since it is all over, how comes it that the hall is still lighted?"

"For another case, which was begun about two hours ago."

"What other case?"

"Oh! this one is a clear case also. It is about a sort of blackguard; a man arrested for a second offence; a convict who has been guilty of theft. I don't know his name exactly. There's a bandit's phiz for you! I'd send him to the galleys on the strength of his face alone."

"Is there any way of getting into the court-room, sir?" said he.

"I really think that there is not. There is a great crowd. However, the hearing has been suspended. Some people have gone out, and when the hearing is resumed, you might make an effort."

"Where is the entrance?"

"Through yonder large door."

The lawyer left him. In the course of a few moments he had experienced, almost simultaneously, almost intermingled with each other, all possible emotions. The words of this indifferent spectator had, in turn, pierced his heart like needles of ice and like blades of fire. When he saw that nothing was settled, he breathed freely once more; but he could not have told whether what he felt was pain or pleasure.

He drew near to many groups and listened to what they were saying. The docket of the session was very heavy; the president had appointed for the same day two short and simple cases. They had begun with the infanticide, and now they had reached the convict, the old offender, the "return horse." This man had stolen apples, but that did not appear to be entirely proved; what had been proved was, that he had already been in the galleys at Toulon. It was that which lent a bad aspect to his case. However, the man's examination and the depositions of the witnesses had been completed, but the lawyer's plea, and the speech of the public prosecutor were still to come; it could not be finished before midnight. The man would probably be condemned; the attorney-general was very clever, and never missed his culprits; he was a brilliant fellow who wrote verses.

An usher stood at the door communicating with the hall of the Assizes. He inquired of this usher:—

"Will the door be opened soon, sir?"

"It will not be opened at all," replied the usher.

"What! It will not be opened when the hearing is resumed? Is not the hearing suspended?"

"The hearing has just been begun again," replied the usher, "but the door will not be opened again."

"Why?"

"Because the hall is full."

"What! There is not room for one more?"

"Not another one. The door is closed. No one can enter now."

The usher added after a pause: "There are, to tell the truth, two or three extra places behind Monsieur le President, but Monsieur le President only admits public functionaries to them."

So saying, the usher turned his back.

He retired with bowed head, traversed the antechamber, and slowly descended the stairs, as though hesitating at every step. It is probable that he was holding counsel with himself. The violent conflict which had been going on within him since the preceding evening was not yet ended; and every moment he encountered some new phase of it. On reaching

369

the landing-place, he leaned his back against the balusters and folded his arms. All at once he opened his coat, drew out his pocket-book, took from it a pencil, tore out a leaf, and upon that leaf he wrote rapidly, by the light of the street lantern, this line: M. Madeleine, Mayor of M. sur M.; then he ascended the stairs once more with great strides, made his way through the crowd, walked straight up to the usher, handed him the paper, and said in an authoritative manner:—

"Take this to Monsieur le President."

The usher took the paper, cast a glance upon it, and obeyed.

CHAPTER VIII

AN ENTRANCE BY FAVOR

Although he did not suspect the fact, the mayor of M. sur M. enjoyed a sort of celebrity. For the space of seven years his reputation for virtue had filled the whole of Bas Boulonnais; it had eventually passed the confines of a small district and had been spread abroad through two or three neighboring departments. Besides the service which he had rendered to the chief town by resuscitating the black jet industry, there was not one out of the hundred and forty communes of the arrondissement of M. sur M. which was not indebted to him for some benefit. He had even at need contrived to aid and multiply the industries of other arrondissements. It was thus that he had, when occasion offered, supported with his credit and his funds the linen factory at Boulogne, the flax-spinning industry at Frevent, and the hydraulic manufacture of cloth at Boubers-sur-Canche. Everywhere the name of M. Madeleine was pronounced with veneration. Arras and Douai envied the happy little town of M. sur M. its mayor.

The Councillor of the Royal Court of Douai, who was presiding over this session of the Assizes at Arras, was acquainted, in common with the rest of the world, with this name which was so profoundly and universally honored. When the usher, discreetly opening the door which connected the council-chamber with the court-room, bent over the back of the President's arm-chair and handed him the paper on which was inscribed the line which we have just perused, adding: "The gentleman desires to be present at the trial," the President, with a quick and deferential movement, seized a pen and wrote a few words at the bottom of the paper and returned it to the usher, saying, "Admit him."

The unhappy man whose history we are relating had remained near the door of the hall, in the same place and the same attitude in which the usher had left him. In the midst of his revery he heard some one saying to him, "Will Monsieur do me the honor to follow me?" It was the same usher who had turned his back upon him but a moment previously, and who was now bowing to the earth before him. At the same time, the usher handed him the paper. He unfolded it, and as he chanced to be near the light, he could read it.

"The President of the Court of Assizes presents his respects to M. Madeleine."

He crushed the paper in his hand as though those words contained for him a strange and bitter aftertaste.

He followed the usher.

A few minutes later he found himself alone in a sort of wainscoted cabinet of severe aspect, lighted by two wax candles, placed upon a table with a green cloth. The last words of the usher who had just quitted him still rang in his ears: "Monsieur, you are now in the council-chamber; you have only to turn the copper handle of yonder door, and you will find yourself in the court-room, behind the President's chair." These words were mingled in his thoughts with a vague memory of narrow corridors and dark staircases which he had recently traversed.

The usher had left him alone. The supreme moment had arrived. He sought to collect his faculties, but could not. It is chiefly at the moment when there is the greatest need for attaching them to the painful realities of life, that the threads of thought snap within the brain. He was in the very place where the judges deliberated and condemned. With stupid tranquillity he surveyed this peaceful and terrible apartment, where so many lives had been broken, which was soon to ring with his name, and which his fate was at that moment traversing. He stared at the wall, then he looked at himself, wondering that it should be that chamber and that it should be he.

He had eaten nothing for four and twenty hours; he was worn out by the jolts of the cart, but he was not conscious of it. It seemed to him that he felt nothing.

He approached a black frame which was suspended on the wall, and which contained, under glass, an ancient autograph letter of Jean Nicolas Pache, mayor of Paris and minister, and dated, through an error, no doubt, the 9th of June, of the year II., and in which Pache forwarded to the commune the list of ministers and deputies held in arrest by them. Any spectator who had chanced to see him at that moment, and who had watched him, would have imagined, doubtless, that this letter struck him as very curious, for he did not take his eyes from it, and he read it two or three times. He read it without paying any attention to it, and unconsciously. He was thinking of Fantine and Cosette.

As he dreamed, he turned round, and his eyes fell upon the brass knob of the door which separated him from the Court of Assizes. He had almost forgotten that door. His glance, calm at first, paused there, remained fixed on that brass handle, then grew terrified, and little by little became impregnated with fear. Beads of perspiration burst forth among his hair and trickled down upon his temples.

At a certain moment he made that indescribable gesture of a sort of authority mingled with rebellion, which is intended to convey, and which does so well convey, "Pardieu! who compels me to this?" Then he wheeled briskly round, caught sight of the door through which he had entered in front of him, went to it, opened it, and passed out. He was no longer in that chamber; he was outside in a corridor, a long, narrow corridor, broken by steps and gratings, making all sorts of angles, lighted here and there by lanterns similar to the night taper of invalids, the corridor through which he had approached. He breathed, he listened; not a sound in front, not a sound behind him, and he fled as though pursued.

When he had turned many angles in this corridor, he still listened. The same silence reigned, and there was the same darkness around him. He was out of breath; he staggered; he leaned against the wall. The stone was cold; the perspiration lay ice-cold on his brow; he straightened himself up with a shiver.

Then, there alone in the darkness, trembling with cold and with something else, too, perchance, he meditated.

He had meditated all night long; he had meditated all the day: he heard within him but one voice, which said, "Alas!"

A quarter of an hour passed thus. At length he bowed his head, sighed with agony, dropped his arms, and retraced his steps. He walked slowly, and as though crushed. It seemed as though some one had overtaken him in his flight and was leading him back.

He re-entered the council-chamber. The first thing he caught sight of was the knob of the door. This knob, which was round and of polished brass, shone like a terrible star for him. He gazed at it as a lamb might gaze into the eye of a tiger.

He could not take his eyes from it. From time to time he advanced a step and approached the door.

Had he listened, he would have heard the sound of the adjoining hall like a sort of confused murmur; but he did not listen, and he did not hear.

Suddenly, without himself knowing how it happened, he found himself near the door; he grasped the knob convulsively; the door opened.

He was in the court-room.

CHAPTER IX

A PLACE WHERE CONVICTIONS ARE IN PROCESS OF FORMATION

He advanced a pace, closed the door mechanically behind him, and remained standing, contemplating what he saw.

It was a vast and badly lighted apartment, now full of uproar, now full of silence, where all the apparatus of a criminal case, with its petty and mournful gravity in the midst of the throng, was in process of development.

At the one end of the hall, the one where he was, were judges, with abstracted air, in threadbare robes, who were gnawing their nails or closing their eyelids; at the other end, a ragged crowd; lawyers in all sorts of attitudes; soldiers with hard but honest faces; ancient, spotted woodwork, a dirty ceiling, tables covered with serge that was yellow rather than green; doors blackened by handmarks; tap-room lamps which emitted more smoke than light, suspended from nails in the wainscot; on the tables candles in brass candlesticks; darkness, ugliness, sadness; and from all this there was disengaged an austere and august impression, for one there felt that grand human thing which is called the law, and that grand divine thing which is called justice.

No one in all that throng paid any attention to him; all glances were directed towards a single point, a wooden bench placed against a small door, in the stretch of wall on the President's left; on this bench, illuminated by several candles, sat a man between two gendarmes.

This man was the man.

He did not seek him; he saw him; his eyes went thither naturally, as though they had known beforehand where that figure was.

He thought he was looking at himself, grown old; not absolutely the same in face, of course, but exactly similar in attitude and aspect, with his bristling hair, with that wild and uneasy eye, with that blouse, just as it was on the day when he entered D—, full of hatred, concealing his soul in that hideous mass of frightful thoughts which he had spent nineteen years in collecting on the floor of the prison.

He said to himself with a shudder, "Good God! shall I become like that again?"

This creature seemed to be at least sixty; there was something indescribably coarse, stupid, and frightened about him.

At the sound made by the opening door, people had drawn aside to make way for him; the President had turned his head, and, understanding that the personage who had just entered was the mayor of M. sur M., he had bowed to him; the attorney-general, who had seen M. Madeleine at M. sur M., whither the duties of his office had called him more than once, recognized him and saluted him also: he had hardly perceived it; he was the victim of a sort of hallucination; he was watching.

Judges, clerks, gendarmes, a throng of cruelly curious heads, all these he had already beheld once, in days gone by, twenty-seven years before; he had encountered those fatal things once more; there they were; they moved; they existed; it was no longer an effort of his memory, a mirage of his thought; they were real gendarmes and real judges, a real crowd, and real men of flesh and blood: it was all over; he beheld the monstrous aspects of his past reappear and live once more around him, with all that there is formidable in reality.

All this was yawning before him.

He was horrified by it; he shut his eyes, and exclaimed in the deepest recesses of his soul, "Never!"

And by a tragic play of destiny which made all his ideas tremble, and rendered him nearly mad, it was another self of his that was there! all called that man who was being tried Jean Valjean.

Under his very eyes, unheard-of vision, he had a sort of representation of the most horrible moment of his life, enacted by his spectre.

Everything was there; the apparatus was the same, the hour of the night, the faces of the judges, of soldiers, and of spectators; all were the same, only above the President's head there hung a crucifix, something which the courts had lacked at the time of his condemnation: God had been absent when he had been judged.

There was a chair behind him; he dropped into it, terrified at the thought that he might be seen; when he was seated, he took advantage of a pile of cardboard boxes, which stood on the judge's desk, to conceal his face from the whole room; he could now see without being seen; he had fully regained consciousness of the reality of things; gradually he recovered; he attained that phase of composure where it is possible to listen.

M. Bamatabois was one of the jurors.

He looked for Javert, but did not see him; the seat of the witnesses was hidden from him by the clerk's table, and then, as we have just said, the hall was sparely lighted.

At the moment of this entrance, the defendant's lawyer had just finished his plea.

The attention of all was excited to the highest pitch; the affair had lasted for three hours: for three hours that crowd had been watching a strange man, a miserable specimen of humanity, either profoundly stupid or profoundly subtle, gradually bending beneath the weight of a terrible likeness. This man, as the reader already knows, was a vagabond who had been found in a field carrying a branch laden with ripe apples, broken in the orchard of a neighbor, called the Pierron orchard. Who was this man? an examination had been made; witnesses had been heard, and they were unanimous; light had abounded throughout the entire debate; the accusation said: "We have in our grasp not only a marauder, a stealer of fruit; we have here, in our hands, a bandit, an old offender who has broken his ban, an ex-convict, a miscreant of the most dangerous description, a malefactor named Jean Valjean, whom justice has long been in search of, and who, eight years ago, on emerging from the galleys at Toulon, committed a highway robbery, accompanied by violence, on the person of a child, a Savoyard named Little Gervais; a crime provided for by article 383 of the Penal Code, the right to try him for which we reserve hereafter, when his identity shall have been judicially established. He has just committed a fresh theft; it is a case of a second offence; condemn him for the fresh deed; later on he will be judged for the old crime." In the face of this accusation, in the face of the unanimity of the witnesses, the accused appeared to be astonished more than anything else; he made signs and gestures which were meant to convey No, or else he stared at the ceiling: he spoke with difficulty, replied with embarrassment, but his whole person, from head to foot, was a denial; he was an idiot in the presence of all these minds ranged in order of battle around him, and like a stranger in the midst of this society which was seizing fast upon him; nevertheless, it was a question of the most menacing future for him; the likeness increased every moment, and the entire crowd surveyed, with more anxiety than he did himself, that sentence freighted with calamity, which descended ever closer over his head; there was even a glimpse of a possibility afforded; besides the galleys, a possible death penalty, in case his identity were established, and the affair of Little Gervais were to end thereafter in condemnation. Who was this man? what was the nature of his apathy? was it imbecility or craft? Did he understand too well, or did he not understand at all? these were questions which divided the crowd, and seemed to divide the jury; there was something both terrible and puzzling in this case: the drama was not only melancholy; it was also obscure.

The counsel for the defence had spoken tolerably well, in that provincial tongue which has long constituted the eloquence of the bar, and which was formerly employed by all advocates, at Paris as well as at Romorantin or at Montbrison, and which today, having become classic, is no longer spoken except by the official orators of magistracy, to whom it is suited on account of its grave sonorousness and its majestic stride; a tongue in which a husband is called a consort, and a woman a spouse; Paris, the centre of art and civilization; the king, the monarch; Monseigneur the Bishop, a sainted pontiff; the district-attorney, the eloquent interpreter of public prosecution; the arguments, the accents which we have just listened to; the age of Louis XIV., the grand age; a theatre, the temple of Melpomene; the reigning family, the august blood of our kings; a concert, a musical solemnity; the General Commandant of the province, the illustrious warrior, who, etc.; the pupils in the seminary, these tender levities; errors imputed to newspapers, the imposture which distills its venom through the columns of those organs; etc. The lawyer had, accordingly, begun with an explanation as to the theft of the apples,—an awkward matter couched in fine style; but Benigne Bossuet himself was obliged to allude to a chicken in the midst of a funeral oration, and he extricated himself from the situation in stately fashion. The lawyer established the fact that the theft of the apples had not been circumstantially proved. His client, whom he, in his character of counsel, persisted in calling Champmathieu, had not been seen scaling that wall nor breaking that branch by any one. He had been taken with that branch (which the lawyer preferred to call a bough) in his possession; but he said that he had found it broken off and lying on the ground, and had picked it up. Where was there any proof to the contrary? No doubt that branch had been broken off and concealed after the scaling of the wall, then thrown away by the alarmed marauder; there was no doubt that there had been a thief in the case. But what proof was there that that thief had been Champmathieu? One thing only. His character as an ex-convict. The lawyer did not deny that that character appeared to be, unhappily, well attested; the accused had resided at Faverolles; the accused had exercised the calling of a tree-pruner there; the name of Champmathieu might well have had its origin in Jean Mathieu; all that was true,—in short, four witnesses recognize Champmathieu, positively and without hesitation, as that convict, Jean Valjean; to these signs, to this testimony, the counsel could oppose nothing but the denial of his client, the denial of an interested party; but supposing that he was the convict Jean Valjean, did that prove that he was the thief of the apples? that was a presumption at the most, not a proof. The prisoner, it was true, and his counsel, "in good faith," was obliged to admit it, had adopted "a bad system of defence." He obstinately denied everything, the theft and his character of convict. An admission upon this last point would certainly have been better, and would have won for him the indulgence of his judges; the counsel had advised him to do this; but the accused had obstinately refused, thinking, no doubt, that he would save everything by admitting nothing. It was an error; but ought not the paucity of this intelligence to be taken into consideration? This man was visibly stupid. Long-continued wretchedness in the galleys, long misery outside the galleys, had brutalized him, etc. He defended himself badly; was that a reason for condemning him? As for the affair with Little Gervais, the counsel need not discuss it; it did not enter into the case. The lawyer wound up by beseeching the jury and the court, if the identity of Jean Valjean appeared to them to be evident, to apply to him the police penalties which are provided for a criminal who has broken his ban, and not the frightful chastisement which descends upon the convict guilty of a second offence.

The district-attorney answered the counsel for the defence. He was violent and florid, as district-attorneys usually are.

He congratulated the counsel for the defence on his "loyalty," and skilfully took advantage of this loyalty. He reached the accused through all the concessions made by his lawyer. The advocate had seemed to admit that the prisoner was Jean Valjean. He took note of this. So this man was Jean Valjean. This point had been conceded to the accusation and could no longer be disputed. Here, by means of a clever autonomasia which went back to the sources and causes of crime, the district-attorney thundered against the immorality of the romantic school, then dawning under the name of the Satanic school, which had been bestowed upon it by the critics of the Quotidienne and the Oriflamme; he attributed, not without some probability, to the influence of this perverse literature the crime of Champmathieu, or rather, to speak more correctly, of Jean Valjean. Having exhausted these considerations, he passed on to Jean Valjean himself. Who was this Jean Valjean? Description of Jean Valjean: a monster spewed forth, etc. The model for this sort of description is contained in the tale of Theramene, which is not useful to tragedy, but which every day renders great services to judicial eloquence. The audience and the jury "shuddered." The description finished, the district-attorney resumed with an oratorical turn calculated to raise the enthusiasm of the journal of the prefecture to the highest pitch on the following day: And it is such a man, etc., etc., etc., vagabond, beggar, without means of existence, etc., etc., inured by his past life to culpable deeds, and but little reformed by his sojourn in the galleys, as was proved by the crime committed against Little Gervais, etc., etc.; it is such a man, caught upon the highway in the very act of theft, a few paces from a wall that had been scaled, still holding in his hand the object stolen, who denies the crime, the theft, the climbing the wall; denies everything; denies even his own identity! In addition to a hundred other proofs, to which we will not recur, four witnesses recognize him—Javert, the upright inspector of police; Javert, and three of his former companions in infamy, the convicts Brevet, Chenildieu, and Cochepaille. What does he offer in opposition to this overwhelming unanimity? His denial. What obduracy! You will do justice, gentlemen of the jury, etc., etc. While the district-attorney was speaking, the accused listened to him open-mouthed, with a sort of amazement in which some admiration was assuredly blended. He was evidently surprised that a man could talk like that. From time to time, at those "energetic" moments of the prosecutor's speech, when eloquence which cannot contain itself overflows in a flood of withering epithets and envelops the accused like a storm, he moved his head slowly from right to left and from left to right in the sort of mute and melancholy protest with which he had contented himself since the beginning of the argument. Two or three times the spectators who were nearest to him heard him say in a low voice, "That is what comes of not having asked M. Baloup." The district-attorney directed the attention of the jury to this stupid attitude, evidently deliberate, which denoted not imbecility, but craft, skill, a habit of deceiving justice, and which set forth in all its nakedness the "profound perversity" of this man. He ended by making his reserves on the affair of Little Gervais and demanding a severe sentence.

At that time, as the reader will remember, it was penal servitude for life.

The counsel for the defence rose, began by complimenting Monsieur l'Avocat-General on his "admirable speech," then replied as best he could; but he weakened; the ground was evidently slipping away from under his feet.

CHAPTER X

THE SYSTEM OF DENIALS

The moment for closing the debate had arrived. The President had the accused stand up, and addressed to him the customary question, "Have you anything to add to your defence?"

The man did not appear to understand, as he stood there, twisting in his hands a terrible cap which he had.

The President repeated the question.

This time the man heard it. He seemed to understand. He made a motion like a man who is just waking up, cast his eyes about him, stared at the audience, the gendarmes, his counsel, the jury, the court, laid his monstrous fist on the rim of woodwork in front of his bench, took another look, and all at once, fixing his glance upon the district-attorney, he began to speak. It was like an eruption. It seemed, from the manner in which the words escaped from his mouth,—incoherent, impetuous, pell-mell, tumbling over each other,—as though they were all pressing forward to issue forth at once. He said:—

"This is what I have to say. That I have been a wheelwright in Paris, and that it was with Monsieur Baloup. It is a hard trade. In the wheelwright's trade one works always in the open air, in courtyards, under sheds when the masters are good, never in closed workshops, because space is required, you see. In winter one gets so cold that one beats one's arms together to warm one's self; but the masters don't like it; they say it wastes time. Handling iron when there is ice between the paving-stones is hard work.

That wears a man out quickly One is old while he is still quite young in that trade. At forty a man is done for. I was fifty-three. I was in a bad state. And then, workmen are so mean! When a man is no longer young, they call him nothing but an old bird, old beast! I was not earning more than thirty sous a day. They paid me as little as possible. The masters took advantage of my age—and then I had my daughter, who was a laundress at the river. She earned a little also. It sufficed for us two. She had trouble, also; all day long up to her waist in a tub, in rain, in snow. When the wind cuts your face, when it freezes, it is all the same; you must still wash. There are people who have not much linen, and wait until late; if you do not wash, you lose your custom. The planks are badly joined, and water drops on you from everywhere; you have your petticoats all damp above and below. That penetrates. She has also worked at the laundry of the Enfants-Rouges, where the water comes through faucets. You are not in the tub there; you wash at the faucet in front of you, and rinse in a basin behind you. As it is enclosed, you are not so cold; but there is that hot steam, which is terrible, and which ruins your eyes. She came home at seven o'clock in the evening, and went to bed at once, she was so tired. Her husband beat her. She is dead. We have not been very happy. She was a good girl, who did not go to the ball, and who was very peaceable. I remember one Shrove-Tuesday when she went to bed at eight o'clock. There, I am telling the truth; you have only to ask. Ah, yes! how stupid I am! Paris is a gulf. Who knows Father Champmathieu there? But M. Baloup does, I tell you. Go see at M. Baloup's; and after all, I don't know what is wanted of me."

The man ceased speaking, and remained standing. He had said these things in a loud, rapid, hoarse voice, with a sort of irritated and savage ingenuousness. Once he paused to salute some one in the crowd. The sort of affirmations which he seemed to fling out before him at random came like hiccoughs, and to each he added the gesture of a wood-cutter who is splitting wood. When he had finished, the audience burst into a laugh. He stared at the public, and, perceiving that they were laughing, and not understanding why, he began to laugh himself.

It was inauspicious.

The President, an attentive and benevolent man, raised his voice.

He reminded "the gentlemen of the jury" that "the sieur Baloup, formerly a master-wheelwright, with whom the accused stated that he had served, had been summoned in vain. He had become bankrupt, and was not to be found." Then turning to the accused, he enjoined him to listen to what he was about to say, and added: "You are in a position where reflection is necessary. The gravest presumptions rest upon you, and may induce vital results. Prisoner, in your own interests, I summon you for the last time to explain yourself clearly on two points. In the first place, did you or did you not climb the wall of the Pierron orchard, break the branch, and steal the apples; that is to say, commit the crime of breaking in and theft? In the second place, are you the discharged convict, Jean Valjean—yes or no?"

The prisoner shook his head with a capable air, like a man who has thoroughly understood, and who knows what answer he is going to make. He opened his mouth, turned towards the President, and said:—

"In the first place—"

Then he stared at his cap, stared at the ceiling, and held his peace.

"Prisoner," said the district-attorney, in a severe voice; "pay attention. You are not answering anything that has been asked of you. Your embarrassment condemns you. It is evident that your name is not Champmathieu; that you are the convict, Jean Valjean, concealed first under the name of Jean Mathieu, which was the name of his mother; that you went to Auvergne; that you were born at Faverolles, where you were a pruner of trees. It is evident that you have been guilty of entering, and of the theft of ripe apples from the Pierron orchard. The gentlemen of the jury will form their own opinion."

The prisoner had finally resumed his seat; he arose abruptly when the district-attorney had finished, and exclaimed:—

"You are very wicked; that you are! This what I wanted to say; I could not find words for it at first. I have stolen nothing. I am a man who does not have something to eat every day. I was coming from Ailly; I was walking through the country after a shower, which had made the whole country yellow: even the ponds were overflowed, and nothing sprang from the sand any more but the little blades of grass at the wayside. I found a broken branch with apples on the ground; I picked up the branch without knowing that it would get me into trouble. I have been in prison, and they have been dragging me about for the last three months; more than that I cannot say; people talk against me, they tell me, 'Answer!' The gendarme, who is a good fellow, nudges my elbow, and says to me in a low voice, 'Come, answer!' I don't know how to explain; I have no education; I am a poor man; that is where they wrong me, because they do not see this. I have not stolen; I picked up from the ground things that were lying there. You say, Jean Valjean, Jean Mathieu! I don't know those persons; they are villagers. I worked for M. Baloup, Boulevard de l'Hopital; my name is Champmathieu. You are very clever to tell me where I was born; I don't know myself: it's not everybody who has a house in which to come into the world; that would be too convenient. I think that my father and mother were people who strolled along the highways; I know nothing different. When I was a child, they called me young fellow; now they call me old fellow; those are my baptismal names; take that as you like. I have been in Auvergne; I have been at Faverolles. Pardi. Well! can't a man have been in Auvergne, or at Faverolles, without having been in the galleys? I tell you that I have not stolen, and that I am Father Champmathieu; I have been with M. Baloup; I have had a settled residence. You worry me with your nonsense, there! Why is everybody pursuing me so furiously?"

The district-attorney had remained standing; he addressed the President:—

"Monsieur le President, in view of the confused but exceedingly clever denials of the prisoner, who would like to pass himself off as an idiot, but who will not succeed in so doing,—we shall attend to that,—we demand that it shall please you and that it shall please the court to summon once more into this place the convicts Brevet, Cochepaille, and Chenildieu, and Police-Inspector Javert, and question them for the last time as to the identity of the prisoner with the convict Jean Valjean."

"I would remind the district-attorney," said the President, "that Police-Inspector Javert, recalled by his duties to the capital of a neighboring arrondissement, left the court-room and the town as soon as he had made his deposition; we have accorded him permission, with the consent of the district-attorney and of the counsel for the prisoner."

"That is true, Mr. President," responded the district-attorney. "In the absence of sieur Javert, I think it my duty to remind the gentlemen of the jury of what he said here a few hours ago. Javert is an estimable man, who does honor by his rigorous and strict probity to inferior but important functions. These are the terms of his deposition: 'I do not even stand in need of circumstantial proofs and moral presumptions to give the lie to the prisoner's denial. I recognize him perfectly. The name of this man is not Champmathieu; he is an ex-convict named Jean Valjean, and is very vicious and much to be feared. It is only with extreme regret that he was released at the expiration of his term. He underwent nineteen years of penal servitude for theft. He made five or six attempts to escape. Besides the theft from Little Gervais, and from the Pierron orchard, I suspect him of a theft committed in the house of His Grace the late Bishop of D—I often saw him at the time when I was adjutant of the galley-guard at the prison in Toulon. I repeat that I recognize him perfectly.'"

This extremely precise statement appeared to produce a vivid impression on the public and on the jury. The district-attorney concluded by insisting, that in default of Javert, the three witnesses Brevet, Chenildieu, and Cochepaille should be heard once more and solemnly interrogated.

The President transmitted the order to an usher, and, a moment later, the door of the witnesses' room opened. The usher, accompanied by a gendarme ready to lend him armed assistance, introduced the convict

Brevet. The audience was in suspense; and all breasts heaved as though they had contained but one soul.

The ex-convict Brevet wore the black and gray waistcoat of the central prisons. Brevet was a person sixty years of age, who had a sort of business man's face, and the air of a rascal. The two sometimes go together. In prison, whither fresh misdeeds had led him, he had become something in the nature of a turnkey. He was a man of whom his superiors said, "He tries to make himself of use." The chaplains bore good testimony as to his religious habits. It must not be forgotten that this passed under the Restoration.

"Brevet," said the President, "you have undergone an ignominious sentence, and you cannot take an oath."

Brevet dropped his eyes.

"Nevertheless," continued the President, "even in the man whom the law has degraded, there may remain, when the divine mercy permits it, a sentiment of honor and of equity. It is to this sentiment that I appeal at this decisive hour. If it still exists in you,—and I hope it does,—reflect before replying to me: consider on the one hand, this man, whom a word from you may ruin; on the other hand, justice, which a word from you may enlighten. The instant is solemn; there is still time to retract if you think you have been mistaken. Rise, prisoner. Brevet, take a good look at the accused, recall your souvenirs, and tell us on your soul and conscience, if you persist in recognizing this man as your former companion in the galleys, Jean Valjean?"

Brevet looked at the prisoner, then turned towards the court.

"Yes, Mr. President, I was the first to recognize him, and I stick to it; that man is Jean Valjean, who entered at Toulon in 1796, and left in 1815. I left a year later. He has the air of a brute now; but it must be because age has brutalized him; he was sly at the galleys: I recognize him positively."

"Take your seat," said the President. "Prisoner, remain standing."

Chenildieu was brought in, a prisoner for life, as was indicated by his red cassock and his green cap. He was serving out his sentence at the galleys of Toulon, whence he had been brought for this case. He was a small man of about fifty, brisk, wrinkled, frail, yellow, brazen-faced, feverish, who had a sort of sickly feebleness about all his limbs and his whole person, and an immense force in his glance. His companions in the galleys had nicknamed him I-deny-God (Je-nie Dieu, Chenildieu).

The President addressed him in nearly the same words which he had used to Brevet. At the moment when he reminded him of his infamy which deprived him of the right to take an oath, Chenildieu raised his head and looked the crowd in the face. The President invited him to reflection, and asked him as he had asked Brevet, if he persisted in recognition of the prisoner.

Chenildieu burst out laughing.

"Pardieu, as if I didn't recognize him! We were attached to the same chain for five years. So you are sulking, old fellow?"

"Go take your seat," said the President.

The usher brought in Cochepaille. He was another convict for life, who had come from the galleys, and was dressed in red, like Chenildieu, was a peasant from Lourdes, and a half-bear of the Pyrenees. He had guarded the flocks among the mountains, and from a shepherd he had slipped into a brigand. Cochepaille was no less savage and seemed even more stupid than the prisoner. He was one of those wretched men whom nature has sketched out for wild beasts, and on whom society puts the finishing touches as convicts in the galleys.

The President tried to touch him with some grave and pathetic words, and asked him, as he had asked the other two, if he persisted, without hesitation or trouble, in recognizing the man who was standing before him.

"He is Jean Valjean," said Cochepaille. "He was even called Jean-the-Screw, because he was so strong."

Each of these affirmations from these three men, evidently sincere and in good faith, had raised in the audience a murmur of bad augury for the prisoner,—a murmur which increased and lasted longer each time that a fresh declaration was added to the proceeding.

The prisoner had listened to them, with that astounded face which was, according to the accusation, his principal means of defence; at the first, the gendarmes, his neighbors, had heard him mutter between his teeth: "Ah, well, he's a nice one!" after the second, he said, a little louder, with an air that was almost that of satisfaction, "Good!" at the third, he cried, "Famous!"

The President addressed him:—

"Have you heard, prisoner? What have you to say?"

He replied:—

"I say, 'Famous!'"

An uproar broke out among the audience, and was communicated to the jury; it was evident that the man was lost.

"Ushers," said the President, "enforce silence! I am going to sum up the arguments."

At that moment there was a movement just beside the President; a voice was heard crying:—

"Brevet! Chenildieu! Cochepaille! look here!"

All who heard that voice were chilled, so lamentable and terrible was it; all eyes were turned to the point whence it had proceeded. A man, placed among the privileged spectators who were seated behind the court, had just risen, had pushed open the half-door which separated the tribunal from the audience, and was standing in the middle of the hall; the President, the district-attorney, M. Bamatabois, twenty persons, recognized him, and exclaimed in concert:—

"M. Madeleine!"

CHAPTER XI

CHAMPMATHIEU MORE AND
MORE ASTONISHED

It was he, in fact. The clerk's lamp illumined his countenance. He held his hat in his hand; there was no disorder in his clothing; his coat was carefully buttoned; he was very pale, and he trembled slightly; his hair, which had still been gray on his arrival in Arras, was now entirely white: it had turned white during the hour he had sat there.

All heads were raised: the sensation was indescribable; there was a momentary hesitation in the audience, the voice had been so heart-rending; the man who stood there appeared so calm that they did not understand at first. They asked themselves whether he had indeed uttered that cry; they could not believe that that tranquil man had been the one to give that terrible outcry.

This indecision only lasted a few seconds. Even before the President and the district-attorney could utter a word, before the ushers and the gendarmes could make a gesture, the man whom all still called, at that moment, M. Madeleine, had advanced towards the witnesses Cochepaille, Brevet, and Chenildieu.

"Do you not recognize me?" said he.

All three remained speechless, and indicated by a sign of the head that they did not know him. Cochepaille, who was intimidated, made a military salute. M. Madeleine turned towards the jury and the court, and said in a gentle voice:—

"Gentlemen of the jury, order the prisoner to be released! Mr. President, have me arrested. He is not the man whom you are in search of; it is I: I am Jean Valjean."

Not a mouth breathed; the first commotion of astonishment had been followed by a silence like that of the grave; those within the hall experienced that sort of religious terror which seizes the masses when something grand has been done.

In the meantime, the face of the President was stamped with sympathy and sadness; he had exchanged a rapid sign with the district-attorney and a few low-toned words with the assistant judges; he addressed the public, and asked in accents which all understood:—

"Is there a physician present?"

The district-attorney took the word:—

"Gentlemen of the jury, the very strange and unexpected incident which disturbs the audience inspires us, like yourselves, only with a sentiment which it is unnecessary for us to express. You all know, by reputation at least, the honorable M. Madeleine, mayor of M. sur M.; if there is a physician in the audience, we join the President in requesting him to attend to M. Madeleine, and to conduct him to his home."

M. Madeleine did not allow the district-attorney to finish; he interrupted him in accents full of suavity and authority. These are the words which he uttered; here they are literally, as they were written down, immediately after the trial by one of the witnesses to this scene, and as they now ring in the ears of those who heard them nearly forty years ago:—

"I thank you, Mr. District-Attorney, but I am not mad; you shall see; you were on the point of committing a great error; release this man! I am fulfilling a duty; I am that miserable criminal. I am the only one here who sees the matter clearly, and I am telling you the truth. God, who is on high, looks down on what I am doing at this moment, and that suffices. You can take me, for here I am: but I have done my best; I concealed myself under another name; I have become rich; I have become a mayor; I have tried to re-enter the ranks of the honest. It seems that that is not to be done. In short, there are many things which I cannot tell. I will not narrate the story of my life to you; you will hear it one of these days. I robbed Monseigneur the Bishop, it is true; it is true that I robbed Little Gervais; they were right in telling you that Jean Valjean was a very vicious wretch. Perhaps it was not altogether his fault. Listen, honorable judges! a man who has been so greatly humbled as I have has neither any remonstrances to make to Providence, nor any advice to give to society; but, you see, the infamy from which I have tried to escape is an injurious thing; the galleys make the convict what he is; reflect upon that, if you please. Before going to the galleys, I was a poor peasant, with very little intelligence, a sort of idiot; the galleys wrought a change in me. I was stupid; I became vicious: I was a block of wood; I became a firebrand. Later on, indulgence and kindness saved me, as severity had ruined me. But, pardon me, you cannot understand what I am saying. You will find at my house, among the ashes in the fireplace, the forty-sou piece which I stole, seven years ago, from little Gervais. I have nothing farther to add; take me. Good God! the district-attorney shakes his head; you say, 'M. Madeleine has gone mad!' you do not believe me! that is distressing. Do not, at least, condemn this man! What! these men do not recognize me! I wish Javert were here; he would recognize me."

Nothing can reproduce the sombre and kindly melancholy of tone which accompanied these words.

He turned to the three convicts, and said:—

"Well, I recognize you; do you remember, Brevet?"

He paused, hesitated for an instant, and said:—

"Do you remember the knitted suspenders with a checked pattern which you wore in the galleys?"

Brevet gave a start of surprise, and surveyed him from head to foot with a frightened air. He continued:—

"Chenildieu, you who conferred on yourself the name of 'Jenie-Dieu,' your whole right shoulder bears a deep burn, because you one day laid your shoulder against the chafing-dish full of coals, in order to efface the three letters T. F. P., which are still visible, nevertheless; answer, is this true?"

"It is true," said Chenildieu.

He addressed himself to Cochepaille:—

"Cochepaille, you have, near the bend in your left arm, a date stamped in blue letters with burnt powder; the date is that of the landing of the Emperor at Cannes, March 1, 1815; pull up your sleeve!"

Cochepaille pushed up his sleeve; all eyes were focused on him and on his bare arm.

A gendarme held a light close to it; there was the date.

The unhappy man turned to the spectators and the judges with a smile which still rends the hearts of all who saw it whenever they think of it. It was a smile of triumph; it was also a smile of despair.

"You see plainly," he said, "that I am Jean Valjean."

In that chamber there were no longer either judges, accusers, nor gendarmes; there was nothing but staring eyes and sympathizing hearts. No one recalled any longer the part that each might be called upon to play; the district-attorney forgot he was there for the purpose of prosecuting, the President that he was there to preside, the counsel for the defence that he was there to defend. It was a striking circumstance that no question was put, that no authority intervened. The peculiarity of sublime spectacles is, that they capture all souls and turn witnesses into spectators. No one, probably, could have explained what he felt; no one, probably, said to himself that he was witnessing the splendid outburst of a grand light: all felt themselves inwardly dazzled.

It was evident that they had Jean Valjean before their eyes. That was clear. The appearance of this man had sufficed to suffuse with light that matter which had been so obscure but a moment previously, without any further explanation: the whole crowd, as by a sort of electric revelation, understood instantly and at a single glance the simple and magnificent history of a man who was delivering himself up so that another man might not be condemned in his stead. The details, the hesitations, little possible oppositions, were swallowed up in that vast and luminous fact.

It was an impression which vanished speedily, but which was irresistible at the moment.

"I do not wish to disturb the court further," resumed Jean Valjean. "I shall withdraw, since you do not arrest me. I have many things to do. The district-attorney knows who I am; he knows whither I am going; he can have me arrested when he likes."

He directed his steps towards the door. Not a voice was raised, not an arm extended to hinder him. All stood aside. At that moment there was about him that divine something which causes multitudes to stand aside and make way for a man. He traversed the crowd slowly. It was never known who opened the door, but it is certain that he found the door open when he reached it. On arriving there he turned round and said:—

"I am at your command, Mr. District-Attorney."

Then he addressed the audience:—

"All of you, all who are present—consider me worthy of pity, do you not? Good God! When I think of what I was on the point of doing, I consider that I am to be envied. Nevertheless, I should have preferred not to have had this occur."

He withdrew, and the door closed behind him as it had opened, for those who do certain sovereign things are always sure of being served by some one in the crowd.

Less than an hour after this, the verdict of the jury freed the said Champmathieu from all accusations; and Champmathieu, being at once released, went off in a state of stupefaction, thinking that all men were fools, and comprehending nothing of this vision.

BOOK EIGHTH.

A COUNTER-BLOW

CHAPTER I

IN WHAT MIRROR M. MADELEINE
CONTEMPLATES HIS HAIR

The day had begun to dawn. Fantine had passed a sleepless and feverish night, filled with happy visions; at daybreak she fell asleep. Sister Simplice, who had been watching with her, availed herself of this slumber to go and prepare a new potion of chinchona. The worthy sister had been in the laboratory of the infirmary but a few moments, bending over her drugs and phials, and scrutinizing things very closely, on account of the dimness which the half-light of dawn spreads over all objects. Suddenly she raised her head and uttered a faint shriek. M. Madeleine stood before her; he had just entered silently.

"Is it you, Mr. Mayor?" she exclaimed.

He replied in a low voice:—

"How is that poor woman?"

"Not so bad just now; but we have been very uneasy."

She explained to him what had passed: that Fantine had been very ill the day before, and that she was better now, because she thought that the mayor had gone to Montfermeil to get her child. The sister dared not question the mayor; but she perceived plainly from his air that he had not come from there.

"All that is good," said he; "you were right not to undeceive her."

"Yes," responded the sister; "but now, Mr. Mayor, she will see you and will not see her child. What shall we say to her?"

He reflected for a moment.

"God will inspire us," said he.

"But we cannot tell a lie," murmured the sister, half aloud.

It was broad daylight in the room. The light fell full on M. Madeleine's face. The sister chanced to raise her eyes to it.

"Good God, sir!" she exclaimed; "what has happened to you? Your hair is perfectly white!"

"White!" said he.

Sister Simplice had no mirror. She rummaged in a drawer, and pulled out the little glass which the doctor of the infirmary used to see whether a patient was dead and whether he no longer breathed. M. Madeleine took the mirror, looked at his hair, and said:—

"Well!"

He uttered the word indifferently, and as though his mind were on something else.

The sister felt chilled by something strange of which she caught a glimpse in all this.

He inquired:—

"Can I see her?"

"Is not Monsieur le Maire going to have her child brought back to her?" said the sister, hardly venturing to put the question.

"Of course; but it will take two or three days at least."

"If she were not to see Monsieur le Maire until that time," went on the sister, timidly, "she would not know that Monsieur le Maire had returned, and it would be easy to inspire her with patience; and when the child arrived, she would naturally think Monsieur le Maire had just come with the child. We should not have to enact a lie."

M. Madeleine seemed to reflect for a few moments; then he said with his calm gravity:—

"No, sister, I must see her. I may, perhaps, be in haste."

The nun did not appear to notice this word "perhaps," which communicated an obscure and singular sense to the words of the mayor's speech. She replied, lowering her eyes and her voice respectfully:—

"In that case, she is asleep; but Monsieur le Maire may enter."

He made some remarks about a door which shut badly, and the noise of which might awaken the sick woman; then he entered Fantine's chamber, approached the bed and drew aside the curtains. She was asleep. Her breath issued from her breast with that tragic sound which is peculiar to those maladies, and which breaks the hearts of mothers when they are watching through the night beside their sleeping child who is condemned to death. But this painful respiration hardly troubled a sort of ineffable serenity which overspread her countenance, and which transfigured her in her sleep. Her pallor had become whiteness; her cheeks were crimson; her long golden lashes, the only beauty of her youth and her virginity which remained to her, palpitated, though they remained closed and drooping. Her whole person was trembling with an indescribable unfolding of wings, all ready to open wide and bear her away, which could be felt as they rustled, though they could not be seen. To see her thus, one would never have dreamed that she was an invalid whose life was almost despaired of. She resembled rather something on the point of soaring away than something on the point of dying.

The branch trembles when a hand approaches it to pluck a flower, and seems to both withdraw and to offer itself at one and the same time. The human body has something of this tremor when the instant arrives in which the mysterious fingers of Death are about to pluck the soul.

M. Madeleine remained for some time motionless beside that bed, gazing in turn upon the sick woman and the crucifix, as he had done two months before, on the day when he had come for the first time to see her in that asylum. They were both still there in the same attitude—she sleeping, he praying; only now, after the lapse of two months, her hair was gray and his was white.

The sister had not entered with him. He stood beside the bed, with his finger on his lips, as though there were some one in the chamber whom he must enjoin to silence.

She opened her eyes, saw him, and said quietly, with a smile:—

"And Cosette?"

CHAPTER II

FANTINE HAPPY

She made no movement of either surprise or of joy; she was joy itself. That simple question, "And Cosette?" was put with so profound a faith, with so much certainty, with such a complete absence of disquiet and of doubt, that he found not a word of reply. She continued:—

"I knew that you were there. I was asleep, but I saw you. I have seen you for a long, long time. I have been following you with my eyes all night long. You were in a glory, and you had around you all sorts of celestial forms."

He raised his glance to the crucifix.

"But," she resumed, "tell me where Cosette is. Why did not you place her on my bed against the moment of my waking?"

He made some mechanical reply which he was never afterwards able to recall.

Fortunately, the doctor had been warned, and he now made his appearance. He came to the aid of M. Madeleine.

"Calm yourself, my child," said the doctor; "your child is here."

Fantine's eyes beamed and filled her whole face with light. She clasped her hands with an expression which contained all that is possible to prayer in the way of violence and tenderness.

"Oh!" she exclaimed, "bring her to me!"

Touching illusion of a mother! Cosette was, for her, still the little child who is carried.

"Not yet," said the doctor, "not just now. You still have some fever. The sight of your child would agitate you and do you harm. You must be cured first."

She interrupted him impetuously:—

"But I am cured! Oh, I tell you that I am cured! What an ass that doctor is! The idea! I want to see my child!"

"You see," said the doctor, "how excited you become. So long as you are in this state I shall oppose your having your child. It is not enough to see her; it is necessary that you should live for her. When you are reasonable, I will bring her to you myself."

The poor mother bowed her head.

"I beg your pardon, doctor, I really beg your pardon. Formerly I should never have spoken as I have just done; so many misfortunes have happened to me, that I sometimes do not know what I am saying. I understand you; you fear the emotion. I will wait as long as you like, but I swear to you that it would not have harmed me to see my daughter. I have been seeing her; I have not taken my eyes from her since yesterday evening. Do you know? If she were brought to me now, I should talk to her very gently. That is all. Is it not quite natural that I should desire to see my daughter, who has been brought to me expressly from Montfermeil? I am not angry. I know well that I am about to be happy. All night long I have seen white things, and persons who smiled at me. When Monsieur le Docteur pleases, he shall bring me Cosette. I have no longer any fever; I am well. I am perfectly conscious that there is nothing the matter with me any more; but I am going to behave as though I were ill, and not stir, to please these ladies here. When it is seen that I am very calm, they will say, 'She must have her child.'"

M. Madeleine was sitting on a chair beside the bed. She turned towards him; she was making a visible effort to be calm and "very good," as she expressed it in the feebleness of illness which resembles infancy, in order that, seeing her so peaceable, they might make no difficulty about bringing Cosette to her. But while she controlled herself she could not refrain from questioning M. Madeleine.

"Did you have a pleasant trip, Monsieur le Maire? Oh! how good you were to go and get her for me! Only tell me how she is. Did she stand the journey well? Alas! she will not recognize me. She must have forgotten me by this time, poor darling! Children have no memories. They are like birds. A child sees one thing today and another thing tomorrow, and thinks of nothing any longer. And did she have white linen? Did those Thenardiers keep her clean? How have they fed her? Oh! if you only knew how I have suffered, putting such questions as that to myself during all the time of my wretchedness. Now, it is all past. I am happy. Oh, how I should like to see her! Do you think her pretty, Monsieur le Maire? Is not my daughter beautiful? You must have been very cold in that diligence! Could she not be brought for just one little instant? She might be taken away directly afterwards. Tell me; you are the master; it could be so if you chose!"

He took her hand. "Cosette is beautiful," he said, "Cosette is well. You shall see her soon; but calm yourself; you are talking with too much vivacity, and you are throwing your arms out from under the clothes, and that makes you cough."

In fact, fits of coughing interrupted Fantine at nearly every word.

Fantine did not murmur; she feared that she had injured by her too passionate lamentations the confidence which she was desirous of inspiring, and she began to talk of indifferent things.

"Montfermeil is quite pretty, is it not? People go there on pleasure parties in summer. Are the Thenardiers prosperous? There are not many travellers in their parts. That inn of theirs is a sort of a cook-shop."

M. Madeleine was still holding her hand, and gazing at her with anxiety; it was evident that he had come to tell her things before which his mind now hesitated. The doctor, having finished his visit, retired. Sister Simplice remained alone with them.

But in the midst of this pause Fantine exclaimed:—

"I hear her! mon Dieu, I hear her!"

She stretched out her arm to enjoin silence about her, held her breath, and began to listen with rapture.

There was a child playing in the yard—the child of the portress or of some work-woman. It was one of those accidents which are always occurring, and which seem to form a part of the mysterious stage-setting of mournful scenes. The child—a little girl—was going and coming, running to warm herself, laughing, singing at the top of her voice. Alas! in what are the plays of children not intermingled. It was this little girl whom Fantine heard singing.

"Oh!" she resumed, "it is my Cosette! I recognize her voice."

The child retreated as it had come; the voice died away. Fantine listened for a while longer, then her face clouded over, and M. Madeleine heard her say, in a low voice: "How wicked that doctor is not to allow me to see my daughter! That man has an evil countenance, that he has."

But the smiling background of her thoughts came to the front again. She continued to talk to herself, with her head resting on the pillow: "How happy we are going to be! We shall have a little garden the very first thing; M. Madeleine has promised it to me. My daughter will play in the garden. She must know her letters by this time. I will make her spell. She will run over the grass after butterflies. I will watch her. Then she will take her first communion. Ah! when will she take her first communion?"

She began to reckon on her fingers.

"One, two, three, four—she is seven years old. In five years she will have a white veil, and openwork stockings; she will look like a little woman. O my good sister, you do not know how foolish I become when I think of my daughter's first communion!"

She began to laugh.

He had released Fantine's hand. He listened to her words as one listens to the sighing of the breeze, with his eyes on the ground, his mind absorbed in reflection which had no bottom. All at once she ceased speaking, and this caused him to raise his head mechanically. Fantine had become terrible.

She no longer spoke, she no longer breathed; she had raised herself to a sitting posture, her thin shoulder emerged from her chemise; her face, which had been radiant but a moment before, was ghastly, and she seemed to have fixed her eyes, rendered large with terror, on something alarming at the other extremity of the room.

"Good God!" he exclaimed; "what ails you, Fantine?"

She made no reply; she did not remove her eyes from the object which she seemed to see. She removed one hand from his arm, and with the other made him a sign to look behind him.

He turned, and beheld Javert.

CHAPTER III

JAVERT SATISFIED

This is what had taken place.

The half-hour after midnight had just struck when M. Madeleine quitted the Hall of Assizes in Arras. He regained his inn just in time to set out again by the mail-wagon, in which he had engaged his place. A little before six o'clock in the morning he had arrived at M. sur M., and his first care had been to post a letter to M. Laffitte, then to enter the infirmary and see Fantine.

However, he had hardly quitted the audience hall of the Court of Assizes, when the district-attorney, recovering from his first shock, had taken the word to deplore the mad deed of the honorable mayor of M. sur M., to declare that his convictions had not been in the least modified by that curious incident, which would be explained thereafter, and to demand, in the meantime, the condemnation of that Champmathieu, who was evidently the real Jean Valjean. The district-attorney's persistence was visibly at variance with the sentiments of every one, of the public, of the court, and of the jury. The counsel for the defence had some difficulty in refuting this harangue and in establishing that, in consequence of the revelations of M. Madeleine, that is to say, of the real Jean Valjean, the aspect of the matter had been thoroughly altered, and that the jury had before their eyes now only an innocent man. Thence the lawyer had drawn some epiphonemas, not very fresh, unfortunately, upon judicial errors, etc., etc.; the President, in his summing up, had joined the counsel for the defence, and in a few minutes the jury had thrown Champmathieu out of the case.

Nevertheless, the district-attorney was bent on having a Jean Valjean; and as he had no longer Champmathieu, he took Madeleine.

Immediately after Champmathieu had been set at liberty, the district-attorney shut himself up with the President. They conferred "as to the necessity of seizing the person of M. le Maire of M. sur M." This phrase, in which there was a great deal of of, is the district-attorney's, written with his own hand, on the minutes of his report to the attorney-general. His first emotion having passed off, the President did not offer many objections. Justice must, after all, take its course. And then, when all was said, although the President was a kindly and a tolerably intelligent man, he was, at the same time, a devoted and almost an ardent royalist, and he had been shocked to hear the Mayor of M. sur M. say the Emperor, and not Bonaparte, when alluding to the landing at Cannes.

The order for his arrest was accordingly despatched. The district-attorney forwarded it to M. sur M. by a special messenger, at full speed, and entrusted its execution to Police Inspector Javert.

The reader knows that Javert had returned to M. sur M. immediately after having given his deposition.

Javert was just getting out of bed when the messenger handed him the order of arrest and the command to produce the prisoner.

The messenger himself was a very clever member of the police, who, in two words, informed Javert of what had taken place at Arras. The order of arrest, signed by the district-attorney, was couched in these words: "Inspector Javert will apprehend the body of the Sieur Madeleine, mayor of M. sur M., who, in this day's session of the court, was recognized as the liberated convict, Jean Valjean."

Any one who did not know Javert, and who had chanced to see him at the moment when he penetrated the antechamber of the infirmary, could have divined nothing of what had taken place, and would have thought his air the most ordinary in the world. He was cool, calm, grave, his gray hair was perfectly smooth upon his temples, and he had just mounted the stairs with his habitual deliberation. Any one who was thoroughly acquainted with him, and who had examined him attentively at the moment, would have shuddered. The buckle of his leather stock was under his left ear instead of at the nape of his neck. This betrayed unwonted agitation.

Javert was a complete character, who never had a wrinkle in his duty or in his uniform; methodical with malefactors, rigid with the buttons of his coat.

That he should have set the buckle of his stock awry, it was indispensable that there should have taken place in him one of those emotions which may be designated as internal earthquakes.

He had come in a simple way, had made a requisition on the neighboring post for a corporal and four soldiers, had left the soldiers in the courtyard, had had Fantine's room pointed out to him by the portress, who was utterly unsuspicious, accustomed as she was to seeing armed men inquiring for the mayor.

On arriving at Fantine's chamber, Javert turned the handle, pushed the door open with the gentleness of a sick-nurse or a police spy, and entered.

Properly speaking, he did not enter. He stood erect in the half-open door, his hat on his head and his left hand thrust into his coat, which was buttoned up to the chin. In the bend of his elbow the leaden head of his enormous cane, which was hidden behind him, could be seen.

Thus he remained for nearly a minute, without his presence being perceived. All at once Fantine raised her eyes, saw him, and made M. Madeleine turn round.

The instant that Madeleine's glance encountered Javert's glance, Javert, without stirring, without moving from his post, without approaching him, became terrible. No human sentiment can be as terrible as joy.

It was the visage of a demon who has just found his damned soul.

The satisfaction of at last getting hold of Jean Valjean caused all that was in his soul to appear in his countenance. The depths having been stirred up, mounted to the surface. The humiliation of having, in some slight degree, lost the scent, and of having indulged, for a few moments, in an error with regard to Champmathieu, was effaced by pride at having so well and accurately divined in the first place, and of having for so long cherished a just instinct. Javert's content shone forth in his sovereign attitude. The deformity of triumph overspread that narrow brow. All the demonstrations of horror which a satisfied face can afford were there.

Javert was in heaven at that moment. Without putting the thing clearly to himself, but with a confused intuition of the necessity of his presence and of his success, he, Javert, personified justice, light, and truth in their celestial function of crushing out evil. Behind him and around him, at an infinite distance, he had authority, reason, the case judged, the legal conscience, the public prosecution, all the stars; he was protecting order, he was causing the law to yield up its thunders, he was avenging society, he was lending a helping hand to the absolute, he was standing erect in the midst of a glory. There existed in his victory a remnant of defiance and of combat. Erect, haughty, brilliant, he flaunted abroad in open day the superhuman bestiality of a ferocious archangel. The terrible shadow of the action which he was accomplishing caused the vague flash of the social sword to be visible in his clenched fist; happy and indignant, he held his heel upon crime, vice, rebellion, perdition, hell; he was radiant, he exterminated, he smiled, and there was an incontestable grandeur in this monstrous Saint Michael.

Javert, though frightful, had nothing ignoble about him.

Probity, sincerity, candor, conviction, the sense of duty, are things which may become hideous when wrongly directed; but which, even when hideous, remain grand: their majesty, the majesty peculiar to the human conscience, clings to them in the midst of horror; they are virtues which have one vice,—error. The honest, pitiless joy of a fanatic in the full flood of his atrocity preserves a certain lugubriously venerable radiance. Without himself suspecting the fact, Javert in his formidable happiness was to be pitied, as is every ignorant man who triumphs. Nothing could be so poignant and so terrible as this face, wherein was displayed all that may be designated as the evil of the good.

CHAPTER IV

AUTHORITY REASSERTS ITS RIGHTS

Fantine had not seen Javert since the day on which the mayor had torn her from the man. Her ailing brain comprehended nothing, but the only thing which she did not doubt was that he had come to get her. She could not endure that terrible face; she felt her life quitting her; she hid her face in both hands, and shrieked in her anguish:—

"Monsieur Madeleine, save me!"

Jean Valjean—we shall henceforth not speak of him otherwise—had risen. He said to Fantine in the gentlest and calmest of voices:—

"Be at ease; it is not for you that he is come."

Then he addressed Javert, and said:—

"I know what you want."

Javert replied:—

"Be quick about it!"

There lay in the inflection of voice which accompanied these words something indescribably fierce and frenzied. Javert did not say, "Be quick about it!" he said "Bequiabouit."

No orthography can do justice to the accent with which it was uttered: it was no longer a human word: it was a roar.

He did not proceed according to his custom, he did not enter into the matter, he exhibited no warrant of arrest. In his eyes, Jean Valjean was a sort of mysterious combatant, who was not to be laid hands upon, a wrestler in the dark whom he had had in his grasp for the last five years, without being able to throw him. This arrest was not a beginning, but an end. He confined himself to saying, "Be quick about it!"

As he spoke thus, he did not advance a single step; he hurled at Jean Valjean a glance which he threw out like a grappling-hook, and with which he was accustomed to draw wretches violently to him.

It was this glance which Fantine had felt penetrating to the very marrow of her bones two months previously.

At Javert's exclamation, Fantine opened her eyes once more. But the mayor was there; what had she to fear?

Javert advanced to the middle of the room, and cried:—

"See here now! Art thou coming?"

The unhappy woman glanced about her. No one was present excepting the nun and the mayor. To whom could that abject use of "thou" be addressed? To her only. She shuddered.

Then she beheld a most unprecedented thing, a thing so unprecedented that nothing equal to it had appeared to her even in the blackest deliriums of fever.

She beheld Javert, the police spy, seize the mayor by the collar; she saw the mayor bow his head. It seemed to her that the world was coming to an end.

Javert had, in fact, grasped Jean Valjean by the collar.

"Monsieur le Maire!" shrieked Fantine.

Javert burst out laughing with that frightful laugh which displayed all his gums.

"There is no longer any Monsieur le Maire here!"

Jean Valjean made no attempt to disengage the hand which grasped the collar of his coat. He said:—

"Javert—"

Javert interrupted him: "Call me Mr. Inspector."

"Monsieur," said Jean Valjean, "I should like to say a word to you in private."

414

"Aloud! Say it aloud!" replied Javert; "people are in the habit of talking aloud to me."

Jean Valjean went on in a lower tone:—

"I have a request to make of you—"

"I tell you to speak loud."

"But you alone should hear it—"

"What difference does that make to me? I shall not listen."

Jean Valjean turned towards him and said very rapidly and in a very low voice:—

"Grant me three days' grace! three days in which to go and fetch the child of this unhappy woman. I will pay whatever is necessary. You shall accompany me if you choose."

"You are making sport of me!" cried Javert. "Come now, I did not think you such a fool! You ask me to give you three days in which to run away! You say that it is for the purpose of fetching that creature's child! Ah! Ah! That's good! That's really capital!"

Fantine was seized with a fit of trembling.

"My child!" she cried, "to go and fetch my child! She is not here, then! Answer me, sister; where is Cosette? I want my child! Monsieur Madeleine! Monsieur le Maire!"

Javert stamped his foot.

"And now there's the other one! Will you hold your tongue, you hussy? It's a pretty sort of a place where convicts are magistrates, and where women of the town are cared for like countesses! Ah! But we are going to change all that; it is high time!"

He stared intently at Fantine, and added, once more taking into his grasp Jean Valjean's cravat, shirt and collar:—

"I tell you that there is no Monsieur Madeleine and that there is no Monsieur le Maire. There is a thief, a brigand, a convict named Jean Valjean! And I have him in my grasp! That's what there is!"

Fantine raised herself in bed with a bound, supporting herself on her stiffened arms and on both hands: she gazed at Jean Valjean, she gazed at

Javert, she gazed at the nun, she opened her mouth as though to speak; a rattle proceeded from the depths of her throat, her teeth chattered; she stretched out her arms in her agony, opening her hands convulsively, and fumbling about her like a drowning person; then suddenly fell back on her pillow.

Her head struck the head-board of the bed and fell forwards on her breast, with gaping mouth and staring, sightless eyes.

She was dead.

Jean Valjean laid his hand upon the detaining hand of Javert, and opened it as he would have opened the hand of a baby; then he said to Javert:—

"You have murdered that woman."

"Let's have an end of this!" shouted Javert, in a fury; "I am not here to listen to argument. Let us economize all that; the guard is below; march on instantly, or you'll get the thumb-screws!"

In the corner of the room stood an old iron bedstead, which was in a decidedly decrepit state, and which served the sisters as a camp-bed when they were watching with the sick. Jean Valjean stepped up to this bed, in a twinkling wrenched off the head-piece, which was already in a dilapidated condition, an easy matter to muscles like his, grasped the principal rod like a bludgeon, and glanced at Javert. Javert retreated towards the door. Jean Valjean, armed with his bar of iron, walked slowly up to Fantine's couch. When he arrived there he turned and said to Javert, in a voice that was barely audible:—

"I advise you not to disturb me at this moment."

One thing is certain, and that is, that Javert trembled.

It did occur to him to summon the guard, but Jean Valjean might avail himself of that moment to effect his escape; so he remained, grasped his cane by the small end, and leaned against the door-post, without removing his eyes from Jean Valjean.

Jean Valjean rested his elbow on the knob at the head of the bed, and his brow on his hand, and began to contemplate the motionless body of

416

Fantine, which lay extended there. He remained thus, mute, absorbed, evidently with no further thought of anything connected with this life. Upon his face and in his attitude there was nothing but inexpressible pity. After a few moments of this meditation he bent towards Fantine, and spoke to her in a low voice.

What did he say to her? What could this man, who was reproved, say to that woman, who was dead? What words were those? No one on earth heard them. Did the dead woman hear them? There are some touching illusions which are, perhaps, sublime realities. The point as to which there exists no doubt is, that Sister Simplice, the sole witness of the incident, often said that at the moment that Jean Valjean whispered in Fantine's ear, she distinctly beheld an ineffable smile dawn on those pale lips, and in those dim eyes, filled with the amazement of the tomb.

Jean Valjean took Fantine's head in both his hands, and arranged it on the pillow as a mother might have done for her child; then he tied the string of her chemise, and smoothed her hair back under her cap. That done, he closed her eyes.

Fantine's face seemed strangely illuminated at that moment.

Death, that signifies entrance into the great light.

Fantine's hand was hanging over the side of the bed. Jean Valjean knelt down before that hand, lifted it gently, and kissed it.

Then he rose, and turned to Javert.

"Now," said he, "I am at your disposal."

CHAPTER V

A SUITABLE TOMB

Javert deposited Jean Valjean in the city prison.

The arrest of M. Madeleine occasioned a sensation, or rather, an extraordinary commotion in M. sur M. We are sorry that we cannot conceal the fact, that at the single word, "He was a convict," nearly every one deserted him. In less than two hours all the good that he had done had been forgotten, and he was nothing but a "convict from the galleys." It is just to add that the details of what had taken place at Arras were not yet known. All day long conversations like the following were to be heard in all quarters of the town:—

"You don't know? He was a liberated convict!" "Who?" "The mayor." "Bah! M. Madeleine?" "Yes." "Really?" "His name was not Madeleine at all; he had a frightful name, Bejean, Bojean, Boujean." "Ah! Good God!" "He has been arrested." "Arrested!" "In prison, in the city prison, while waiting to be transferred." "Until he is transferred!" "He is to be transferred!" "Where is he to be taken?" "He will be tried at the Assizes for a highway robbery which he committed long ago." "Well! I suspected as much. That man was too good, too perfect, too affected. He refused the cross; he bestowed sous on all the little scamps he came across. I always thought there was some evil history back of all that."

The "drawing-rooms" particularly abounded in remarks of this nature.

One old lady, a subscriber to the Drapeau Blanc, made the following remark, the depth of which it is impossible to fathom:—

"I am not sorry. It will be a lesson to the Bonapartists!"

It was thus that the phantom which had been called M. Madeleine vanished from M. sur M. Only three or four persons in all the town remained faithful to his memory. The old portress who had served him was among the number.

On the evening of that day the worthy old woman was sitting in her lodge, still in a thorough fright, and absorbed in sad reflections. The factory had been closed all day, the carriage gate was bolted, the street was deserted. There was no one in the house but the two nuns, Sister Perpetue and Sister Simplice, who were watching beside the body of Fantine.

Towards the hour when M. Madeleine was accustomed to return home, the good portress rose mechanically, took from a drawer the key of M. Madeleine's chamber, and the flat candlestick which he used every evening to go up to his quarters; then she hung the key on the nail whence he was accustomed to take it, and set the candlestick on one side, as though she was expecting him. Then she sat down again on her chair, and became absorbed in thought once more. The poor, good old woman bad done all this without being conscious of it.

It was only at the expiration of two hours that she roused herself from her revery, and exclaimed, "Hold! My good God Jesus! And I hung his key on the nail!"

At that moment the small window in the lodge opened, a hand passed through, seized the key and the candlestick, and lighted the taper at the candle which was burning there.

The portress raised her eyes, and stood there with gaping mouth, and a shriek which she confined to her throat.

She knew that hand, that arm, the sleeve of that coat.

It was M. Madeleine.

It was several seconds before she could speak; she had a seizure, as she said herself, when she related the adventure afterwards.

"Good God, Monsieur le Maire," she cried at last, "I thought you were——"

She stopped; the conclusion of her sentence would have been lacking in respect towards the beginning. Jean Valjean was still Monsieur le Maire to her.

He finished her thought.

"In prison," said he. "I was there; I broke a bar of one of the windows; I let myself drop from the top of a roof, and here I am. I am going up to my room; go and find Sister Simplice for me. She is with that poor woman, no doubt."

The old woman obeyed in all haste.

He gave her no orders; he was quite sure that she would guard him better than he should guard himself.

No one ever found out how he had managed to get into the courtyard without opening the big gates. He had, and always carried about him, a pass-key which opened a little side-door; but he must have been searched, and his latch-key must have been taken from him. This point was never explained.

He ascended the staircase leading to his chamber. On arriving at the top, he left his candle on the top step of his stairs, opened his door with very little noise, went and closed his window and his shutters by feeling, then returned for his candle and re-entered his room.

It was a useful precaution; it will be recollected that his window could be seen from the street.

He cast a glance about him, at his table, at his chair, at his bed which had not been disturbed for three days. No trace of the disorder of the night before last remained. The portress had "done up" his room; only she had picked out of the ashes and placed neatly on the table the two iron ends of the cudgel and the forty-sou piece which had been blackened by the fire.

He took a sheet of paper, on which he wrote: "These are the two tips of my iron-shod cudgel and the forty-sou piece stolen from Little

Gervais, which I mentioned at the Court of Assizes," and he arranged this piece of paper, the bits of iron, and the coin in such a way that they were the first things to be seen on entering the room. From a cupboard he pulled out one of his old shirts, which he tore in pieces. In the strips of linen thus prepared he wrapped the two silver candlesticks. He betrayed neither haste nor agitation; and while he was wrapping up the Bishop's candlesticks, he nibbled at a piece of black bread. It was probably the prison-bread which he had carried with him in his flight.

This was proved by the crumbs which were found on the floor of the room when the authorities made an examination later on.

There came two taps at the door.

"Come in," said he.

It was Sister Simplice.

She was pale; her eyes were red; the candle which she carried trembled in her hand. The peculiar feature of the violences of destiny is, that however polished or cool we may be, they wring human nature from our very bowels, and force it to reappear on the surface. The emotions of that day had turned the nun into a woman once more. She had wept, and she was trembling.

Jean Valjean had just finished writing a few lines on a paper, which he handed to the nun, saying, "Sister, you will give this to Monsieur le Cure."

The paper was not folded. She cast a glance upon it.

"You can read it," said he.

She read:—

"I beg Monsieur le Cure to keep an eye on all that I leave behind me. He will be so good as to pay out of it the expenses of my trial, and of the funeral of the woman who died yesterday. The rest is for the poor."

The sister tried to speak, but she only managed to stammer a few inarticulate sounds. She succeeded in saying, however:—

"Does not Monsieur le Maire desire to take a last look at that poor, unhappy woman?"

"No," said he; "I am pursued; it would only end in their arresting me in that room, and that would disturb her."

He had hardly finished when a loud noise became audible on the staircase. They heard a tumult of ascending footsteps, and the old portress saying in her loudest and most piercing tones:—

"My good sir, I swear to you by the good God, that not a soul has entered this house all day, nor all the evening, and that I have not even left the door."

A man responded:—

"But there is a light in that room, nevertheless."

They recognized Javert's voice.

The chamber was so arranged that the door in opening masked the corner of the wall on the right. Jean Valjean blew out the light and placed himself in this angle. Sister Simplice fell on her knees near the table.

The door opened.

Javert entered.

The whispers of many men and the protestations of the portress were audible in the corridor.

The nun did not raise her eyes. She was praying.

The candle was on the chimney-piece, and gave but very little light.

Javert caught sight of the nun and halted in amazement.

It will be remembered that the fundamental point in Javert, his element, the very air he breathed, was veneration for all authority. This was impregnable, and admitted of neither objection nor restriction. In his eyes, of course, the ecclesiastical authority was the chief of all; he was religious, superficial and correct on this point as on all others. In his eyes, a priest was a mind, who never makes a mistake; a nun was a creature who never sins; they were souls walled in from this world, with a single door which never opened except to allow the truth to pass through.

On perceiving the sister, his first movement was to retire.

But there was also another duty which bound him and impelled him imperiously in the opposite direction. His second movement was to remain and to venture on at least one question.

This was Sister Simplice, who had never told a lie in her life. Javert knew it, and held her in special veneration in consequence.

"Sister," said he, "are you alone in this room?"

A terrible moment ensued, during which the poor portress felt as though she should faint.

The sister raised her eyes and answered:—

"Yes."

"Then," resumed Javert, "you will excuse me if I persist; it is my duty; you have not seen a certain person—a man—this evening? He has escaped; we are in search of him—that Jean Valjean; you have not seen him?"

The sister replied:—

"No."

She lied. She had lied twice in succession, one after the other, without hesitation, promptly, as a person does when sacrificing herself.

"Pardon me," said Javert, and he retired with a deep bow.

O sainted maid! you left this world many years ago; you have rejoined your sisters, the virgins, and your brothers, the angels, in the light; may this lie be counted to your credit in paradise!

The sister's affirmation was for Javert so decisive a thing that he did not even observe the singularity of that candle which had but just been extinguished, and which was still smoking on the table.

An hour later, a man, marching amid trees and mists, was rapidly departing from M. sur M. in the direction of Paris. That man was Jean Valjean. It has been established by the testimony of two or three carters who met him, that he was carrying a bundle; that he was dressed in a blouse. Where had he obtained that blouse? No one ever found out. But an aged workman had died in the infirmary of the factory a few days before, leaving behind him nothing but his blouse. Perhaps that was the one.

One last word about Fantine.

We all have a mother,—the earth. Fantine was given back to that mother.

The cure thought that he was doing right, and perhaps he really was, in reserving as much money as possible from what Jean Valjean had left for the poor. Who was concerned, after all? A convict and a woman of the town. That is why he had a very simple funeral for Fantine, and reduced it to that strictly necessary form known as the pauper's grave.

So Fantine was buried in the free corner of the cemetery which belongs to anybody and everybody, and where the poor are lost. Fortunately, God knows where to find the soul again. Fantine was laid in the shade, among the first bones that came to hand; she was subjected to the promiscuousness of ashes. She was thrown into the public grave. Her grave resembled her bed.

[The end of Volume I. "Fantine"]